URBAN HIKES SOUTHERN CALIFORNIA

HELP US KEEP THIS GUIDE UP TO DATE

Every effort has been made by the author and editors to make this guide as accurate and useful as possible. However, many things can change after a guide is published—trails are rerouted, regulations change, facilities come under new management, and so forth.

We would love to hear from you concerning your experiences with this guide and how you feel it could be improved and kept up to date. While we may not be able to respond to all comments and suggestions, we'll take them to heart, and we'll also make certain to share them with the author. Please send your comments and suggestions to the following address:

Globe Pequot Press
Reader Response/Editorial Department
246 Goose Lane, Suite 200
Guilford, CT 06437

Or you may e-mail us at:

editorial@GlobePequot.com

Thanks for your input, and happy trails!

URBAN HIKES
SOUTHERN
CALIFORNIA

A GUIDE TO THE STATE'S GREATEST
URBAN HIKING ADVENTURES

Bob Inman

FALCONGUIDES

GUILFORD, CONNECTICUT

*I dedicate this book to people everywhere who express love
for their cities by going out and walking in them.*

FALCONGUIDES®

An imprint of The Rowman & Littlefield Publishing Group, Inc.
4501 Forbes Blvd., Ste. 200
Lanham, MD 20706
www.rowman.com

Falcon and FalconGuides are registered trademarks and Make Adventure Your Story is a
trademark of The Rowman & Littlefield Publishing Group, Inc.

Distributed by NATIONAL BOOK NETWORK

British Library Cataloguing-in-Publication Information available

Library of Congress Cataloging-in-Publication Data

Names: Inman, Robert, 1950– author.
Title: Urban hikes Southern California : a guide to the area's greatest urban hiking adventures /
    Bob Inman.
Description: Guilford, Connecticut : FalconGuides, [2021] | Includes index. | Summary: "Features
    easy-to-follow urban trails that allow hikers of all levels to discover the landmarks that shape
    the Golden State's cities and towns"— Provided by publisher.
Identifiers: LCCN 2020053175 (print) | LCCN 2020053176 (ebook) | ISBN 9781493052578
    (paperback) | ISBN 9781493052585 (epub)
Subjects: LCSH: Hiking—California, Southern—Guidebooks. | Trails—California, Southern—
    Guidebooks. | California, Southern—Guidebooks.
Classification: LCC GV199.42.C22 I57 2021 (print) | LCC GV199.42.C22 (ebook) | DDC
    796.5109794/9—dc23
LC record available at https://lccn.loc.gov/2020053175
LC ebook record available at https://lccn.loc.gov/2020053176

∞™ The paper used in this publication meets the minimum requirements of American National
Standard for Information Sciences—Permanence of Paper for Printed Library Materials, ANSI/
NISO Z39.48-1992.

CONTENTS

ACKNOWLEDGMENTS

I want to express my thanks to the several thousand people who have participated in the urban hikes that I have led. I endeavor to show them new places and provide some new information. Ultimately, what I learn from my walking friends is greater than what I teach them. Particular thanks go to three of these fellow walkers. Gabrielle Mandola and Mark Thomas filled me with ideas for the hikes in Whittier and Claremont. Scott Taylor gave me the blueprint for two of the San Diego hikes.

This project would have wandered off into oblivion without the support and patience of my wife, Barbara May.

LOS PADRES NATIONAL FOREST

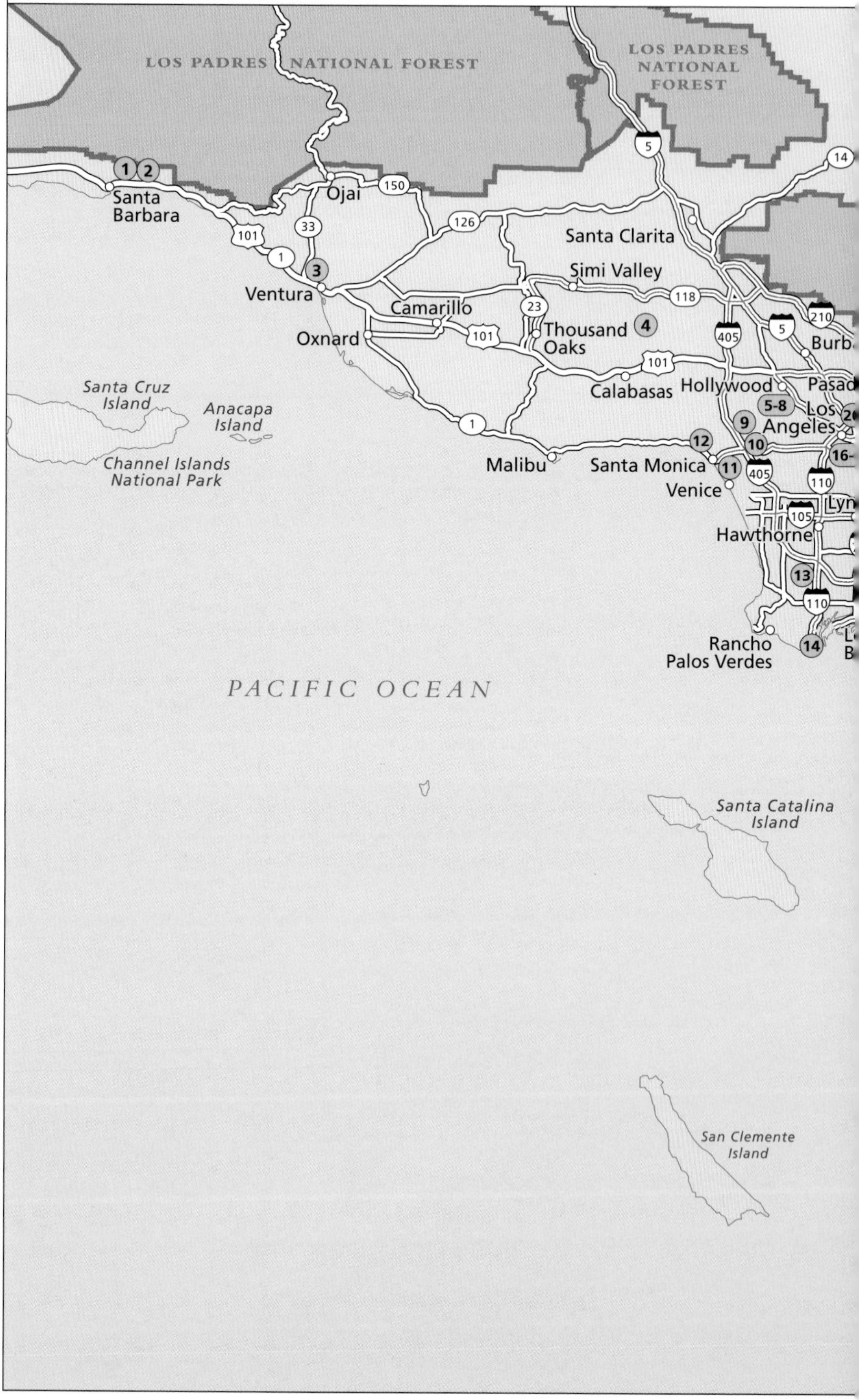

LOS PADRES NATIONAL FOREST

5

14

① ②
Santa
Barbara

Ojai

150

101

33

126

Santa Clarita

Simi Valley

Ventura

③

Camarillo

23

118

Thousand ④
Oaks

405

5

Burb

210

Oxnard

101

101

Calabasas

Hollywood

Pasad

5-8

Los

2

Santa Cruz
Island

Anacapa
Island

9

Angeles

12

10

16-

Channel Islands
National Park

1

Malibu

Santa Monica

11

405

Venice

110

Lyn

105

Hawthorne

13

110

PACIFIC OCEAN

Rancho
Palos Verdes

14

L
B

*Santa Catalina
Island*

*San Clemente
Island*

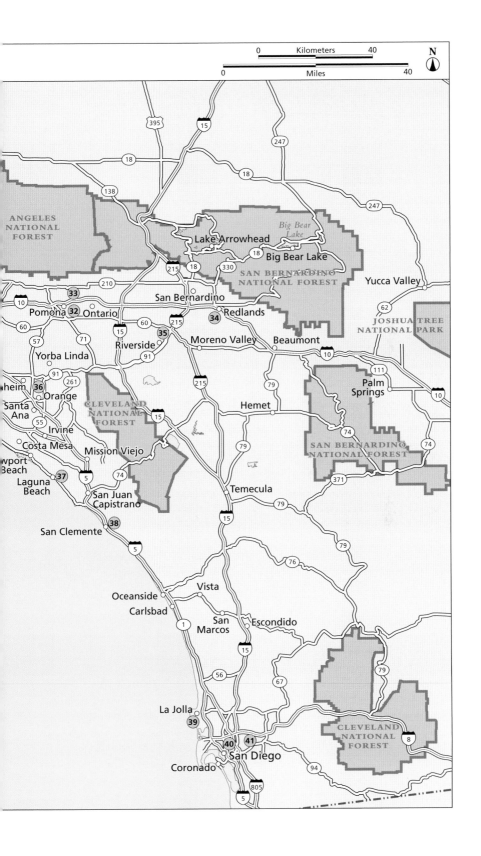

BEFORE YOU HIT THE TRAIL

Come hike with me in the urban areas of Southern California. The hike could be a serene stroll on the sidewalks of the historic district of Orange. It could be an up, down, and repeat traverse across three canyons in the Hollywood Hills. It might be a brewery crawl in Torrance or a taco crawl in Boyle Heights. We will enjoy some great views: the view from Mount Nebo in San Diego after a breathtaking stair climb, the view across Angels Gate and the seaport from the end of 40th Street in San Pedro, and the view out to Anacapa and Santa Cruz Islands from Ventura's Grant Park. There will be intimate, quiet places as well: Orcutt Ranch in West Hills, Cedar Grove in Griffith Park, and the Ennisbrook Trail in Montecito. Memorable moments are triggered by a countless variety of waypoints on these hikes: the wholesale floral mart in the Downtown markets, a historic campus graffiti wall in Claremont, flowers and lipstick smudges on Marilyn Monroe's crypt in Westwood, dinosaurs on a rooftop in Studio City. All these experiences and many more can be had on the hikes in this book.

Southern California lends itself perfectly to urban hiking. There is no question about its metropolitan nature. This book provides hiking suggestions for seven California counties. If just the urban parts of those counties were broken away from California, they would compose a new state second only to Texas in population. These are places with thriving cultures, enormous diversity, great physical beauty, and wonderful weather. These hikes are designed to provide a fun and invigorating experience as you discover the rich cultural landscape. Yes, there are locations within this urban region that are ugly, banal, and overloaded with social ills. If I were to design these routes to avoid any sight of these ills, your experience of hiking them would be both dishonest and very dull.

In 2010 I started organizing urban hikes as an avocation. I embraced my home city of Los Angeles and self-published two books about walking in it. My hikes are free, and I lead about twenty a year. More than 6,000 people have joined these events. The forty-one hikes in this book do not just come from a notion in my head. The methodology has been team tested.

WHAT ARE THESE HIKES LIKE?

The urban hikes in this guide showcase the diversity of both the physical and the built environment of Southern California. The greatest portion of this hiking is done in residential neighborhoods. This could suggest to some people an activity on monotonous blocks of boring tract houses. That is just not the case. Try hiking Rolando Village's catwalks, Pomona's Lincoln Park District, Pasadena's Bungalow Heaven, or Ventura's soulful Simpson Tract. These are residential streets that engage your curiosity and lighten your step. Other environments covered in these hikes range from municipal parks to

A great blue heron on the Los Angeles River

downtowns; from coastlines to sage-covered hillside; from cafe-lined blocks to college campuses; from tourist zones to woodland.

Very few of the 220 miles of these hikes are done on wide boulevards; most are done on sidewalks, but many miles occur on streets with no sidewalks, paved pathways, dirt trails, and public stairways. In the mountains or the woods, a narrow, crooked trail that goes up and down is always more interesting than a flat wide trail where you can see what's coming from half a mile away. That sentiment also applies to the streets and blocks selected for these hikes. Much of urban Southern California is not flat. All but eight of these forty-one hikes have at least a few hilly spots. The hikes that gain a moderate 300 to 500 feet do not undertake it all in one go; climbing is typically spread through the course of the activity.

I've discussed the physical experience of these hikes; what about the process? First and foremost, this is a book about recreation, about getting some exercise in an intriguing mix of environments. There is simple pleasure following a basic trail through mountain and meadow without thinking about which way to go except for the occasional junction. Using a guidebook to urban hikes inevitably means that you need to read the script and stay on it. Every street corner is a potential trail junction. The reason that a turn is instructed will typically not be apparent. Sometimes you are told to turn rather than go straight to guide you to a block that has restrooms or a place to get a cold drink. To use a mountaineering expression, sometimes turns are instructed so that a hiker does not "wall out," meaning to get into a situation where there are no signals or crosswalks to safely bridge a river of automobile traffic. Very often the turns in the text are simply to get you to see something that I think you will enjoy. My urban hikes will never be the shortest distance between two points.

Hikers take pleasure in mobility; they want to cover ground at a pace that provides some health benefit. A good urban hike should have a flow, and too many turns hinder that flow. While I lead you through turns to enjoy something special, I aim to provide a hike, not a tour. Good guidebooks for rustic trail hikes provide context about geology, flora, fauna, and other topics. An urban hikes guidebook is going to focus less on natural phenomena and more on people and their achievements. You should review the "What to See" segment of each hike description, but the routes should satisfy you even without the background stories that I provide.

USING THE TRAIL FINDER

The Trail Finder at the end of the front matter in this book is mostly self-explanatory, but Southern California urban hikes are a new concept and a few additional words might be helpful. The Trail Finder has five categories. A grid displays which of the forty-one hikes fall under those categories.

Best Photos: Any hike with great views fits this category. I also include hikes with a lot of color and visual personality under Best Photos.

Family Friendly: Most of the hikes get checked under this category. Ten of these hikes are between 3 and 4 miles; the others are longer. A hike that seems repetitive is going to raise more of a red flag to a healthy young person than a hike that is physically challenging. When an event with their elders starts feeling more like school than like fun, youthful resistance kicks in. Reflecting on my own years of parenting, I know that young people love to explore, they love surprises, and they often enjoy feeling personally invested in an activity. Let them be first up that stairway or trail that you can't see the end of. See if they want to take over reading the Miles and Directions and instructing their elders where the turns are. There are 9- and 10-year-olds who will ace all of the hikes in this book. For others, it will just be too much. More than half of these hikes could be completed while pushing a stroller, though you probably need to filter out the ones that mention stairs.

Water Features: Southern California is an arid environment, so this category is checked only where you encounter ocean views, reservoir lakes, channeled rivers and creeks, or cooling fountains.

Dog Friendly: Only two of the hikes have spots where your dog is unlawful and where it would be difficult to detour. Some reasons that other hikes are not listed as dog friendly are because of potential transit rides after point-to-point routes or because there are so many good interiors or free museums along the way that are good for the hiker and not so good for the dog. Those choices are up to you. The text for the Boyle Heights and Northeast Los Angeles Hilltops hikes cites other issues why I think your dog should stay home. On the whole, a healthy dog with a responsible human companion will just love these hikes.

Finding Solitude: What you will find is many places where the experience is similar to walking on a quiet country lane, even if there are houses around. Maybe you just need to go on a few of these hikes to see what I mean.

URBAN HIKES AS A RESOURCE FOR NEW RESIDENTS AND TRAVELERS

Southern California is a magnet for tourists. This is also a place that attracts enterprising people who move here to see how they like it. Urban hikes are perfect for both. I know that many are adventurous, inquisitive people who would like some other ideas about seeing the *real* Southern California. These hikes are for you. You will feel that you are getting a unique experience that you can tailor to your own interests and time frame, and the price is right.

Many people move here with an eagerness to learn about their new home. They've been here long enough to know there is something special happening in places like La Jolla, Laguna, Claremont, Highland Park, or Ventura. This book lays out ways to discover these places without a lot of trial and error or expense.

THE SOCIAL VALUE OF URBAN HIKES

Urban hikes will never be a substitute for that trip to Yosemite or Zion, but they don't have to be. Here are opportunities to get outside, exercise, have fun, and to do so with minimal expense or global impact. Are you conditioning for climbing Mount Whitney or hiking the John Muir Trail? Instead of driving back and forth to the Southern California national forests, try some vigorous up and down urban hikes someplace closer to home. Get out of the bubble of your immediate neighborhoods and get to know more about the city around you. Urban hikes will give you greater appreciation and understanding of places and people that you share your region with. That will benefit you and everyone around you.

WEATHER

Southern California has a Mediterranean climate that the world envies. The urban areas have no snow, and most of the annual rainfall is limited to January to March. Humidity is rarely an issue. Ninety-degree days generally cool to the 60s at night. Downsides are frequent triple-digit-temperature summer days inland and periods of unhealthful air quality.

Variables in temperature and cloud cover in Southern California are the very nature of this topography with a cool ocean on one side, a savanna or desert environment on the other, and unbroken bands of mountains 5,000 to 10,000 feet high in between. Quick forecasts always boil the expected daytime temperatures down to three groups: coastal, metropolitan, and inland valley, where each bracket is a 10-degree change. These are projections void of nuance, but average summertime highs of 70s on the coast, 80s in the city, and 90s in the inland valleys is a good rule of thumb. Add 10 degrees to each bracket during a heat wave. There are always exceptions: days when everywhere inland is perfect and the coast is uncomfortably foggy, or summer days when an invigorating Santa Ana wind leaves an inland valley hot but crystal clear.

The hike goes through a dreamy double row of palm trees in Pomona.

FLORA AND FAUNA

Fauna? You may not frequently see coyotes, but they are everywhere. Your urban hike on the edge of the undeveloped hills might be enhanced by deer sightings. Many mammals inhabit the urban areas but only appear at night. Bears do wander down into our hiking areas of Monrovia and Altadena, but that is very infrequent. And of course, when you are in Griffith Park you are in the home of our favorite mountain lion, P-22. The urban areas of Southern California have incredible biodiversity. Large swaths of land have never been developed because of their terrain. The temperate climate combines with a wide variety of both native and non-native vegetation to make Southern California an accommodating home to many animal species. Los Angeles County has over 500 recorded species of birds; no county in the United States has more.

Even if it is an invented landscape, the flora of Southern California is a major source of pleasure on an urban hike. Trees include the classics, western sycamore and coast live oak that belong here, Peruvian peppers and eucalyptus that do not. Mexican fan palm trees are iconic, and useless when a hiker needs shade. Ficus trees are great for shade, but their roots can make sidewalks unusable. In Southern California, there is always vegetation with color. The indigo-colored flowers of the South American jacaranda will dress entire neighborhoods in late spring. Peak summer heat brings the color of oleander, bougainvillea, and crape myrtle. Hiking here is fragrant with the scent of sage, citrus, fig, and star jasmine.

STAYING SAFE

Urban hiking is generally injury free. One of the attractions of hiking in the city is that you are not alone in a remote location with no cellular service. But there are a few things you need to watch out for. Your biggest worry is a fall on a hard surface that is caused by a bad sidewalk, pothole, or uneven curb or stairway step. Watch out for automobiles and their distracted drivers, particularly at stop signs and on empty roads where cars seem to come out of nowhere. People will invariably ask if the streets are "safe" to walk in with a reference to dangers from other people. I would tell you that most of the worry in this department is purely anecdotal and urban legend. I have walked thousands of miles in the past dozen years by myself in the urban areas of Southern California and I have never had an issue. But my situation might not be your situation. I want you to be comfortable and to have a good time. People with elevated urban anxieties should try some of the hikes in the other six sections before some of the hikes in Metro Los Angeles. As with anywhere, be aware of your surroundings.

RULES OF THE URBAN TRAIL

Walking represents one of our most pure forms of personal freedom. I hesitate to constrain your activity to a list of rules, but there are a few things to think about. When you do these hikes, you leave your neighborhood to hike in someone else's. Be a good guest. Don't trespass. Don't pick fruit off their trees. Control your dog, and give plenty of space to that local dog walker and dog who are not used to strangers. Keep voices down and think about possible misunderstandings before you point your camera at something. Give drivers space to pass you on narrow roads and get over to the side quickly if a car approaches while you are hiking in the roadway. People will typically be proud that they live in these cool neighborhoods and happy that you are passing through. Don't give them reasons not to be.

WHAT TO BRING ON AN URBAN HIKE

Carry enough water to last you at least an hour. The text will advise if you should carry a snack or rely on places that you pass. The forecast and time of day will dictate if you need a backup layer for warmth.

Sun is a major concern, so think about a hat, sunscreen, and sunglasses. Some people like to use an ultralight umbrella as a parasol. Hand sanitizer may prove to be useful. Besides your phone/camera, a backup battery for phone and camera is essential after 3 or 4 hours. Think about your getaway plan if you need to leave the hike. Having a ride-sharing app loaded on your device as well as a transit card with value preloaded are both really good ideas.

Everything comes down to your feet. Expensive padded socks are a great investment. Your shoes should be solid with usable tread. You won't be boulder hopping or slogging through bogs. You will be walking on surface that is much harder than a rustic trail. Do a few of the longer hikes in this book and you will understand the value of shoes that are breathable and lightweight but heavily padded.

HOW TO USE THIS GUIDE

The hikes are presented in an easy-to-read format with at-a-glance information at the start. Each hike description contains the following information:

Hike number and name: The hike number is also shown on the location map to help you visualize the general location of the hike.

Overview: Each hike is introduced with a general description, including some reasons you should do it.

Start: Each hike begins at a location that everyday maps will identify as well as a physical street address that your devices will be able to navigate to.

Elevation gain: The total number of feet to be ascended on this activity is provided as measured by the Gaia GPS mobile app and cross-checked by the AllTrails mobile app.

Distance: This is the total distance of the hike in miles. Distances were carefully measured using a Garmin GPS handheld device. The structure of the hike is listed after the distance. The hikes in this guide will be a nonrepeating loop; a lollipop, where the end briefly overlaps the beginning; or a point-to-point, where the end point is not the same as the start point.

Hiking time: This is a bracket of how much time the hike might consume. Someone who walks at an average pace and spends only a moderate amount of time doing additional exploring of the features along the way will finish their hike in the middle of this bracket.

Difficulty: All the hikes are rated as easy, moderate, or difficult. This is a subjective rating, but in general easy hikes can be done by nearly anyone and take less than 3 hours. Moderate hikes are very doable but will take a bit longer. They are more than 4.5 miles in length or climb more than 500 feet. Difficult hikes might become an ordeal for some hikers and are more than 7.0 miles in length or climb more than 750 feet.

Best season: All the hikes in this book can physically be undertaken on any day of the year. For some hikes, historical averages predict excessive heat or poor air quality during some months. Those months are excluded, and the rest of the year is expressed as best season.

Best days and times: This section is provided for some of the hikes where an important feature is not open all day, every day. This is also where you are alerted that a key passage point closes at a certain hour. Overall recommendations for these hikes assume that you will be hiking during daytime hours, finishing no later than 8 p.m. on summer nights.

Trail surface: This is what to plan for: sidewalks, pavement without sidewalks, paved path, dirt, sand, stairs. Most of the hikes will take place on more than one of these surfaces.

Other trail users: Since our hikes take place on public right-of-way in populated areas, assume that you will be sharing the "trail" during the hike. This list gives you a heads-up for what to watch for and what level of patience might be required.

Restroom availability: This indicates at what mileage points you can expect to find an accessible public restroom. At some of these locations, you are expected to make a nominal purchase.

Canine compatibility: This section tells you if bringing your dog(s) will be compatible with the nature of the hike. If a hike is dog friendly, keeping your pet on a leash will always be required.

Contact: On several of the hikes, a phone number is provided that will be useful for status updates or for making reservations at a suggested feature.

Parking status: This briefly summarizes what sort of parking will be available at or near the start point and if you will have to pay for it.

Rail transit accessibility: Eighteen of these hikes can be easily reached by using public rail transit, and this section identifies the agency, line, and station and the distance to the route. "N/A" indicates that there is no viable rail transit option. Each of these hikes can be reached by a public transit bus, but that topic is too complicated to cover in this guidebook.

Trailhead GPS: The coordinates are provided for where you will begin the hike.

Finding the trailhead: These are generic driving directions from well-known highways. In an urban environment, hikers will likely use their devices to chart their approach to the trailhead, customized for where they are coming from and for the current traffic conditions.

What to See: This section includes background on the hike or perhaps a prevailing theme. Information is also provided about features that are certain to catch your attention. Since the path of an urban hike has an infinite number of blocks to choose from, here is where the author explains why you have been sent this particular way.

Miles and Directions: This is a listing of the turns that need to be made to stay on the route matched to the distance, in miles and tenths, measured from the start of the hike. In many cases, a few turns are bunched together before the next elapsed mileage figure is given. Important landmarks and transition points are also listed with elapsed mileage from the start of the hike. If you wander off route to explore something, to get food or beverage, or to locate a restroom, that will add to the elapsed mileage figure provided. You should be able to follow the route by referring to this section; however, Miles and Directions are not a substitute for thoroughly reading the What to See narrative before taking the trip.

TRAIL FINDER

	BEST PHOTOS	FAMILY FRIENDLY	WATER FEATURES	DOG FRIENDLY	FINDING SOLITUDE
01 Santa Barbara	•	•	•	•	•
02 Montecito		•	•	•	•
03 Ventura	•	•	•	•	•
04 West Hills	•	•	•	•	
05 Studio City	•	•	•	•	
06 Universal City to Hollywood	•	•	•		
07 Three Hollywood Hills Canyons	•	•	•	•	
08 Whitley and Hollywood Heights	•	•	•	•	
09 Westwood and UCLA	•	•	•	•	
10 Cheviot Hills–Rancho Park	•	•			
11 Venice	•	•	•	•	•
12 Santa Monica Canyons	•	•	•	•	•
13 Torrance	•				
14 San Pedro	•	•	•	•	•
15 Long Beach	•	•	•	•	•
16 West Adams	•	•			
17 University Park and USC	•				
18 Downtown Markets	•				
19 Little Tokyo–Bunker Hill	•	•	•		
20 Boyle Heights	•				
21 Elysian Park–Elysian Heights	•	•	•	•	
22 Silver Lake	•	•	•	•	•
23 Griffith Park–Los Feliz	•	•	•	•	
24 Northeast Los Angeles Hilltops	•	•	•		
25 Highland Park	•	•			

	BEST PHOTOS	FAMILY FRIENDLY	WATER FEATURES	DOG FRIENDLY	FINDING SOLITUDE
26 Eagle Rock	●	●	●	●	
27 Pasadena–Arroyo Seco	●	●	●	●	
28 Pasadena–Oak Knoll	●	●			
29 Altadena	●	●	●	●	
30 Monrovia	●	●	●		
31 Whittier	●	●			
32 Pomona	●	●			
33 Claremont	●	●	●	●	
34 Redlands	●	●			
35 Riverside	●	●	●	●	
36 City of Orange	●	●			
37 Laguna Beach	●	●	●	●	●
38 San Clemente	●	●	●	●	●
39 La Jolla	●	●	●	●	●
40 Bankers Hill–Balboa Park	●	●	●	●	
41 Rolando Village–La Mesa	●	●	●		

MAP LEGEND

Municipal

🛡️5	Interstate Highway
101	US Highway
33	State Road
━━━━	County/Forest/Local Road
= = = =	Unpaved Road
────────	Pedestrian Road/Paved Trail
‑‑‑‑‑‑‑	Trail
├───┼───┤	Railroad

Featured Routes

═══════	Featured Road
───────	Featured Pedestrian Road/ Paved Trail
•‑‑‑‑‑‑	Featured Trail

Water Features

◯	Lake/Body of Water
∴∴∴	Beach
∿	River/Creek

Symbols

⌣	Bridge
†	Cemetery
○	City/Town
▬	Dam
•━•	Gate
🗼	Lighthouse
▭	Lodging
▲	Mountain/Peak
🅿	Parking
⛩	Picnic Area
■	Point of Interest
🍴	Restaurant
🚻	Restrooms
🧗	Scenic View
▥	Steps
🗼	Tower
①	Trailhead

Land Management

▬	National Park/Forest
▲	State/City Park
⬚	Nature Preserve

SANTA BARBARA AND VENTURA COUNTIES

Santa Barbara and Ventura Counties compose the northwest corner of the urban area that this guidebook covers. Beyond Santa Barbara, widespread urban concentration does not begin again until the Salinas–Monterey area, 200 miles north.

The sea and the mountains define this subregion, and you are aware of one or both every moment that you hike here. The Santa Barbara Channel is the northern part of the curved Pacific Ocean coastline of Southern California. When they are not shrouded by fog, feast on the view of tiny and low Anacapa and broad and mountainous Santa Cruz, two of the northern islands of the Channel Islands archipelago. Compared to the other regional sections in this guidebook, the urban zone is very narrow here before it gives way to the Santa Ynez Mountains. Very near to the hiking areas in this section are some of the richest fields and orchards of strawberries, lemons, avocados, and flowers in the United States.

The weather in this area always seems perfect. Directions are sometimes counterintuitive, because this region includes the longest segment of the Pacific coastline in the

Anacapa and Santa Cruz Islands come into view over the Santa Barbara Channel from Brakey Road on the Ventura hike.

Fog conceals Santa Cruz Island and the Santa Barbara Channel looking from Ferro Drive on the Ventura hike.

continental United States that runs east to west rather than south to north. You are more aware here of the era when Southern California was owned by Spain than in other sections. Only two of the hikes in this book include the historic Spanish missions, and both are in this section. Nowhere else in Southern California stayed as faithful as Santa Barbara to the Spanish Laws of the Indies that prescribed that towns in the New World lay out their streets diagonally to cardinal north and south. Historic appreciation is also heightened in this section for the presence of the indigenous Chumash people who maintained a large population here circulating from island to floodplain to mountain. Favorite hike in this section? The Santa Barbara hike is the best for mixing the cultural landscape, old and new, with a variety of landscapes and views, from the flats to the steep hills.

1 **SANTA BARBARA**

Santa Barbara is the American Riviera. It's a perfect scenario: a lovely seacoast, then a narrow band of flat streets filled with parks and landmark buildings, then steep residential hillsides with great views, then a raw wilderness with 3,500-foot ridgetops. This urban hike stays inland from the beach and down from the mountain slopes, but it visits the best that is in between.

Start: Santa Barbara Amtrak Station, 209 State St., Santa Barbara 93101
Elevation gain: 750 feet
Distance: 7.8-mile loop
Hiking time: 3.5 to 4.5 hours
Difficulty: Difficult
Best season: Year-round
Trail surface: Sidewalks, pavement without sidewalks, dirt, stairs
Other trail users: Tourists, shoppers, and diners
Restroom availability: Miles 0.4, 1.9, 3.0, 6.9

Canine compatibility: Dogs must remain on leash.
Contact: Mission Santa Barbara, (805) 682-4149
Parking status: Pay lot at transit station
Rail transit accessibility: Amtrak Pacific Surfliner, Santa Barbara station is the start point.
Trailhead GPS: N34° 24.83′ W119° 41.50′

FINDING THE TRAILHEAD

Take Highway 101 north. Take exit 96B for Garden Street. Turn left onto Garden Street. Turn right onto Yanonali Street. The station entrance is on the west side of State Street where it meets Yanonali Street.

WHAT TO SEE

Begin this clockwise loop on State Street. Downtown Santa Barbara is jam-packed with Spanish-style buildings ranging from well-restored pre-1850 artifacts to faithful replicants from the 1920 to 1935 era. After a half-mile, the hike examines the interior of a few city blocks. The grassy oval of Plaza de la Guerra has figured strongly in the town's social history. Here in the early 1800s, you might have encountered a pre–American era bullfight or fiesta. Across the street, the low U-shaped Casa de la Guerra was home to an important local family of that era. The retail alleys of "Street in Spain" and El Paseo are 1920s creations themed to the historical precedents. The Presidio was founded in 1782 as the last of four military outposts built by the Spanish along the coast of Alta California.

Santa Barbara decided that it would not be an industrial town, and the late 1800s saw the inception of a movement to maintain a strong visual and cultural connection with its Spanish heritage. Santa Barbara would be a "Santa Fe on the Pacific." That sentiment was in full flourish when the 1925 Santa Barbara earthquake struck. Most of a 36-block downtown area suffered heavy damage, and a new ordinance restricted rebuilding to conform to the Spanish milieu. The most notable post-earthquake achievement is the amazing county courthouse building. Completed in 1929 as designed by architect William Mooser, it has been referred to as both the finest example of the Spanish Colonial

"Street in Spain"
commercial alley from the 1920s

Revival style and as the most extraordinary public building in the country. Wander through it a bit and climb the steps for the rooftop view.

After the courthouse comes the Upper East neighborhood. Garden Street displays a catalog of excellent domestic architecture, including some houses from a couple of decades before the Spanish style became all the rage. 1624 Garden is an interesting bungalow court with an arched screen; El Nido at 1900 is an example of a Victorian-era mansion that was made Spanish to keep up with the trends; 2010–2050 is Crocker Row, a set of five 1890s homes in the Mission Revival style; 232 Los Olivos at the southwest corner of Garden is a 1922 example of the work of George Washington Smith, Santa Barbara's preeminent Andalusian Spanish–style architect.

Mission Santa Barbara comes at 3.0 miles. Founded in 1786, there were three chapels before this one built after an 1812 earthquake ruined what came before. The Classical facade surprises many viewers; among his possessions from Spain, the mission's Pastor Ripoll had an illustrated treatise on architecture written by the Roman architect Vitruvius. Beyond the rose garden, Plaza Rubio is a lovely string of 1920s Spanish Revival homes that frame the open space. One legend says that this way through these homes is a trace from an 18th-century footpath that connected the mission to the Presidio.

The route climbs into the Riviera neighborhood via a passage with 116 steps. Alameda Padre Serra was once the path of a streetcar line that serviced State Normal School. Pass below what remains of that Mediterranean-style campus walking above Lasuen Road. This was the precursor to UCSB. The Riviera was laid out for luxury living and the quiet streets were planted with eucalyptus, acacia, and oak. The views are sensational. Before Dover Road, watch on the left side of Paterna for an indescribable collection of frog figures. The Mission Steps and the landscaping around them are the crowning achievement of your hike.

Follow the well-named Olive Street for a mile in lower east side Santa Barbara. The corner of Olive and Cota Streets comes at mile 6.8 and the legendary La Super-Rica Taqueria is just 0.4 mile to the left; read the reviews. If you are just looking for a public restroom, head 1 block to the left to Ortega Park. At Haley Street, enter an area with craft breweries and cafes. The final 0.4 mile of the hike along Yanonali Street is the heart of the Funk Zone, an eclectic cluster of wine tasting rooms, galleries, shops, and restaurants.

MILES AND DIRECTIONS

0.0 START at Santa Barbara Amtrak station where the platform meets State Street. Turn left to walk away from the waterfront. After Ortega Street, turn right into a pedestrian way just after 718 State St.

0.6 Turn left into Plaza de la Guerra. Walk on pavement or grass. Cross De La Guerra Street in the crosswalk. Proceed straight from the crosswalk into a pedestrian way signed as "Street in Spain." Turn right into the arcaded pedestrian mall of El Paseo. This leads out to 813 Anacapa St. Turn left on Anacapa.

0.8 Turn right on Cañon Perdido Street. Turn left on Santa Barbara Street. Turn left on Figueroa Street. Turn right on Anacapa Street.

1.3 Santa Barbara County Courthouse. Enter through the arch at the base of the clock tower. Explore the gardens, the halls, and climb the 144 steps to the tower.

1.5 Leave the courthouse the way that you came in. Turn right on Anacapa Street.

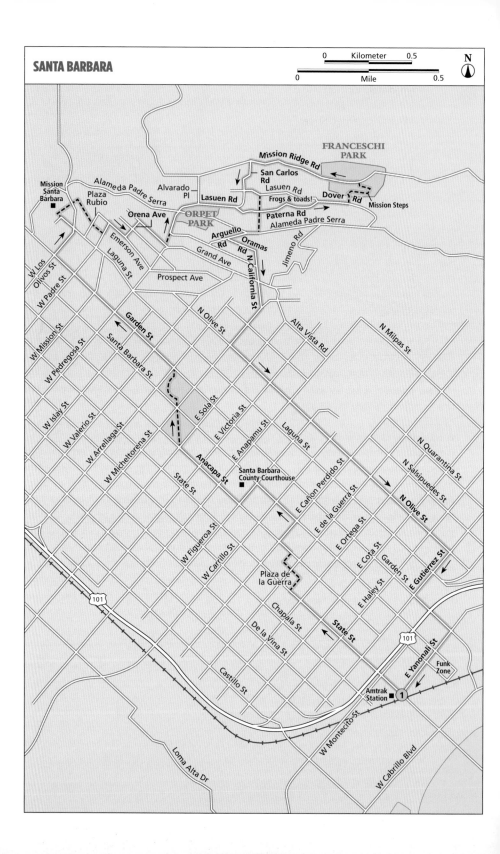

SANTA BARBARA

FRANCESCHI PARK

Mission Ridge Rd

San Carlos Rd

Lasuen Rd

Alvarado Pl

Lasuen Rd

Frogs & toads!

Dover Rd

Mission Steps

Mission Santa Barbara

Alameda Padre Serra

Plaza Rubio

Orena Ave

ORPET PARK

Paterna Rd

Alameda Padre Serra

Emerson Ave

Laguna St

Arguello Rd

Oramas Rd

N California St

Jimeno Rd

W Los Olivos St

W Padre St

Grand Ave

Prospect Ave

Garden St

N Olive St

Alta Vista Rd

N Milpas St

W Mission St

Santa Barbara St

W Pedregosa St

W Islay St

W Valerio St

W Arrellaga St

E Sola St

E Victoria St

E Anapamu St

Laguna St

N Quarantina St

W Micheltorena St

Anacapa St

Santa Barbara County Courthouse

E Cañon Perdido St

N Salsipuedes St

N Olive St

State St

W Figueroa St

W Carrillo St

E de la Guerra St

E Ortega St

E Cota St

Garden St

E Gutierrez St

Plaza de la Guerra

E Haley St

Chapala St

De la Vina St

State St

101

Castillo St

E Yanonali St

Funk Zone

Amtrak Station

1

Loma Alta Dr

W Montecito St

W Cabrillo Blvd

101

0   Kilometer   0.5

0   Mile   0.5

N

1.7 Enter Alameda Park on the right at the corner of Anacapa and Sola Streets. Walk diagonally to the corner of Santa Barbara and Micheltorena Streets. There are restrooms on the east corner. Cross to the north corner and turn right on Micheltorena. Immediately turn left into a park path of the Keck Park gardens. Find your way on paths to the diagonal corner of the gardens at Arrellaga and Garden Streets.

2.1 Turn left on Garden Street.

2.7 Turn right on Los Olivos Street. Turn left on Laguna Street.

3.0 Mission Santa Barbara. Leaving the mission, walk past the front door of the sanctuary and turn left on Los Olivos. Take the crosswalk to the northeast side of Los Olivos and then turn right. Walk across the grassy park, aiming for the center of the rose garden at the southeast corner. Pass a fountain to enter Plaza Rubio. Turn into a semi-secret public path between the houses at 414 and 420 Plaza Rubio. Turn left where it ends at Padre Street.

3.3 Turn right on Emerson Avenue. Turn left on Orena Avenue. Turn right on Grand Avenue.

3.6 Turn left up a pedestrian stairway-path that begins at the utility pole across from where Pedregosa Street intersects Grand Avenue. After this, cross the street and veer left to enter a long stair-sidewalk that climbs to the left of Pedregosa Street.

3.8 Turn right from the stair-sidewalk onto Alameda Padre Serra. Walk to the corner and turn left on Lasuen Road, which is a continuation of Pedregosa. Locate the paved path on the left side of Lasuen. This path ends at Alvarado Place. Continue on Lasuen where there is no sidewalk.

4.0 Veer right by an ornamental light post onto Paterna Road.

4.3 Frogs and toads assembly on the left side of Paterna Road.

4.4 Turn right on Dover Road.

4.5 Turn left up the Mission Steps, which begin next to a speed limit sign. Climb these 150 or so steps in several zigzags to Mission Ridge Road. There are several spur paths. When in doubt, keep going up.

4.7 Turn left on the unsigned street, which is Mission Ridge Road.

5.0 Turn left on San Carlos Road. This curves right to briefly turn into Mira Vista Avenue. Turn left to regain San Carlos Road.

5.2 Turn left on Lasuen Road. Pass a single house on the right then watch for several stone steps from Lasuen that indicate the start of a pedestrian path going downhill from the utility pole. Follow to the next street (Paterna Road) and find the continuation of the pedestrian path going downhill. Just before the next street, the path meets an elevated sidewalk. Turn right, intersect Alameda Padre Serra, and then veer left on Arguello Road.

5.5 Turn sharp left on Oramas Road. Turn right on California Street.

5.8 Turn right on Micheltorena Street.

5.9 Turn left on Olive Street.

7.1 Turn right on Gutierrez Street.

7.3 Turn left on Garden Street.

7.5 Turn right on Yanonali Street.

7.6 Funk Zone.

7.8 End of hike at Santa Barbara Amtrak station.

2 MONTECITO

This green and peaceful hike blurs the lines between an "urban hike" and something else. The route walks on beach sand and nature trails. Even the street walking often gives a feeling of walking on a country road. Throw in an optional stop in an expensive beach resort hotel and you get an idea of how varied an urban hike can be.

Start: Montecito Country Mart, 1028 Coast Village Rd., Santa Barbara 93108
Elevation gain: 400 feet
Distance: 8.1-mile lollipop
Hiking time: 3.5 to 5 hours
Difficulty: Difficult
Best season: January–December
Trail surface: Sidewalks, pavement without sidewalks, dirt, sand, stairs
Other trail users: Shoppers and diners

Restroom availability: Miles 2.2 (no dogs), 5.4
Canine compatibility: Dogs must remain on leash.
Parking status: Free curb parking on the street outside Montecito Country Mart
Rail transit accessibility: N/A
Trailhead GPS: N34° 25.36' W119° 39.08'

FINDING THE TRAILHEAD

From Highway 101 northbound, take exit 94B for Hermosillo Road. Turn left on Coast Village Road. Turn right on Hot Springs Road.

WHAT TO SEE

Check the tides: If the tide will be higher than 2.5 feet, your feet and lower legs will get wet at the 1.0-mile mark. This lollipop hike with a counterclockwise loop begins with a pleasant pedestrian tunnel and quiet lane walk to Butterfly Beach and the Biltmore. When the Santa Barbara Biltmore opened in 1927, the hotel personified Santa Barbara as a wealthy resort destination. The 1937 Moderne-style Coral Casino has a feature that resembles an octagonal lighthouse.

On the beach, the hike goes around a point to reach Hammond's Beach, a noted surfing spot. The open space with the monument is Shalawa Meadow. This may have been a burial site for Chumash people, who have been active in this coastal area for at least 13,000 years.

The Miramar hotel has a 130-year history of guest accommodation. By 1910, they had already expanded to twenty-nine guest cottages. Rebuilt and reopened in 2019, the property has the historical oddity that it is sliced by railroad tracks and frequent trains. They do have several daytime restaurants where the dress code is described as "resort casual." If you are hiking with a dog, you'll have to skip this spot.

The quiet streets give way to the Ennisbrook Trail, which runs south to north within the San Ysidro Creek Preserve. There are a couple of quaint rock bridges over the sometimes-flowing creek, a healthy oak woodland, and displays of yellow and orange nasturtiums. Sitting on the enchanting split-log Rebecca Riskin bench, it is hard to imagine that less than 1,000 feet due west of here is Oprah Winfrey's palatial home on a 40-acre estate. Leaving the Ennisbrook Trail, East Valley Lane displays evidence of the horrific

Path to Eucalyptus Lane
from Montecito Creek

January 2018 mudflow. Two dozen people were killed, and more than one hundred homes were destroyed when San Ysidro Creek was inundated by a flood through an area that had recently suffered a wildfire.

The route spends as little time as possible on walker-unfriendly East Valley Road. Moore and El Bosque Roads provide immediate relief with quiet lanes under canopies of oak. For the architecture scholar, Montecito promises much but delivers little to the passerby. Many sublime structures from some of California's best architects are hidden behind lush vegetation or are too far back on a lot to be seen.

Montecito Village Shopping Center at 5.4 miles has the only facilities on this hike besides the Miramar resort. There is a market/deli, some sit-down eateries, and a public library in this vicinity. Some important architecture that can be appreciated from the road occurs at the 7-mile mark on Mesa and Middle Roads. 1250 Mesa, 1200 Mesa, and 240 Middle are all works built between 1916 and 1925 and designed by George Washington Smith. Smith perfected a picturesque image that Santa Barbara thoroughly adopted. Tile roofs, courtyards, and geometric white stucco with little or no ornamentation were the Andalusian ideal that he worked to re-create.

MILES AND DIRECTIONS

0.0   START at Montecito Country Mart. From the restrooms in the outdoor plaza, exit passing to the right of Union Bank. Turn left on Coast Village Road.

0.3   Turn right by the Chevron, where it reads "Butterfly Lane" to the left and "Coast Village Circle" to the right. Pass the Chevron and take the pedestrian underpass of the highway with signs pointing for the beach. From the underpass, cross the railroad tracks carefully and proceed down Butterfly Lane.

0.6   Turn left on Channel Lane. Ignore (for now) steps or paths for the beach, and walk on the right side of the street.

0.9   Pivot right down a ramp to the beach that begins next to the Coral Casino Beach and Cabana Club, recognizable by its Art Deco lantern. At the bottom of the ramp, pivot left and begin walking on the sand of Hammonds Beach heading east.

1.4   Shalawa Meadow. Look at the monument then return to the beach and continue east.

1.5   Leave the beach at Montecito Creek. Turn left to pass a log seat with a memorial plaque and walk to the left of the channel. Turn right over a footbridge. Enter a path that begins to the right of the residential gateway with the two lampposts. The path occupies a narrow corridor between two fence lines.

1.8   Turn left as the path ends at Eucalyptus Lane. Cross the train tracks. Turn right on Jameson Lane.

2.1   Rosewood Miramar Beach hotel. Return to junction of Jameson and Eucalyptus Lanes.

2.3   Turn right on Eucalyptus Lane and pass over the highway. The street name is now San Ysidro Road. Turn right on San Leandro Lane. As Hixon Road intersects from the right, go straight, now on Jacaranda Lane.

2.7   Turn left on Pomar Lane. Turn right to regain San Leandro Lane. After passing private Tiburon Bay Lane on the right, watch on the left for a small parking area and a trail sign.

3.0   Leave San Leandro Lane for the Ennisbrook Open Space Trail. Pass an old green utility building and follow the obvious trail which immediately goes to the right over a stone bridge. Across the bridge, there is a T trail junction. Take the trail going up

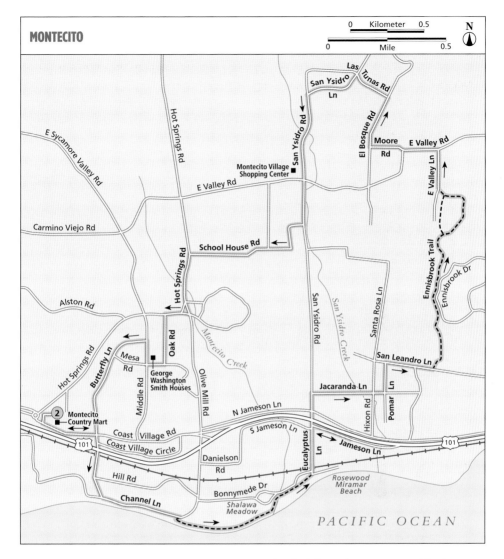

0   Kilometer   0.5

0   Mile   0.5

N

the creek on the left. At mile 3.3, the route briefly follows the pavement of Ennisbrook Drive. As the paved street curves right, it will be clear where the dirt trail departs to the left. At mile 3.5, pass over a second stone footbridge.

3.7 Trail junction at wooden bench. The full Ennisbrook Trail is a lollipop in shape, and up to here the route has followed up the "stick" of the lollipop. Now turn right at the more obvious trail sign to begin going counterclockwise around the top of the lollipop. You will be leaving Ennisbrook Trail before circling back to the "stick."

4.0 Exit the trail to the first paved road encountered in the last 0.5 mile. The location should be apparent even if it is not signed. This is East Valley Lane. Turn right from the trail to take it.

4.2 Turn left on East Valley Road. Walk on the left side facing traffic, as the road is sometimes busy and the space for walking off pavement is narrow. This only lasts 800 feet. East Valley Road curves left at Moore Road. Cross to the other side where

Shalawa Meadow monument at Hammond's Beach

you are visible to traffic approaching on either side of the curve. Continue straight on Moore Road.

4.5 Turn right on El Bosque Road. Turn left on Las Tunas Road. Turn left on San Ysidro Lane.

5.1 Turn left on San Ysidro Road.

5.4 Montecito Village Shopping Center. Most of the amenities are to the right, including the village grocery, which is beyond the Wells Fargo Bank. Restrooms are also available at the library (open Tues–Sat) across from the gas station. Leave this area by continuing south on the right side of San Ysidro Road.

5.8 Turn right on School House Road.

6.4 Turn left on Hot Springs Road. Walk on the left side of the road, pass the Casa Dorinda residential complex, and come to a stop sign. Cross twice to reach the southwest corner, and turn right to stay on Hot Springs Road.

6.8 Turn left on Oak Road.

7.0 George Washington Smith houses. Turn right on Mesa Road. Turn right on Middle Road.

7.3 Turn left on Butterfly Lane.

7.8 Turn right on Coast Village Road. Turn right into the parking lot across from Union Bank.

8.1 Hike ends at Montecito Country Mart.

3 VENTURA

Laid-back Ventura has a sensational town center that many beach-goers never even see. Here is a grid of streets full of great buildings, including some from the early 19th century. You'll find parks and squares, impressive trees, iconic buildings, and a casual vibe. A highlight is a loop in the hilly park behind downtown with views of the coastline and the Channel Islands.

Start: Court of Appeal Building, 200 E Santa Clara St., Ventura 93001
Elevation gain: 450 feet
Distance: 5.1-mile loop
Hiking time: 2.5 to 3 hours
Difficulty: Moderate
Best season: January–December
Trail surface: Sidewalks, pavement without sidewalks, paved path, dirt
Other trail users: Tourists, shoppers, and diners

Restroom availability: Miles 1.1, 3.5
Canine compatibility: Dogs must remain on leash.
Parking status: Paid lot parking
Rail transit accessibility: Amtrak Pacific Surfliner, Ventura Station; walk 0.3 mile to trailhead on Figueroa Street.
Trailhead GPS: N34° 16.77' W119° 17.87'

FINDING THE TRAILHEAD

From Highway 101 northbound, take exit 70A for California Street. Turn right onto California Street. Turn left on Santa Clara Street. Pass Palm Street, and there is a municipal parking lot on the right.

WHAT TO SEE

The Court of Appeal building where this counterclockwise loop hike begins has no significance; it is just a good landmark. Across Figueroa Street, note how some 19th-century houses have been recycled for use as offices. In the pedestrian mall there is a 50-foot-wide acrylic mural commemorating China Alley. A flourishing Chinese settlement was here in the 1880s made up of merchants, laborers, and families. The present mission church was built in 1809 and restored after an earthquake in 1816. The mission complex, including a garden, is open daily; enter from the gift shop to the right of the church. You turn right in front of the mission and pass under two immense Norfolk pines. There is a story that a sea captain planted them to serve as future ship masts, but he never returned to claim them. When the Spanish first arrived by land to this vicinity in 1769, a scribe reported the presence of "a regular town, the most populous and best laid-out of all that we had seen on the journey." The Chumash people created a village here as early as AD 1000. With a situation at the mouth of two free-flowing rivers, this was a prime location for prehistoric settlement.

Three blocks of Main Street have some wonderful old buildings as well as shops, bars, and eateries. Look at the 1879 Franz House a few feet up Oak Street. This Italianate style was all the rage in American domestic architecture before tastes turned to Queen Anne. Also check out the 1927 El Jardin courtyard at 461 Main, designed as one of the earliest outdoor malls in Southern California. Turning the corner to California Street, a

Eucalyptus tree
on Ferro Drive

plaque at the doorway of 21 S. notes the history here of author Erle Stanley Gardner, the creator of the Perry Mason books. Across the street, Lure Fish House is highly regarded.

Turn left on Santa Clara Street and the eye is immediately caught by the huge Moreton Bay fig tree, planted almost 150 years ago. Across from the south end of Plaza Park is the National Register–listed Mitchell block, a cluster of eight splendid homes built between 1886 and 1905. The route goes around the block with the park in the center. Make sure to look inside the post office at the corner of Fir and Santa Clara. In the great tradition of New Deal–era post office murals, these are some of the best anywhere, created by artist Gordon Grant in 1936. Pass near two movie theaters: the Spanish Colonial Revival Ventura Theatre from 1928 and the Century Downtown, where Art Deco wave imagery suggests that it is older than its 1998 date. Limon y Sal restaurant occupies the sensational brick and tile 1928 Groene Building. Consider a pit stop in Starbucks before starting over the hill, because this is the last chance for an hour or so. Ventura's famous hilltop Beaux-Arts city hall was designed in 1912 by architect Albert C. Martin.

The walking on a narrow two-lane road going up the south side into Grant Park and the Serra Cross and coming back down the west side will be the best part of the hike if the weather is good. Views are dominated by Ventura-Oxnard coastline and Anacapa and Santa Cruz Islands. Heading downhill, the left side of the road has a beautiful eucalyptus tree with perfect proportions. The Westside neighborhood along Ventura Avenue has lots of appeal, including a burgeoning arts district. After a dry spell, the vicinity of Ventura Avenue and Simpson Street including the Avenue Branch Library should have restroom availability. From here to the bicycle path, you walk through the Simpson Tract Historic District. This was built in the late 1920s as inexpensive housing for workers in the nearby oil fields.

The proximity to the 33 Freeway is a downside to the Ventura River trail bike path, and you won't spend long on it. The assembly of rocks at the end of the bike path is related to Art City Gallery and Studios at 197 Dubbers St. The Ortega Adobe, built 1855, on Main west of Olive, is worth a look. Great Pacific Iron Works and Patagonia are interwoven names whose products are known well to outdoors people. Founded in 1970 by Yvon Chouinard, their headquarters and first store are here on Olive Street, in the old Hobson Brothers Meat Packing building. Near hike's end, Real Cheap Sports has discounts on Patagonia clothing and gear. One block south, Topa Topa has been ranked by RateBeer as Ventura's top brewery.

MILES AND DIRECTIONS

0.0   START at the doorway of the Court of Appeal building. Cross Santa Clara Street to the north and enter the pedestrian mall that is an extension of Figueroa Street.

0.2   San Buenaventura Mission. Turn right on Main Street in front of the mission. Turn left up Oak Street. Walk a few feet to see the 1870s dwelling at 31 Oak. Return to Main and turn left.

0.5   Turn right on California Street. Turn left on Santa Clara Street.

0.7   Plaza Park. Turn right on Chestnut Street. Turn left on Thompson Boulevard.

0.9   Continue fully around the block. Turn left on Fir Street. Turn left on Santa Clara Street.

1.1   Turn right on Chestnut Street.

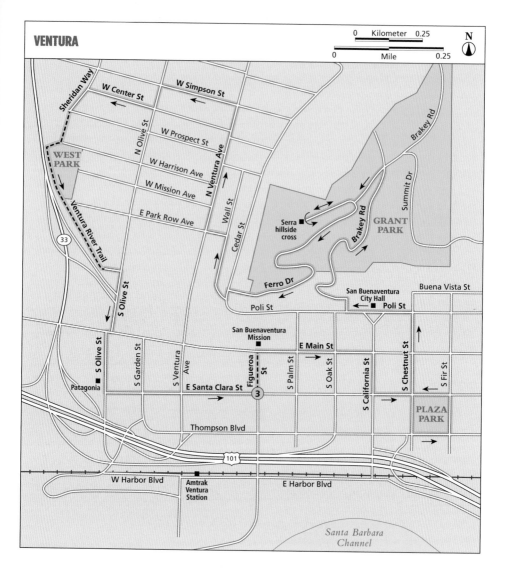

1.2 Turn left on Poli Street.

1.3 San Buenaventura City Hall. Turn right on Brakey Road, which then curves left. In this section of the hike there are no road signs and there is no sidewalk; walk carefully on the left, facing any oncoming cars. Pass the arched entry to Grant Park.

1.9 Turn left at a stop sign.

2.0 At a T intersection, continue straight for the access road to the landmark cross. A walking path to the cross begins to the left of the parking lot.

2.2 Serra hillside cross. Walk out to the cross and return to the same T intersection the same way that you came.

2.4 At the T turn right on Ferro Drive.

3.0 Turn left on Cedar Street. Use the median to assist crossing to the other side, watching traffic. Immediately turn right on Wall Street.

Ventura Post Office mural (1936), Gordon Grant artist

3.1 Stay to the right on Wall Street to follow a long pedestrian ramp that parallels Wall.

3.2 Turn left on East Park Row Avenue. Turn right on Ventura Avenue.

3.5 Turn left on Simpson Street. Turn left on Olive Street. Turn right on Center Street.

3.7 Turn left on Sheridan Way. Leave Sheridan at a curve and enter West Park. Walk between the community center and the parking lot. The entry to the Ventura River Trail is on the right just beyond the colorful children's play equipment.

4.0 Ventura River Trail. Turn left into the bicycle trail.

4.4 Trail ends at Dubbers and Rex Streets. Take Rex to Olive Street and turn right.

4.5 Main Street. The route takes the crosswalk here to continue south on Olive Street. Before crossing, walk to the right to look at the Ortega Adobe, then return to use this crosswalk.

4.7 Patagonia. Turn left on Santa Clara Street.

5.1 End of hike at Court of Appeal building.

SAN FERNANDO VALLEY AND THE HOLLYWOOD HILLS

For almost half of their 50-mile length, the Santa Monica Mountains compose the great wall of the city of Los Angeles. Here the range reaches 1,820 feet at Cahuenga Peak near the Hollywood Sign. North of this range is the San Fernando Valley. To the south are the Hollywood Hills and the great flat basin of Hollywood and beyond. Four of the hikes in this section are within or right up against these mountains. The West Hills hike occurs at the west edge of the San Fernando Valley.

The development of Los Angeles on either side of the Santa Monica Mountains is entangled with the origin story of Los Angeles as we know it. It is a story of displaced people, speculation, greed, vast plantings of grain and citrus, booms and busts, importation of water, and the development of the movie industry and the aviation industry.

Up from the flats of the valley floor or Hollywood, any hiking brings a constant reminder of what a nearly insurmountable barrier the Santa Monica Mountains can be. Except for the major passes, nearly every road gets cut off by topography at some point. Streets and trails are wickedly curved. Streets can be steep, and most don't have sidewalks; walkers need to stay aware of cars. Happily, the mountains create isolation, meaning that there are many infrequently driven streets to choose from to make an enjoyable hike. These can be places where both the views and the quality of the built environment are extraordinary.

Those mountains create another barrier; they keep ocean-influenced air flow out and they keep the desert-influenced air in. This will impact the best time to do these hikes, particularly the West Hills and Studio City hikes. Favorite hike in this section? The Three Hollywood Hills Canyons hike is a wonderful experience mixing the bustling culture of Hollywood with quiet walking and the amazing neighborhood character of the hills and canyons.

A view across to the Hollywood Hills with the San Gabriel Mountains beyond them on the Universal City to Hollywood hike

4 WEST HILLS

The streets of the far west San Fernando Valley still have in places an open feel, and the rustic mood is enhanced by the nearness of the boulder-covered hills of the old Rancho El Escorpion. This hike loops from the marvelous oak woodland of Orcutt Ranch to climb into rustic lanes in the eastern Simi Hills. A clear day will yield incredible views over the Valley floor.

Start: Orcutt Ranch, 23600 Roscoe Blvd., West Hills 91304
Elevation gain: 350 feet
Distance: 4.0-mile loop
Hiking time: 2 to 2.5 hours
Difficulty: Easy
Best season: November–June
Trail surface: Sidewalks, pavement without sidewalks, dirt
Other trail users: None aside from other walkers

Restroom availability: Only at the start point
Canine compatibility: Dogs must remain on leash.
Contact: Orcutt Ranch, (818) 346-7449
Parking status: Parking lot inside park entrance
Rail transit accessibility: N/A
Trailhead GPS: N34° 13.15' W118° 38.47'

FINDING THE TRAILHEAD

From Highway 101 take exit 27 for Shoup Avenue. Merge onto Ventura Boulevard. Go northbound on Shoup Avenue. Turn left onto Roscoe Boulevard. The park is on the left side west of Woodlake Avenue.

WHAT TO SEE

Start this clockwise loop hike early on a hot day. The park around the trailhead is a highlight of this hike, and you should saunter through it on whatever path you choose before or after the loop outside the park. These 24 acres of Orcutt Ranch are barely a tenth the size of the cattle ranch and citrus orchard that was here a century ago. This was the leisure residence of a petroleum geologist named William Orcutt. Orcutt named his estate Rancho Sombra del Roble, which is Spanish for Ranch of the Shaded Oak. He hired Arizona architect L. G. Knipe to design the beautiful Early California–style adobe house in the 1920s. The house, courtyard, and gardens are now a popular wedding venue and, unless an event is booked for the same day, you will typically have the fabulous grounds to yourself. The dense oak woodland includes one tree that is 700 years old. There is one design element on the house and some gateposts that come as a shock unless you understand the context. The swastika symbol is displayed in block form, left facing, and not diagonally rotated. The geometric pattern is an ancient religious icon that long predates a modified form that was adopted by the Nazi Party in the 1920s.

Although lacking in individual highlights, the loop west of Valley Circle Boulevard in the eastern Simi Hills is a reminder of the amazing diversity of both the landscape and the built environment of the city of Los Angeles. The boulder-lined hillsides remind you immediately of the old Western movies, which is not surprising because you are less than 3 miles from the historic locations of Spahn Ranch and Corriganville. When the Europeans arrived in the late 1700s, the Chumash Native American settlement of Momonga

A Bob Inman-led hike opts outside on Black Friday to explore dirt roads above West Hills. *Joni Yung*

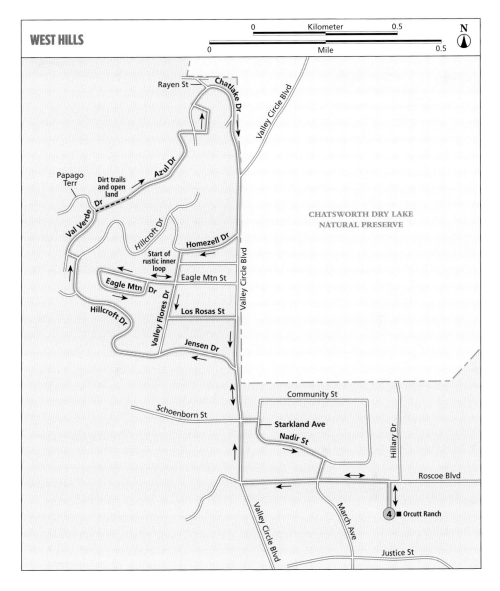

was nearby. This is the heart of the historic Rancho El Escorpión that was granted in 1845 by Governor Pio Pico to three Chumash: Odón Chijulla, Urbano, and Mañuel.

A distinctive physical feature you see today is a broad treeless basin that is the remains of Chatsworth Reservoir. It was built in 1918 as storage for the new Los Angeles aqueduct. The local name for this hiking area today is Lakeside Park. The reservoir was taken out of service after the 1971 San Fernando Earthquake and dedicated as a natural habitat that opens to the public 1 day a year. Hillcroft Drive has a wealth of droopy Peruvian pepper trees. At the dirt road T at mile 1.3, a short detour to the left is recommended where the route turns right. You can walk just to the little rise, or you could walk for miles! Due west from here 2.5 miles is the location of the Santa Susana Field Laboratory. This was where Rocketdyne tested liquid-propellant rocket engines for the space program for a half-century after 1950. The loop of Eagle Mountain Street and Drive is a small rustic, secluded hollow—every bit the definition of a dell.

MILES AND DIRECTIONS

0.0 START at Orcutt Ranch. Go out the gate and turn left on Roscoe Boulevard.

0.4 Cross twice at the signals to reach the northwest corner of Roscoe and Valley Circle Boulevards. Head north on Valley Circle, walking on dirt on the left-hand side of the street.

0.6 Veer left on Jensen Drive.

0.9 Turn right on Hillcroft Drive.

1.2 Turn left at a Y on Val Verde Drive as Hillcroft goes right. Walk uphill past a "No Outlet" sign and quickly turn right to remain on Val Verde.

1.3 Dirt trails and open land. The pavement of Val Verde Drive ends. Turn right at a dirt road T that maps identify as Papago Terrace going left and Azul Drive going right. Follow Azul Drive, which soon will be pavement again.

1.6 Go straight through an unmarked crossroads to take Azul Circle. This bends left. Turn right when it meets Azul Drive.

1.8 Turn right at a Y onto Chatlake Drive. Chatlake is the widest road here, although the signpost only indicates Azul Drive behind you and Rayen Drive going left.

2.0 Turn right on Valley Circle Boulevard. Walk on the narrow right margin of the sometimes-busy road.

2.1 Veer right on Homezell Drive. Turn left on Valley Flores Drive.

2.3 Start of rustic inner loop. Turn right on Eagle Mountain Street. Pass Eagle Mountain Drive on left and go straight. This is a short counterclockwise loop on a narrow rustic road that comes back on itself.

2.7 Turn right from Eagle Mountain Drive to Eagle Mountain Street. Turn right on Valley Flores Drive. Turn left on La Rosas Street.

2.9 Cross Valley Circle Boulevard and turn right. Walk on the wide dirt margin.

3.1 Turn left on Schoenborn Street. Turn right on Starkland Avenue. Turn left on Nadir Street.

3.4 Turn right on March Avenue. Cross Roscoe Boulevard when it is safe and turn left. Turn right into the driveway of Orcutt Ranch.

3.6 Orcutt Ranch Parking lot. Wander the grounds however you like.

4.0 End of hike.

5 **STUDIO CITY**

Studio City is an affluent section of the San Fernando Valley with many connections to the film industry, including a studio that was established by Mack Sennett in 1928. You will pass some of the thriving retail district along Ventura Boulevard, yet this hike also spends quiet miles along Los Angeles River walking paths and along some beautiful tree-lined residential streets.

Start: Moorpark Park, 12061 Moorpark St., Studio City 91604
Elevation gain: 50 feet
Distance: 5.6-mile loop
Hiking time: 2.5 to 3 hours
Difficulty: Moderate
Best season: October–June
Trail surface: Sidewalks, pavement without sidewalks, paved path, dirt

Other trail users: Shoppers and diners
Restroom availability: Miles 3.0 through 4.4
Canine compatibility: Dogs must remain on leash.
Parking status: Free curb parking
Rail transit accessibility: N/A
Trailhead GPS: N34° 09.02' W118° 23.78'

FINDING THE TRAILHEAD

Take the 101 Freeway to exit 14 for Laurel Canyon Boulevard toward Studio City. Turn south onto Laurel Canyon Boulevard. Turn left onto Moorpark Street. The park is at the northeast corner of Moorpark Street and Laurel Canyon Boulevard. Note that there are no restrooms at the starting point or in the first 3 miles, so a stop nearby before parking at the trailhead is advised. Coffee Fix and the Studio City branch library are options located 0.6 mile west on Moorpark.

WHAT TO SEE

Moorpark Park backs up to Tujunga Wash, a major tributary of the Los Angeles River. Begin this counterclockwise loop by heading down Laurel Canyon Boulevard. A dental office with comical signage is a fine example of the Streamline Moderne style with portholes, ship-like handrails, and rounded building corners. And almost hiding in plain sight on the east side of this street is the small 1966 Richard Neutra–designed Virzintas Penthouse. Look above the brown wood fence.

Between miles 0.4 and 2.0 and between miles 4.7 and 5.0, this hike has four developed sections of Los Angeles River walking. Even though the river here is a basic concrete channel of vertical walls, each of these path segments provides a tranquil experience with birdlife and surrounding trees. An obvious drawback to walking along the river in this area is that each north–south cross street (Fulton, Coldwater Canyon, Whitsett, Laurel Canyon) requires leaving the riverbank, since the paths have not (yet) been developed to pass under these streets. The paths between Radford Street and Whitsett Avenue are older and display less flair than the newer paths between Whitsett Avenue and Fulton Avenue, which are newer and blessed with a lot of craftsmanship. Notice how this well-to-do neighborhood integrates itself here and there with the parklike aspects of the river.

Ventura is one of the great boulevards of Los Angeles. At 18 miles, it is said to be the world's longest continuous avenue of businesses. Much of that mileage is banal, but on

Laurel Canyon Boulevard entry
to the Valleyheart Greenway

Ventura Boulevard in Studio City, there is enough commercial authenticity expressed in a semi-village scale to keep the urban hiker engaged. Between mile 3 and mile 4.4 there is a wide variety of food and drink businesses plus several grocery stores. The old-school traditions include Western Bagel, Carney's Hot Dogs, and Art's Delicatessen.

Several Ventura Boulevard locations deserve special attention. Right after Coldwater Canyon, the venerable Sportsmen's Lodge Hotel has tons of entertainment business cachet. It is on the wrong side of the street but certainly worthy of a look inside. The eclectic Coldwater Curve Shops, on the right side of Ventura past Fairway Avenue, were a totally out of the ordinary concept from master architect Rudolph Schindler. In 1940 he was dabbling with what a strip mall might entail. At the corner of Laurel Canyon Boulevard, the Chase Bank is a good example of the architecture and mosaic mural work that Millard Sheets produced during his mid-20th-century collaboration with Home Savings.

Before turning north at Radford Avenue, there is an excellent 0.6-mile out-and-back excursion you should consider adding to your hike. Architect Rudolph Schindler designed an apartment courtyard that is marvelously evocative of Los Angeles just after World War II. To reach the Laurelwood Apartments at 11837 Laurelwood Dr., simply remain on Ventura east of Radford to Carpenter Avenue and turn right. Turn left at Laurelwood Drive and admire the double row of two-story austere sculpted dwellings. Then turn around and return to Radford and Ventura.

CBS Studio Center dominates the neighborhood along Radford Avenue near Ventura Boulevard. Mack Sennett moved his production over the mountain from Hollywood in 1928 when this area was just a lettuce patch and a ranch. This was Republic Studios in the cinema heyday of the 1940s and 1950s. Since the early 1960s, the complex has been mostly associated with TV shows. Gilligan's Island is back there somewhere, closer to Tujunga Wash than to the Pacific Ocean.

The Agnes Avenue Historic District has five adorable American Colonial Revival homes built before 1940 when the Sennett studio lot was being subdivided. Architect Rudolph Schindler designed the home at 4255 Agnes Ave. in 1945. Notice the clerestory window running along a tilted roofline. Finally, a house on Gentry Avenue just north of Woodbridge Street is sure to amuse just before the hike gets back to Moorpark Park.

MILES AND DIRECTIONS

0.0 START at Moorpark Park. From the intersection of Moorpark Street and Laurel Canyon Boulevard, cross to reach the southwest corner by the Mobil station. Head south on Laurel Canyon Boulevard and pass above the Los Angeles River.

0.4 Turn right into the Los Angeles River Greenway path. After just 0.3 mile, veer left on a ramp leading to a footbridge over the river.

0.8 Turn right on the Laurelgrove Pedestrian Bridge. Turn left on Valleyheart Drive. Cross Whitsett Avenue with great care. Whitsett and Valleyheart compose a legal *unmarked crosswalk*. If you find yourself doing this hike at a peak traffic hour, don't push it. Turn left, cross at Ventura Boulevard, and walk back to the other side. Take Valleyheart beyond Whitsett Avenue.

1.1 Enter the Yaroslavsky LA River Greenway Trail.

1.5 Leave the river path to the right, walking up to a clumsy exit to Valleyheart Drive and Alcove Avenue, then go north on Alcove. Turn left on Woodbridge Street. Cross to the west side of Coldwater Canyon Avenue and turn left. As with the previous

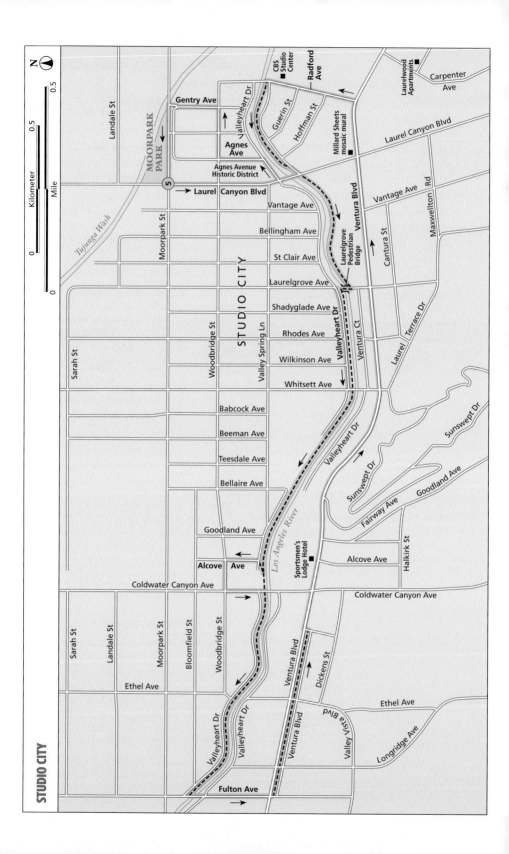

San Fernando Valley domestic eclecticism on Gentry Avenue

legal *unmarked crosswalk*, don't push it. If necessary, turn right, cross at Moorpark Street and walk back to the other side.

1.8 Turn right into the ramp leading down to the North Valleyheart Riverwalk. Exit the river path at a ramp leading up to Valleyheart Drive near a descriptive nature sign for the Oak Hotel. Turn left on Fulton Avenue. Cross to the southside of Ventura Boulevard.

2.6 Turn left into a footpath on the south side of Ventura Boulevard.

3.0 Leave the footpath for sidewalk at Van Noord Avenue and continue east on Ventura Boulevard.

3.2 Sportsmen's Lodge Hotel.

4.2 Millard Sheets mosaic mural.

4.4 Turn left on Radford Avenue. Departure point for hike extension to the Laurelwood Apartments.

4.5 CBS Studio Center. Turn left into the Valleyheart Greenway path near Radford Avenue and Valleyheart Drive.

5.0 Take the ramp out of the Valleyheart Greenway and turn right on Laurel Canyon Boulevard. Cross above the river. Turn right on Valleyheart Drive. Turn left on Agnes Avenue.

5.1 Agnes Avenue Historic District. Turn right on Woodbridge Street.

5.3 Turn left on Gentry Avenue. Take the passage to Moorpark Avenue at the cul-de-sac. Turn left on Moorpark. At Laurel Canyon, cross to the north of the street.

5.6 End of hike at Moorpark Park.

6 UNIVERSAL CITY TO HOLLYWOOD

This hike is a workout up and over the Santa Monica Mountains that also experiences two of the region's most touristy Hollywood-oriented locations. There is a smug satisfaction to getting in and out of these tourist zones somewhat painlessly, and there is a special feeling to walking down the popular Runyon Canyon Trail after a mostly solitary climb on quiet streets with Valley views to reach the top.

Start: Metro Universal City/Studio City Station, 3901 Lankershim Blvd., Studio City 91604
Elevation gain: 850 feet
Distance: 5.5-mile point-to-point
Hiking time: 2.5 to 3.5 hours
Difficulty: Difficult
Best season: October–June
Best days and times: The passage gate into Runyon Canyon at 3.1 miles is locked at dark.
Trail surface: Sidewalks, pavement without sidewalks, paved path, dirt, stairs

Other trail users: Tourists, dogs off-leash
Restroom availability: Miles 0.9, 1.6
Canine compatibility: No. You may not walk your dog through CityWalk.
Parking status: Pay lot at transit station or at Universal Studios
Rail transit accessibility: Metro B (Red) Line, Metro Universal City/Studio City Station is the start point.
Trailhead GPS: N34° 08.38' W118° 21.75'

FINDING THE TRAILHEAD

From the west and north, take 101 or 170 Freeway south to exit 12A toward Lankershim Boulevard/Universal City. Turn right onto Cahuenga Boulevard. Continue onto Ventura Boulevard. Turn right onto Campo De Cahuenga. The station parking entrance is on the right side. From the south, take exit 12A for Lankershim Boulevard toward Universal City. Turn left onto Lankershim Boulevard.

WHAT TO SEE

Understand as you begin this point-to-point hike that it anticipates a one-stop subway ride to return to the starting point. The shortest walking routes from end point to start point have some safety issues. Also note that the Runyon Canyon Trail entry gate at 3.1 miles is locked soon after dark.

A surprisingly stiff climb takes you into the west end of the retail pedestrian alley that is CityWalk. This feature opened in 1993, and the eye is naturally drawn to the glitz and the people. This themed retail mall concept came a decade before comparable locations such as Downtown Disney and The Grove. It is pure invention of course, incorporating design vignettes borrowed from the "real" city. The way out from the east end of CityWalk down to usable sidewalk along Universal Studios Boulevard seems impossibly contrived and reflects how planners failed to anticipate this type of walking.

Soon after the left turn onto Cahuenga Boulevard West, there are some remaining fragments of the former Hanna-Barbera animation studios building built in 1963. The perforated concrete screen is pure Mid-Century Modern and productions like *Scooby*

A road and trail in Runyon Canyon Park link the heart of Hollywood to Mulholland Drive at the rim of the Santa Monica Mountains.

A pink trumpet tree in El Paseo De Cahuenga Park

Doo, *The Flintstones*, and *The Jetsons* were born here. El Paseo De Cahuenga Park is a tiny jewel centered by a pink trumpet tree. Consider taking advantage of the Starbucks or one of the few food places around here. After this, the residential streets and the trail offer no restrooms.

On the left side of the steep hill, 3132 Oakcrest Dr. was designed by famous local International Style architect Gregory Ain. It was commissioned in 1939 by Harry Hay for his mother. Hay was an important early organizer for the gay rights movement. Soon after the stairway comes the first of two clusters of boat houses. These were designed by architect Harry Gesner and mostly built around 1959. Each is a small cottage hanging dramatically over the canyon below it, and it is said that Gesner employed Norwegian seamen to do the labor. Soon after the boat houses comes the utterly amazing expression-istic tile work that craftsman George Ehling performed on his own house by working over a half-century. Approaching the junction of Pacific View Drive and Hockey Trail (mile 2.6), the John Lautner–designed Foster Carling House sits dramatically atop a knoll that has been planted with succulents.

"Serious hikers" often deride the Runyon Canyon Trail. For many, this sometimes-crowded trail is much too popular with would-be celebrities. They say that it is too obvi-ous a choice when there are many alternative trails to sample. But it works wonderfully for what is needed on this hike. The route sticks to the main line of the trail since you are only doing it downhill. Ignore several trail options to the left and right.

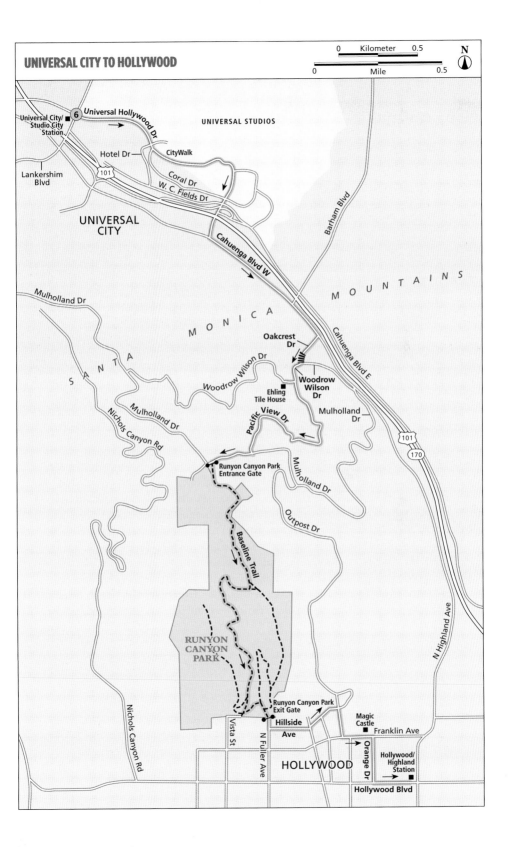

Suddenly you are walking past some cool courtyard apartments and below Yamashiro restaurant and the Magic Castle, all Hollywood icons. Orange Drive drops you into all the glory, madness, legend, and cliché of Hollywood Boulevard.

MILES AND DIRECTIONS

0.0 START at Universal City/Studio City Station. From the top of the escalators for the subway, walk up and over the pedestrian bridge to Universal Hollywood Drive east of Lankershim Boulevard. Head uphill.

0.4 Go left at Hotel Drive, taking the steps and pedestrian bridge over the park access road. Remain a few steps below the Universal City ticketing/entrance area while passing to the left of a small parking lot. After the ticketing area, cross to the left and enter CityWalk by the far side of the Billabong store.

0.6 CityWalk. Follow the main line of CityWalk, but stay to the right at the Hard Rock Cafe. Follow the signs for the E.T. parking structure.

0.9 Cross over a pedestrian bridge into the garage and turn right to pass in front of a bank of elevators. Immediately past the elevators take the stairs all the way down; there are seven flights of ten steps. Arrive at the bottom and walk past a bicycle rack. Here is the beginning of an exterior sidewalk.

1.1 Veer right into sidewalk, walking down the left side of Universal Studios Boulevard. Turn left on Cahuenga Boulevard West.

1.6 Starbucks. Cross in front of Starbucks to the west side of Cahuenga Boulevard West and resume travel uphill on Cahuenga.

1.8 Turn right on Oakcrest Drive. On the left side of the cul-de-sac of Oakcrest Drive, turn left up a steep stairway. Turn right on Woodrow Wilson Drive. Pass the junction of Pacific View Drive and stay on Woodrow Wilson for just 150 feet to the Tile House.

2.1 Ehling Tile House (7110 Sycamore Trail). Turn around on Woodrow Wilson and go back to the corner of Pacific View Drive. Turn right.

2.9 Just before the "No Outlet" sign across from 7257 Pacific View Dr., turn left onto a street that connects to Mulholland Drive. Cross to the other side of Mulholland when it is safe and turn right.

3.1 Runyon Canyon Park. Turn left through a passage gate.

4.4 Veer left to avoid the right-hand side exit to Vista Street. Follow the obvious trail (now dirt, not tarmac) to the exit gate for Fuller Avenue.

4.6 Exit Runyon Canyon Park at the Fuller Avenue gate. From Fuller, turn left on Hillside Avenue. At La Brea Avenue, turn left then right to remain on Hillside Avenue. Turn right on Outpost Drive. At the traffic signal, cross to the south side of Franklin Avenue.

5.1 Turn left on Franklin Avenue.

5.2 Magic Castle. Turn right on Orange Drive. Turn left on Hollywood Boulevard.

5.5 End of hike at Hollywood/Highland Station, 6815 Hollywood Blvd. To return to the start, board any train in the North Hollywood direction and get off at the next stop, Metro Universal City/Studio City Station.

7 THREE HOLLYWOOD HILLS CANYONS

Beginning in the heart of Hollywood, this hike is a clockwise loop exploring three distinct canyons which are folded into the impenetrable wall of the Santa Monica Mountains. This is an area of streets with dramatic views, diverse and eclectic homes, and lush plantings and tree cover. There are ever-changing sightlines of the Hollywood Sign, the Griffith Observatory, and the vast, densely populated basin below.

Start: Hollywood Pantages Theatre, 6233 Hollywood Blvd., Hollywood 90028
Elevation gain: 750 feet
Distance: 6.3-mile loop
Hiking time: 3 to 4 hours
Difficulty: Difficult
Best season: October–June
Best days and times: The passage gate into Hollywood Reservoir at 2.1 miles may be locked as early as 5 p.m.
Trail surface: Sidewalks, pavement without sidewalks, stairs, dirt trail

Other trail users: Tourists, shoppers and diners
Restroom availability: Miles 0.7 (maybe), 2.5, 3.6, 5.6
Canine compatibility: No; dogs are forbidden in a key passage.
Contact: Hollywood Reservoir, (323) 463-0830
Parking status: Pay parking lots
Rail transit accessibility: Metro B (aka Red) Line, Hollywood/Vine Station is across Hollywood Boulevard from the start point.
Trailhead GPS: N34° 06.08' W118° 19.54'

FINDING THE TRAILHEAD

From any direction, find your way to the 101–Hollywood Freeway south of the 134 and north of I-110. From the north or the south, take exit 8C for Gower Street. Turn south onto Gower Street. Turn right on Hollywood Boulevard. The destination is on the right.

WHAT TO SEE

You begin this clockwise loop hike in the heart of Hollywood. The Pantages opened in 1930 as a vaudeville theater. The Academy Awards were held here from 1949 to 1959. The Walk of Fame and the Capitol Records tower are symbols of the media world this area is associated with. Almost immediately, all that Hollywood media activity is over. The Hollywood Dell is your first of three canyons on this hike. The Vedanta Society has been here since 1930, and the temple may be visited; take off shoes and turn off devices. A restroom by the office/bookstore is sometimes accessible to the public. Reaching Quebec Drive, the gorgeous corner Spanish-style house was a featured location in the 1944 film noir classic *Double Indemnity*. Lake Hollywood still actively enforces a ban against dogs, even though the city drinking water has been moved to underground storage. A short over-and-back walk across the Mulholland Dam is a great addition to this hike.

Beachwood Canyon begins at Durand Drive. Norman castle–like Wolf's Lair is a good introduction to Beachwood, because this neighborhood will provide more examples of

Doing an over-and-back detour at the Mulholland Dam is a worthy addition to this hike.

the eclectic and imaginative styles that 1920s builders used in this area, with plenty of castellated walls, domes, and turrets. The upper third of Beachwood Canyon is Hollywoodland, a tract that was promoted in 1924 with the sign with billboard letters and flashing lights. Part of the personality of this area is the bold and repeated use of distinctive stone; you see it in foundation walls, in the entry gate posts near the cafe, and in the fabulous public stairways. You get to do five of those stairways, two down and three up. They average 136 steps each. Some locals have named the classic double stairway for the prolific Armenian-American writer William Saroyan. That's fitting because Hollywoodland has always been a mecca for writers and because the author once lived at the foot of the canyon in the Villa Carlotta Apartments. In Beachwood Village, the market has sandwiches and sundries, and they may let you use the restroom if you buy something. There is also a village cafe that closes late afternoons.

Leave Beachwood Canyon at mile 4.1 with the ascent of a stairway to Hollyridge Drive. Here begins a ridge walk before the descent into the third drainage, Bronson Canyon. Five hundred feet after reaching Hollyridge Drive there is a good overview. Bronson is an entry point to a remote part of Griffith Park. Looking to the left of the observatory in this view, a historic stone quarry can be seen near the head of the canyon. Excavation started here in 1903 to obtain rock for early Los Angeles road building and for use as the ballast for the streetcar tracks.

A mind-numbing series of curving streets bring you down to the base of Bronson Canyon. If you were to climb up and over the next ridge ahead of you, that hike would take you through the Oaks neighborhood and into Ferndale in Griffith Park. Today's hike turns south on Canyon Drive. South of Foothill Drive is classic flatland Hollywood with lovely bungalows under giant palm trees. This is part of the Hollywood Grove preservation zone. The house at 1972 Canyon Dr. was where Evelyn Mulwray kept her sister/daughter Katherine hidden with her butler and maid in the movie *Chinatown*. Fascinating Franklin Village is 0.7 mile from the end of the hike with an unusual blend of apartment towers, shops, and restaurants.

MILES AND DIRECTIONS

0.0 START at Pantages Theatre. Looking at the marquee, turn left (west) on Hollywood Boulevard. Turn right on Vine Street. Turn left on Yucca Street. Turn right on Ivar Avenue. Turn left down a pedestrian passage by Chateau Alto Nido, and at the bottom go west on Franklin Avenue.

0.4 Turn right on Cahuenga Boulevard. Turn right on Dix Street. Turn left on Ivar Avenue and walk under the freeway. Turn right on Vedanta Terrace and then right on Vedanta Place.

0.7 Vedanta Temple. Walk around the left side of the temple and turn right on Vedanta Terrace. Turn left on Vine Street. Take the next right (perhaps unsigned) for Vine Way. Go up a stairway and turn left on Alcyona Drive. Remain on Alcyona as Primrose Avenue intersects from the right and Ivarene Avenue intersects from the left.

1.1 Turn right on El Contento Drive. Turn left on Quebec Drive.

1.4 *Double Indemnity* House. Stay to the left twice to follow Quebec to its dead end.

1.6 Hollywood Dell trail. Follow this trail from the cul-de-sac of Quebec Drive until it reaches the pavement of La Rocha Drive. Turn right on Deep Dell Place.

1.9 Turn left on Weidlake Drive.

2.3 Mulholland Dam and Hollywood Reservoir trailhead. With the dam on the left, look right and go through the pedestrian gate that is built into a larger vehicle gate. Maps indicate this wide dirt and tarmac trail as Mulholland Highway.

2.7 Trail junction; turn right and head up the trail along an impressive stone retaining wall. Maps indicate this trail as Wetona Drive.

2.9 Wolf's Lair. Turn left from the trail onto Durand Drive.

3.0 Veer left at a road split. Turn right down an easy-to-miss stairway near 2954 Durand. At the bottom turn left on Belden Drive. Bypass Rodgerton Drive.

3.3 Turn right down a double stairway near 2950 Belden Dr. and identified on some maps as the Saroyan Stairs. At the bottom, remain above Beachwood Drive and turn right on Woodshire Drive.

3.4 Turn right up a stairway located across from 2786 Woodshire. Turn left on top of Belden Drive. Follow curves of Belden down to Beachwood Market.

3.7 Beachwood Village. Directly in front of the cafe, take the crosswalk across Beachwood Drive leading to Westshire Drive. Immediately turn left on Woodhaven Drive. Turn right on Beachwood Drive.

3.9 Just before 2810 Beachwood, turn right up a stairway. Turn right on Westshire Drive.

4.1 Near 2744 Westshire, turn left up a stairway.

4.2 At top of stairway, turn right on Hollyridge Drive, avoiding Pelham Place. Bypass connecting streets that lead to the right, first for Rutherford Drive and then Verbena Drive.

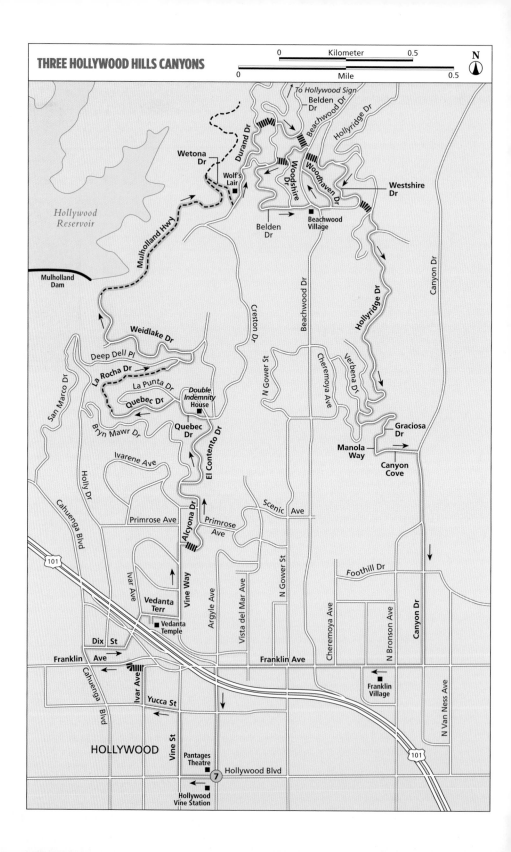

The Vedanta Society of Southern California has been in Hollywood since 1930.

4.8 Turn left to head down Graciosa Drive. The sign might be missing, but this is the first left after passing Verbena on the right. As Graciosa bends left, leave it for Manola Way. Immediately after that, Manola goes straight; leave it to follow Canyon Cove to the left.

5.1 Turn right on Canyon Drive. Go straight on Canyon as Bronson cuts off to the right.

5.5 Turn right on Franklin Avenue.

5.6 Franklin Village at Franklin and Tamarind Avenues.

6.0 Turn left on Argyle Avenue. Turn right on Hollywood Boulevard.

6.3 End of hike at Pantages Theatre.

8 WHITLEY AND HOLLYWOOD HEIGHTS

The urban scene changes quickly when you leave the maelstrom of tourists in the heart of Hollywood and climb just a little way into nearby hills. On this hike you'll curve through streets that dead-end for cars but have passages for walkers to squeeze through, you'll pass a Frank Lloyd Wright house as well as the iconic High Tower, and you'll stroll through an isolated neighborhood that Valentino, Gloria Swanson, and W. C. Fields once called home.

Start: Hollywood and Highland Center, 6801 Hollywood Blvd., Hollywood 90028
Elevation gain: 500 feet
Distance: 3.0-mile loop
Hiking time: 1.5 to 2 hours
Difficulty: Moderate (short but steep)
Best season: October–June. During Academy Awards season, a major film premiere, or the holiday season, parking or even approaching this complex by car would be difficult and you should use rail transit.

Trail surface: Sidewalks, pavement without sidewalks, stairs
Other trail users: None aside from other walkers
Restroom availability: Mile 1.4
Canine compatibility: Dogs must remain on leash.
Parking status: Pay parking lot, validation possible
Rail transit accessibility: Metro B (aka Red) Line, Hollywood/Highland Station is downstairs from the start point.
Trailhead GPS: N34° 06.17' W118° 20.36'

FINDING THE TRAILHEAD

From the 101/170 going south take exit 9C for the Hollywood Bowl. This will channel you without turning onto Cahuenga Boulevard then Highland Avenue. From the 101 going north, take exit 9B toward the Hollywood Bowl. Turn right on Odin Street. Turn left on Highland Avenue. Then from either direction, pass Franklin Avenue. Turn right into the parking garage by the Loews Hollywood Hotel. The Hollywood and Highland Center is a multifaceted entertainment complex. The hike begins in the back corner of outdoor level two near California Pizza Kitchen.

WHAT TO SEE

This hike is a clockwise loop with a lot of wrinkles. The Assyrian gate at Hollywood and Highland Center repeats an image that was portrayed in the 1916 D.W. Griffith film, *Intolerance*. The original filming location was three miles east of here. The steep slog up Hillcrest Road is the worst part of the hike, but all is forgiven with the right turn onto Glencoe Way. The 1924 Frank Lloyd Wright textile block Freeman House occupies the slope at the curve. It was given to the USC School of Architecture in the 1980s, and the expense to merely stabilize the structure has been staggering.

With all the books out about stairway exploring in Los Angeles, you might think that the secret is out about this enclave of Hollywood Heights located west of Highland Avenue. Not the case: Even many longtime Angelenos get caught off guard when they experience this warren of narrow streets, stairways, paved paths, and houses that can only

The High Tower was built in 1923 and is the centerpiece of Hollywood Heights.

be reached by walking some distance from the vehicular streets. The tract was subdivided in 1923. Pedestrian-only streets were built with steps as the only means to connect some building lots to vehicle streets. The elevator, built into a tower with an image of Bologna, was built the same year as a mix of promotion and utility. Today this is a fascinating labyrinth to visit. The Moderne house to the right of the tower stood in as Philip Marlowe's pad (played by Elliott Gould) in the Robert Altman film *The Long Goodbye*.

Before crossing Highland Avenue at Camrose/Milner, you should inspect the cute cluster of recycled bungalows behind the hedge at the northwest corner. There is a picnic area geared to Hollywood Bowl events, and reliable restrooms. Across Highland is the Hollywood Heritage Museum, in a barn that has been moved to this location but was where Jesse Lasky and Cecil B. DeMille collaborated in the very early Hollywood days in 1913.

Whitley Heights is a residential knob that faces Hollywood Heights from the east side of Highland. This enclave was developed in the 1920s as a thematically organized tract where lot buyers were given big incentives to adhere to a Mediterranean style. You will see a lot of Tudor Revival here as well. Circulating through it, you should understand that you are only seeing half of what was built here. A wide swath was demolished to build the freeway in 1951, and a piece of Whitley Heights sits in isolation on the other side.

Leaving Milner Road, 2049 Las Palmas is the oldest (1913) remaining house in the district. It displays several bull's-eye windows. Near the top of the Whitley Terrace steps, Beulah Bondi and Rosalind Russell each once lived at address 6660. Janet Gaynor lived at 6666. Barbara La Marr lived at 6672. Maurice Chevalier lived at 6680. Walking up Milner Road, Watsonia Terrace is a cozy dead-end street going left. Gloria Swanson once lived down there at address 2058, and the same house was once rented as a studio by William Faulkner. 2074 Watsonia was at different times the residence of writer Ben Hecht, musician Leonard Bernstein, and actor Danny Thomas. Blocks away from the path of this hike, Whitley Terrace was the onetime home to Rudolph Valentino, W. C. Fields, Charlie Chaplin, Francis X. Bushman, Tyrone Power, Carmen Miranda, Jane Fonda with Tom Hayden, and many others.

MILES AND DIRECTIONS

0.0 START at Starbucks Hollywood and Highland Center under the faux Assyrian archway. Go down the thirty steps behind California Pizza Kitchen. Turn out to Highland Avenue by Johnny Grant Way. Turn left on Highland, heading for the hills. Walk past the Valero station and cross Franklin Avenue. Turn left on Franklin.

0.2 Turn right on Hillcrest Road. Walk on the left, facing traffic, when the sidewalks end.

0.3 Turn right on Glencoe Way. Follow Glencoe to the "End" sign by address 1983.

0.4 Enter a seemingly random (but public) combination of steps and path that regains the drivable part of Glencoe Way. Next to the 2033 address sign, turn left into the zigzag beginning of what is otherwise a straight, steep stairway. Turn right from the dead end of Paramount Drive.

0.7 Turn right on Camrose Drive. Turn right on Glencoe Way, returning to a point that you recently passed. This time turn left down from the mailbox reading "2021" down a stairway to the dead end of High Tower Drive.

0.9 Turn left on High Tower Drive. Cross Camrose Drive and Yeager Place.

1.1 Turn left up the steps and path that is signed at Los Altos Place. At a pathway T turn right on the stairway that is (probably not signed) Broadview Terrace. Climb past the High Tower. At a pathway junction, turn right down the signposted Alta

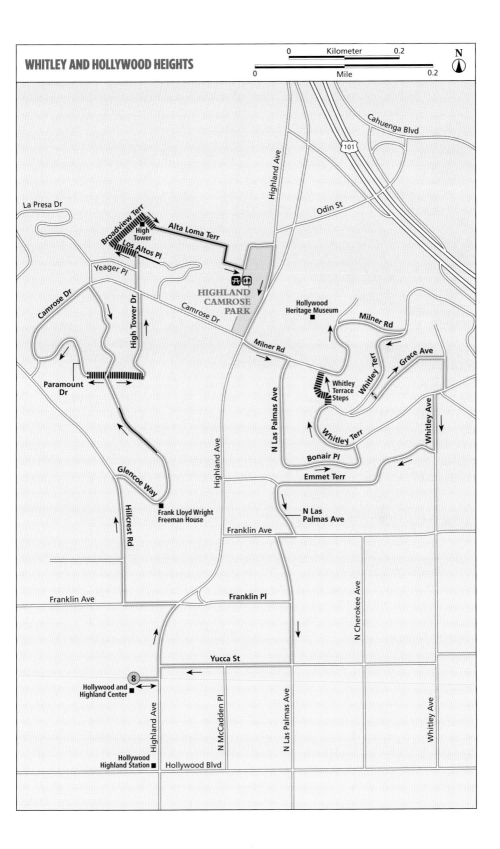

One of several hairpin turns in the landmarked residential enclave of Whitley Terrace

Loma Terrace. These steps and path will dogleg right then left near the bottom. The bottom is a driveway and a cluster of carports. Turn left in the driveway and exit out to Highland Avenue.

1.3 Turn right on Highland Avenue. Stop at the corner of Camrose Drive. Restrooms are typically open inside Highland Camrose picnic area, 300 feet to the right. Turn right on Camrose and enter the bungalow village through the gate. The restroom building is straight back.

1.4 Cross Highland Avenue at the signal that connects Camrose Drive on the west side and Milner Road on the east. Proceed up Milner. Turn right on Las Palmas Avenue. The street name changes to Bonair Place as the road curves left.

1.7 Turn left on Whitley Terrace. Just past address 6666, turn left down the well-signed Whitley Terrace Steps.

1.9 Turn right at the bottom onto Milner Road. Make a hairpin right turn from Milner to Whitley Terrace. Watch on the left for 6687 Whitley Terrace. The next house on the left does not have an address sign. Right after that, before a cluster of garages, there is a hidden wood stairway with a plaque. Turn left up these steps. On top, turn left on Grace Avenue.

2.3 Five-point junction. Take the third street from the left to walk straight down Whitley Avenue. Turn right on Emmet Terrace.

2.5 Turn left on Las Palmas Avenue where Emmet Terrace ends. Cross Franklin Avenue in the crosswalk; turn right then left to resume south on Las Palmas Avenue.

2.8 Turn right on Yucca Street. Turn left on Highland Avenue. Immediately cross Highland at the signal. Walk toward the garage exit and turn left up the steps to the second level of the Hollywood and Highland Center.

3.0 End of hike at the Hollywood and Highland Center.

COASTAL LOS ANGELES COUNTY

Four of the hikes in this section are done within immediate reach of the coast, and three are in communities that are 4 to 5 miles inland. These three areas have coastal-like weather, and they share many more associations with their coastal neighbors than they do with communities farther inland.

Los Angeles County faces two distinct bays. The long crescent of Santa Monica Bay is west facing. Framed by lightly populated and mountainous areas on the north and south end, the middle is a very densely populated coastal plain that is loaded with creative content. Silicone Beach and SpaceX are both located here. The other Los Angeles County exposure to the Pacific Ocean is San Pedro Bay. This is south facing with Palos Verdes Peninsula on the west end and Orange County to the southeast. The outstanding physical and cultural features of San Pedro Bay are the adjacent seaports that combine to form the fifth-busiest port facility in the world. This area is also densely populated, primarily by the unique and fiercely independent communities of San Pedro and Long Beach.

In Palisades Park, looking over the Santa Monica Bay with the Palos Verdes peninsula in the distance

There is much variety in the seven hikes of this section. The Westwood and UCLA hike features a beautiful university campus. The Venice hike combines marvelous canal paths and walk streets with a gaudy beach strip. The Torrance hike is a craft brewery crawl in a charming old town district. The Long Beach hike has a fantastic variety of architectural features from the first 40 years of the 20th century. The weather is great throughout these hikes, although you should know that starting early isn't always a good idea because of morning fog and chill. Long Beach in summer is 13 degrees warmer daily than Santa Monica, but still more refreshing than inland Los Angeles County. Five of these hikes have mild hill climbing, but nothing so dramatic as some of this guide's inland hikes. Favorite hike in this section? Try the Santa Monica Canyons hike. The ups and downs are fun, the quiet green residential canyons are captivating, and the view from Palisades Park will cause you to sigh with delight.

9 WESTWOOD AND UCLA

Outside the campus, Westwood is a neighborhood with a fabulous 1920s commercial center, an excellent free art museum, an iconic tiny cemetery, and serene streets with homes and apartments. The UCLA campus itself is a beautiful hillside greenspace covered with 90 years of architectural styles in buildings. This hike will sample the best of both and visit the UCLA Mathias Botanical Garden.

Start: 1015 Hilgard Ave. Garage, 1015 Hilgard Ave., Los Angeles 90024
Elevation gain: 250 feet
Distance: 4.7-mile loop
Hiking time: 3 to 4 hours
Difficulty: Moderate
Best season: Year-round
Trail surface: Sidewalks, paved pathways

Other trail users: Shoppers and diners, scooters, students
Restroom availability: Miles 0.5, 0.8 to 1.5, 3.1
Canine compatibility: Not a good hike for the dog
Parking status: Pay lot parking
Rail transit accessibility: N/A
Trailhead GPS: N34° 03.70′ W118° 26.50′

FINDING THE TRAILHEAD

From I-405 north of I-10 and south of the 101, take exit 55 for Wilshire Boulevard east. From Wilshire Boulevard, turn left on Malcolm Avenue. Turn left on Weyburn Avenue. Pass Hilgard Avenue and turn left into the pay parking lot. This is currently the best parking for this hike so far as location and cost.

WHAT TO SEE

Begin this clockwise loop hike walking down Hilgard Avenue and immediately come to the entrance of the delectable Lindbrook Village Courtyard. This is a landmarked Monterey-style residential enclave built in 1935, and you may discreetly enter it. Pierce Brothers Westwood is a remarkable cemetery in a small space. Interred here are writers from Ray Bradbury to Truman Capote and singers from Peggy Lee to Roy Orbison. It is the crypt of Marilyn Monroe that draws the most attention. The cemetery is a nice place to pause and use the restroom. It might be too soon in the hike to talk about eating, but you should be aware of the rich assortment of Persian food available on Westwood Boulevard near the right turn from Wellworth. Of the one million Iranian Americans, half live in the Los Angeles area. The heaviest concentration of this population is in the immediate vicinity, something that you may have already observed in the cemetery memorials. The city has assigned the name Persian Square to identify this neighborhood characteristic; more colloquial and wider used is the term *Tehrangeles*. Saffron and Rose Ice Cream is just one of the several great Persian–themed eateries in the 3 blocks south of Wellworth. The austere mixed Art Deco–Moderne style Crest Theatre opened in 1940 as the UCLAN Theatre. It was acquired recently by the UCLA School of the Arts and Architecture, so a revitalization is anticipated.

Reenter Westwood Village at Wilshire and Westwood. The excellent Hammer Museum is free and open daily except Monday. Once the Regents of UCLA selected Italian and Romanesque architecture for the original campus, the planners of Westwood

Pierce Brothers Westwood is a remarkable cemetery in a small space.

Village also sought a cohesive Mediterranean image. Both the campus and the Village opened in 1929. From the start, the Village was to be the fashionable centerpiece of a new residential neighborhood. On the right after the Hammer Museum, the building with the colonnades and the fat center tower was originally a Ralph's Grocery Store. The Janss Investment Corporation invented and managed Westwood from the dome where Westwood, Kinross, and Broxton come together. You should look inside the retail courtyards that are meant to follow the design theme. The first you pass is located by the Verizon store; the second is a block farther by California Pizza Kitchen. Where Broxton ends at Weyburn, other Village icons include the two historic movie theaters and the

The Janss Dome embodies the Mediterranean-inspired architecture throughout the Village center.

nearby clock tower of Holmby Hall. Farther on is the not-to-be-missed Postmodern In-N-Out Burger.

At the 1.5-mile point, the hills start to take over and the commercial zone gives way to a fascinating collection of mostly mid-20th-century apartments, including Richard Neutra's landmarked Strathmore Apartments at 10005 Strathmore and other work by this architect at 638 to 648 Kelton and 507 Landfair. Most outlandish is a John Lautner–designed apartment building at 10901 Strathmore, which has not fared well with fraternity life.

Our loop through UCLA begins at the 2.6-mile mark. This tour is just a taste of a huge campus with many beautiful quads and intimate spaces. The site is very hilly, and students get a workout going to and from the residence hall villages above you to the left and the academic campus on your right. Bruin Walk is one major link. Pauley Pavilion and the statue of John Wooden symbolize the most dominant dynasty in the history of major American collegiate sports. UCLA was the NCAA Men's basketball champion ten times in a 12-year period beginning in 1964. Turning left from the Bruin Bear, you arrive at an open space where six of the oldest campus buildings (1929–1932) face each other along the main axis. Four are located on the terrace above Janss Steps, which is the centerpiece of that axis. Dickson Court is actually a bridge and was one of the original campus features. It is still there, but the arroyo that it was built to cross has been filled in. The captivating Inverted Fountain sits in a plaza with the music quad. From here, the path goes west then south through the Court of the Sciences to reach the peaceful Mathias Botanical Garden. These diverse 7.5 acres are a perfect place to wander, and there are maps posted. The hike ends shortly after leaving the garden.

MILES AND DIRECTIONS

0.0 START at 1015 Hilgard Ave. Garage. Exit the parking facility steps to the corner of Weyburn and Hilgard Avenues. Cross to the east side of Hilgard Avenue and turn right. Cross Lindbrook Drive where Hilgard ends.

0.1 Lindbrook Village Courtyard, 10830 Lindbrook Dr. Look into the landmarked apartment courtyard, then continue to the right on the left-hand side of Lindbrook. Turn left on Glendon Avenue.

0.2 Cross Wilshire Boulevard at the signal. Take Glendon past the office building on your left then turn left following signs to enter Pierce Brothers Westwood Village. Explore the cemetery.

0.6 Leave Pierce Brothers. Turn left in the alley. Turn left on Glendon Avenue. Turn right on Wellworth Avenue.

0.8 Turn right on Westwood Boulevard. Cross Wilshire Boulevard. Consider a visit to the free Hammer Museum on the right. Otherwise, cross to the northwest corner of Wilshire and Westwood Boulevards. Walk north on the left side of Westwood Boulevard.

1.2 Corner of Westwood with Kinross and Broxton Avenues. Cross Kinross. Look in the courtyard occupied by Verizon. Continue northwest on Broxton.

1.3 Corner of Broxton and Weyburn Avenues. Look in the courtyard occupied by California Pizza Kitchen. At Weyburn Avenue, cross toward the Fox Theatre tower and turn left on Weyburn. Turn right on Gayley Avenue.

1.5 Turn left on Le Conte Avenue. Turn right on Levering Avenue. Cross Strathmore Drive, then turn left so you are walking on the right side of Strathmore Drive.

1.8 Strathmore Apartments, 10005 Strathmore Dr. Turn right on Kelton Avenue.

2.3 Turn right on Ophir Drive. Turn right on Landfair Avenue. Turn left on Strathmore Drive.

2.6 Enter UCLA campus at Strathmore and Gayley. Cross Charles Young Drive, then turn left to walk uphill on the right side of Charles Young. Pass a stop sign, then come to a traffic signal.

2.9 Turn right into Bruin Walk.

3.1 Bruin Bear. Turn left, walking to the right of the Ashe Student Health Center. Come into a large quad area with grass and paths. Turn right toward the Janss Steps.

3.3 Janss Steps. Climb the steps to a fountain on the level above with Dickson Court beyond the fountain. Turn left at the fountain, then turn right to walk through the arcaded passage along Royce Hall. When the arcade ends, turn right, go down eight steps, then turn left to walk eastward across Dickson Court. As the vehicle-free quad ends with Portola Plaza, angle toward the center of the court on your right.

3.6 Turn right into Dickson Court South. Pick any of the pathways in this below-grade grassy square and aim for Schoenberg Hall, which displays a collection of friezes honoring world music. Veer right to pass to the right side of Schoenberg Hall.

3.8 Inverted Fountain. Turn right at the fountain and walk with Franz Hall on your left. Turn left (south) at a crossroads that signs identify as Court of the Sciences. If you are back among cars, you went too far.

4.0 Orthopaedic Hospital Building. After passing the bulbous extension of this building, veer left into the narrow passage between Orthopaedic Hospital Building and the Life Sciences Building. This passage goes down thirty steps. At the bottom of the steps, jog left then right to enter the well-signed ramp for the Mathias Botanical Garden.

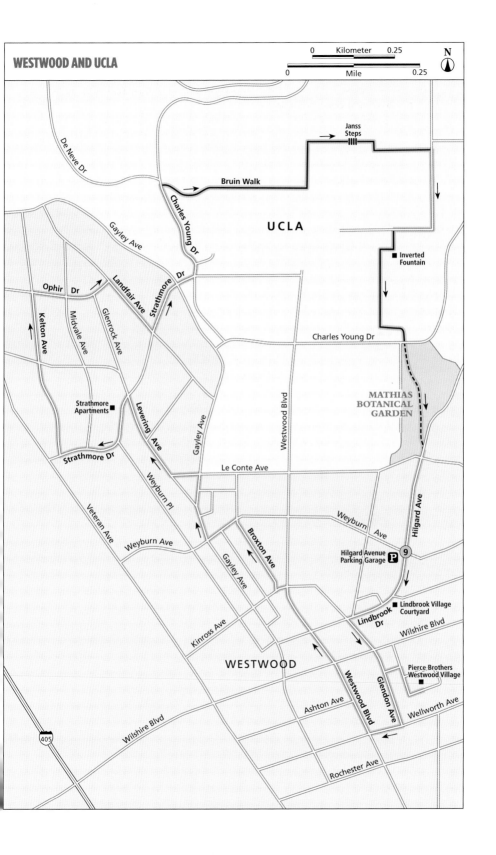

0   Kilometer   0.25

0   Mile   0.25

N

De Neve Dr

Janss Steps

Bruin Walk

Gayley Ave

Charles Young Dr

UCLA

Inverted Fountain

Ophir Dr

Landfair Ave

Strathmore Dr

Kelton Ave

Midvale Ave

Glenrock Ave

Charles Young Dr

Strathmore Apartments

Levering Ave

Gayley Ave

Westwood Blvd

MATHIAS BOTANICAL GARDEN

Strathmore Dr

Le Conte Ave

Weyburn Pl

Hilgard Ave

Veteran Ave

Weyburn Ave

Weyburn Ave

Broxton Ave

Gayley Ave

Hilgard Avenue Parking Garage

9

Lindbrook Village Courtyard

Kinross Ave

Lindbrook Dr

Wilshire Blvd

WESTWOOD

Pierce Brothers Westwood Village

405

Ashton Ave

Westwood Blvd

Glendon Ave

Wellworth Ave

Wilshire Blvd

Rochester Ave

UCLA's Mildred E. Mathias Botanical Garden is a peaceful place a short distance from the notorious traffic of the Village.

4.1 Enter Mathias Botanical Garden through a gate. You are entering at the northwest, uphill corner and will depart through a different gate at the southeast, downhill corner. There are many paths to choose from. Wander at will and follow your intuition to find the exit. The noise of vehicle traffic in that direction will be apparent.

4.5 Exit the gardens near the junction of Hilgard and Le Conte Avenues. Turn right on Hilgard Avenue, walking downhill.

4.7 End of hike at 1015 Hilgard Ave. Garage.

10 CHEVIOT HILLS-RANCHO PARK

This hike explores an area where lovely and prestigious residential districts exist cheek by jowl with an intensely commercial zone of office towers and production studios. The hike goes over hill and dale where beautiful houses are mostly free of privacy fences and express themselves nicely to the passing walker. You will pass architectural highlights, go under soothing trees, and walk in or along handsome public parks and golf courses.

Start: Metro Expo Westwood/Rancho Park Station, 2600 Westwood Blvd., Rancho Park 90064
Elevation gain: 300 feet
Distance: 4.9-mile loop
Hiking time: 2 to 3 hours
Difficulty: Moderate
Best season: Year-round
Trail surface: Sidewalks, park paths
Other trail users: None aside from other walkers
Restroom availability: Mile 3.1
Canine compatibility: Dogs must remain on leash.

Parking status: Free curb parking along Westwood Boulevard between National and the underpass of I-10. This is a 0.4-mile walk from the trailhead, but the hike goes near here and you could catch what was missed at the end of your hike. Free parking lot at Palms Park at the 0.9-mile mark of the hike.
Rail transit accessibility: Metro E (Expo) Line, Westwood/Rancho Park Station is the start point.
Trailhead GPS: N34° 02.20' W118° 25.53'

FINDING THE TRAILHEAD

From I-10 between the 110 Freeway and I-405, take exit 4 for Overland Avenue. From the east, go straight from the exit ramp onto National Boulevard. From the west, turn right on Overland Avenue, turn left on National Boulevard. In either case, turn right on Westwood Boulevard. The trailhead is a light rail station at the corner of Exposition and Westwood Boulevards.

WHAT TO SEE

Avoid commute hours. Most of this counterclockwise loop hike is quiet at any hour, but the brief mileage spent on boulevards would be unpleasant when there is an onslaught of automobiles Almost immediately the hike passes the Petal House on two sides. This is an early 1980s work by architect Eric Owen Moss to deconstruct and reimagine a generic 1945-built house. *Petal* in this case refers to how the house opens up and out around the roof.

The footbridge over the Metro line provides a pedestrian-only passage into Cheviot Hills, an enclave of about 1,400 homes that was developed in the 1920s. There is a great inventory of mature street trees; watch for the red ironbark eucalyptus trees. Notice how the streets follow the contours; the planners of this neighborhood did well not to try to force a grid upon it. Most of the homes are pleasant examples of the prevailing period styles of the 1920s. After turning left onto Queensbury Drive at the 1.6-mile mark, there are several notable architectural landmarks. A natural wood–clad house with a knife-edge corner at the intersection of Bannockburn and Queensbury Drives is the Strauss House. This is a 1941 work by architect Raphael Soriano. At the northwest corner of Queensbury and Club Drives, Pritzker Architecture Prize–winning Thom Mayne built a home

A pedestrian bridge at Palms Park goes over the Metro E Line.

for his family in 2017. An ordinary house was demolished to make room for the new one, but extraordinary author Ray Bradbury had lived in that house for 50 years. A tribute to Bradbury—a great walker who never learned to drive—is incorporated in the entry-area of the new house. 2926 Club Dr. is a wonderful 1956 Mid-Century Modern home from architect A. Quincy Jones. The signature feature is the broad wingspan roofline.

Cheviot Hills Recreation Center, at 3.1 miles, is the obvious choice for a pause and a restroom break. This spot is centered between two golf courses. Well hidden on the right side of the direction of travel is Hillcrest Country Club. It was founded in the 1920s as the first Los Angeles country club for the city's Jewish community, and it has a century-long association with personalities from the movie business. On the left side of travel is the public, city-run Rancho Park Golf Course.

The route passes historic 20th Century Fox Studios. That name reflects an amalgamation of two film companies in the 1930s. An amalgamation of Fox with Disney in the 21st century perhaps means that this studio will soon give way to a residential village. The first connection this land had to the film industry was when silent cowboy star Tom Mix established a 176-acre ranch here in the 19-teens which he later sold to William Fox. The 1950s brought television as well as a trend that did not favor backlot production. 20th Century Fox hired consultants and planners including architect Welton Becket to invent a *city within the city* on the studio lot. By the mid-1960s, this plan was realized as Century City. You walk outside the corner of the historic studio where production facilities remain.

The Rancho Park neighborhood is a great area for the purple bloom of the jacaranda trees in late spring. Saint Timothy's Catholic Church on Pico has a beautiful bell tower. The extravagantly decorated design around the doorway is *Churrigueresque*. That term indicates a style popularized during the Baroque era of Spanish architecture. Pico

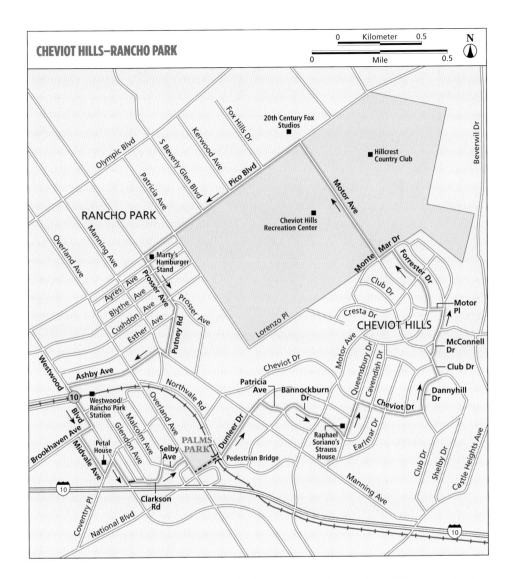

Kilometer

Mile

N

20th Century Fox
Studios

Hillcrest
Country Club

Fox Hills Dr

Kenwood Ave

S Beverly Glen Blvd

Patricia Ave

Olympic Blvd

Pico Blvd

Beverwil Dr

RANCHO PARK

Cheviot Hills
Recreation Center

Motor Ave

Overland Ave

Manning Ave

Marty's
Hamburger
Stand

Prosser Ave

Ayres Ave

Blythe Ave

Cushdon Ave

Esther Ave

Prosser Ave

Putney Rd

Lorenzo Pl

Monte Mar Dr

Forrester Dr

Club Dr

Cresta Dr

Motor
Pl

CHEVIOT HILLS

McConnell
Dr

Club Dr

Westwood

Ashby Ave

Northvale Rd

Cheviot Dr

Patricia
Ave

Bannockburn
Dr

Motor Ave

Queensbury Dr

Cavendish Dr

Cheviot Dr

Dannyhill
Dr

Westwood/
Rancho Park
Station

Overland Ave

Malcolm Ave

Glendon Ave

Dunleer Dr

Raphael
Soriano's
Strauss
House

Earlmar Dr

Club Dr

Shelby Dr

Castle Heights Ave

Brookhaven Ave

Midvale Ave

Petal
House

Selby
Ave

PALMS
PARK

Pedestrian Bridge

Manning Ave

10

Coventry Pl

Clarkson
Rd

National Blvd

10

Boulevard near Prosser Avenue is 1 mile from the end of the walk and has some food options. Marty's is a rare surviving walk-up hamburger-sandwich stand that has been in business at this location for more than 60 years. If you wanted to alter the end of the hike without adding distance, foodies might select to just keep going west on Pico, and then turn left on Westwood Boulevard. Among other choices, this alternative route would pass the venerable Apple Pan restaurant.

MILES AND DIRECTIONS

0.0 START at Metro Expo Westwood/Rancho Park Station. From the light rail platform, the exits lead to the east side of Westwood Boulevard. Cross to the west side of the street and turn left (south) on Westwood Boulevard. Turn right on Brookhaven Avenue. Turn left on Midvale Avenue.

The Petal House by architect Eric Owen Moss deconstructs and reimagines a typical post–World War II house.

0.3 Petal House, 2828 Midvale Ave. Turn left on Coventry Place. Cross to the east side of Westwood Boulevard and turn right. Just before walking under the freeway, turn left into a pedestrian passage. Go straight (east) from this passage to Clarkson Road. Follow Clarkson through a curve and turn right on Selby Avenue. Turn left to regain Clarkson. Turn right on Overland Avenue. At National Boulevard, cross to the northeast corner.

0.9 Palms Park. From the crosswalk, follow a walkway parallel to the freeway that passes to the right of the park. Cross the pedestrian bridge. On the other side of the tracks, cross Northvale Road and head straight on Dunleer Drive. Turn right on Patricia Avenue. Turn left on Haddington Drive. Turn right on Bannockburn Drive. Cross Motor Avenue.

1.6 Strauss House. Turn left on Queensbury Drive. Turn right on Cheviot Drive. Turn left on Dannyhill Drive. Turn left on Club Drive. Turn right on McConnell Drive.

2.5 Turn left on Motor Place. Turn right on Forrester Drive. Turn left on Monte Mar Drive and cross to the west side of Motor Avenue. Turn right on Motor and walk to the right side of the tennis courts. Enter the recreation area using steps on the other side of the courts.

3.1 Cheviot Hills Recreation Center. After the tennis courts, locate a park path and walk parallel to Motor Avenue. You will pass the pool, the gym, and the ball fields. Where the path terminates at the golf course, shift right to follow the sidewalk on the left side of Motor Avenue. Cross to north side of Pico Boulevard.

3.4 20th Century Fox Studios. Turn left on Pico Boulevard.

4.1 Marty's Hamburger Stand. Turn left on Prosser Avenue. Veer right on Putney Road.

4.5 Turn right on Manning Avenue. Turn left on Ashby Avenue. Cross Overland Avenue and continue on Ashby. Turn left on Westwood Boulevard.

4.9 End of hike at Expo Westwood/Rancho Park Station.

11 VENICE

Venice has a fascinating history from the early 1900s, and there are many features that show off this history if you know where to look. Venice has been home to architectural experimentation in the past 40 years and this hike points out many examples, including the work of Frank Gehry. The canal paths and walk streets of Venice present a residential culture and walking environment unlike anywhere else in Southern California.

Start: Rainbow Crosswalk, 1305 Abbot Kinney Blvd., Venice 90291
Elevation gain: 50 feet
Distance: 5.5-mile loop
Hiking time: 2.5 to 3.5 hours
Difficulty: Moderate
Best season: Year-round
Trail surface: Sidewalks, paved paths
Other trail users: Tourists, shoppers and diners, cyclists, scooters

Restroom availability: Miles 2.0 through 2.8
Canine compatibility: Dogs must remain on leash.
Parking status: Mixture of difficult to find free and metered parking nearby. Pay parking lots on Electric Avenue 0.3 mile distant.
Rail transit accessibility: N/A
Trailhead GPS: N33° 59.47′ W118° 28.08′

FINDING THE TRAILHEAD

Driving on I-10 west of I-405, take exit 1B for CA 1/Lincoln Boulevard. Turn left on Lincoln Boulevard. Turn right on California Street. Turn right on Abbot Kinney Boulevard.

WHAT TO SEE

If it is a dreary, foggy day, or if it is a peak beach day when crowds will diminish the experience, save this hike for another day. The Rainbow Crosswalk was dedicated in 2019 to commemorate the 50th anniversary of the Stonewall uprising in New York City. Abbot Kinney's Venice of America opened in 1905 with a network of canals interlaced with peninsulas and islands of residential, social, and commercial buildings. The first mile of this route passes through the heart of these ghost canals. The waterways in this part of Venice were mostly filled in by the city by 1930. Wide streets are a tip-off; Cabrillo Avenue was Cabrillo Canal and Windward Avenue was Lion Canal. South of Cabrillo, Andalusia Avenue traces the course of a small bridge that once connected triangular St. Mark's Island to surrounding fingers of land. The matching bungalows on either side of Andalusia were built circa 1913 as a holiday camp called United States Island. Each bungalow was named for a state. Since the 1980s, Venice has been fertile ground for architectural experimenting, and the tiny building lots mean that those experiments can be seen clearly from the street. The Vienna firm of Coop Himmelb(l)au built the house at 513 Grand Blvd. in 2002.

Windward Circle was once the central lagoon and bathing lake that connected to three of the canals. Working in the Postmodern style in the 1980s, local architect Steven Ehrlich created three buildings which present an homage to the history of the area, including a callout to the *Race Through the Clouds* roller coaster, which was once here.

The walking path along Howland Canal near its intersection with Grand Canal

The Arnoldi Studio on the left, where Indiana intersects Hampton, is always a good mural wall. The most recent display features portraits of Jim Morrison, Teena Marie, and Arnold Schwarzenegger.

The Binoculars Building is a three-building composition begun by Frank Gehry with artists Claes Oldenburg and Coosje van Bruggen in 1985. The original client was a major ad agency; now it is home to Google Los Angeles. At the corner of Rose, a clown fronts the Postmodern Renaissance Building meant to emulate the buildings of Venice in the early 1900s. Paloma Avenue is the first of the *walk streets* on this hike, and Venice has the best concentration of such features in Southern California. Picture a typical avenue where small homes with front yards line sidewalks on both sides of a drivable street. Then subtract one sidewalk and the center motorway. The remaining sidewalk framed by front yards and homes is the classic Southern California walk street. At the end of Paloma Avenue an inscrutable house of glass corners and metal roof is the only US residential work by architect Arata Isozaki. Isozaki would later win the Pritzker Prize.

Leaving the boardwalk, 39 Horizon Ave. is a three-story house in galvanized corrugated metal designed by Frank Gehry. There is more Frank Gehry work to be seen 20 minutes further on at the Norton House. Here, a study has the semi-comical look of a lifeguard tower. To the right of this, the lavender-colored Snipper House by architect Miguel Angelo Flores is also notable.

The recommended route for touring the canal paths is just a suggestion. If you want to wander more, understand that the described route meets the canals near the southwest corner and is planned to leave near the northeast corner. These canals survived because,

A mural just off Abbot Kinney Boulevard by Tel Aviv artist PILPELED

in the 1930s, this group was considered too low rent to be entitled to city "improvements" that filled in the original Kinney canals. A Los Angeles canal restoration was completed here in 1993.

In the 0.7-mile stretch between the canals and the best of the Venice walk streets, the route passes SPARC, which is a mural conservancy operating out of the old Art Deco Venice jail building. It is worth a stop when open. The final walk streets are magical; observe how each one has a circular planter mid-block. On Amoroso Place, a gnarled pittosporum supports a swing. Except for the two motorist streets that it crosses, Nowita Place is a pedestrian–only corridor that extends 0.4 mile. From here, the cafes and shops of Abbot Kinney beckon at the end of the hike.

MILES AND DIRECTIONS

0.0 START at the Rainbow Crosswalk and cross Abbot Kinney Boulevard heading south (from address 1305 to 1302). Enter alley-like Cadiz Court from the crosswalk. Turn left on Cabrillo Avenue. Turn right on Andalusia Avenue. Turn left on Grand Boulevard. Walk only far enough to see address 513.

0.3 Turn around and take Grand Boulevard west to Windward Circle. Go counterclockwise along the circle and turn right on Main Street and go northwest on the right side of Main.

0.9 Cross Abbot Kinney, then turn right. Make two quick left turns, first on Brooks Avenue, then on Hampton Drive.

1.2 Turn left on Sunset Avenue. Turn right on Main Street.

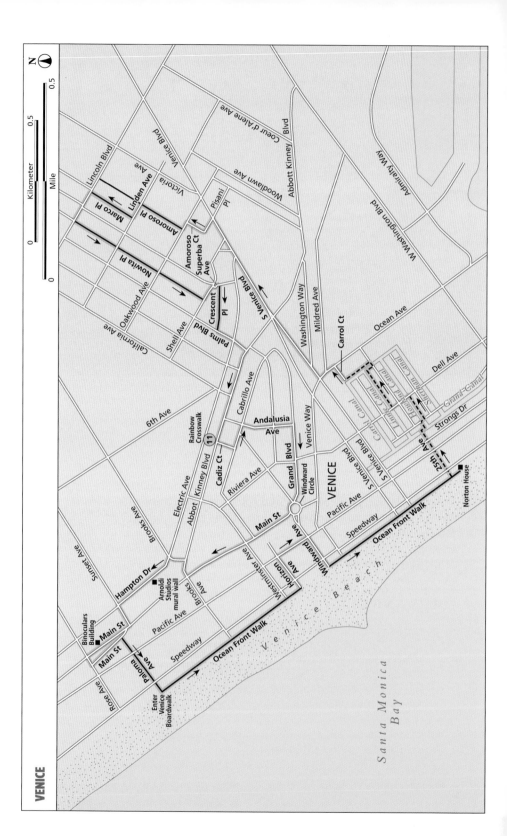

1.3 Binoculars Building. Turn left on Rose Avenue. Cross Main Street and pass beyond a parking lot. Turn left into smaller South Main Street (one way, perhaps unsigned). Turn right into the Paloma Avenue walk street.

1.6 Turn left on Pacific Avenue. At Sunset Avenue, use the crosswalk to get across Pacific and turn right. Turn left to reenter the Paloma Avenue walk street.

1.8 Turn left into the Venice Boardwalk—aka Ocean Front Walk.

2.3 Turn left on Horizon Avenue. Turn right on Pacific Avenue. Turn right on Windward Avenue.

2.6 Windward Avenue at Venice Boardwalk. Turn left to follow the boardwalk down the coast (southeast) to just beyond 25th Avenue.

3.0 Norton House, 2509 Ocean Front Walk. From the Norton House, turn around. Come back to 25th Avenue and turn right. This turns into a walk street. Cross Pacific Avenue and follow the serpentine walking path. Cross Strongs Drive and stay on path to reach Grand Canal.

3.2 Grand Canal. Cross the humpback bridge over Grand Canal and turn right on the canal path. Turn left to follow path on the left side of Howland Canal. Immediately take the pedestrian bridge going to the right side of Howland Canal and then turn left. Turn left over the vehicle bridge (Dell Avenue) to cross over Howland Canal. At Linnie Canal, turn right onto the path before Dell Avenue crosses that canal. Walk as far as you can on the right side of Linnie Canal. Turn right and then left into a humpback bridge over the waterway.

3.5 Off this bridge, turn left to walk on the northeast side of the canal network. Leave the water turning right on Carrol Court. Turn left on Ocean Avenue.

3.7 Turn right on South Venice Boulevard and walk along the right side of the wide street.

4.1 At Shell Avenue, take the crosswalk to the other side of Venice Bouleyard toward the fire station and Beyond Baroque arts center. Turn right on Venice Boulevard. Turn left on Pisani Place.

4.2 Pass between SPARC on the left and a parking lot on the right. Turn right in the alley, which is unsigned Amoroso Court. Turn left on Oakwood Avenue.

4.3 Turn right into the Amoroso Place walk street. Turn left at the first cross street, unsigned Linden Avenue. Turn right into the Marco Place walk street.

4.6 Turn left on Lincoln Boulevard. Turn left into the sketchy beginning of Nowita Place walk street. Follow this walk street past two vehicle streets until it ends at a third, which is Shell Avenue.

5.1 Turn left on Shell Avenue. Walk wide right of the traffic circle and look for a grassy triangular area. Turn right on the path here to enter the Crescent Place walk street.

5.2 Turn left where Crescent Place exits to Palms Boulevard. Turn right on Abbot Kinney Boulevard.

5.5 End of hike at the Rainbow Crosswalk.

A skateboarder coasts by a Frank Gehry–designed beach house on the Venice Boardwalk.

12 SANTA MONICA CANYONS

This hike is a beautiful exercise done in intimate canyons and on the palisades overlooking Santa Monica Bay. In Palisades Park, this jaunt occurs with the company of scores of locals and visitors. In the canyons, there is quiet solitude. Here there is a rare combination of affluence with eclecticism, and a tradition of architectural excellence in a remarkable physical environment.

Start: Rustic Canyon Recreational Park, 102-178 Latimer Rd., Pacific Palisades 90402
Elevation gain: 400 feet
Distance: 5.8-mile loop
Hiking time: 2.5 to 3.5 hours
Difficulty: Moderate
Best season: Year-round
Trail surface: Sidewalks, pavement without sidewalks, paved path, dirt, stairs

Other trail users: Stairway climbers
Restroom availability: Miles 1.5, 4
Canine compatibility: Dogs must remain on leash.
Parking status: Free lot parking in the park, street parking outside the lot
Rail transit accessibility: N/A
Trailhead GPS: N34° 02.27' W118° 30.89'

FINDING THE TRAILHEAD

From any direction, access I-10 west of I-405. Continue onto CA 1 North. Turn right onto Entrada Drive. Turn left onto Mesa Road. Turn left onto Latimer Road. The destination will be on the left.

WHAT TO SEE

The route is shaped like a figure 8; it begins with a counterclockwise loop that returns to the starting point after 1.5 miles. Then the larger loop goes clockwise. The recreation center building was created as the clubhouse for the Uplifters Club, an invite-only association of the male power elite of 1920s Los Angeles. They were associated most with polo, amateur theatrics, and insobriety. Some of the homes found in the first 10 minutes of the walk began as camp-like dwellings for club members. Brooktree Road has many houses that carry the woodsy feel of the Rustic Canyon. Architect Ray Kappe, a co-founder of SCI-Arc (the Southern California Institute of Architecture), was one of the major contributors here with examples at 755, 739, 737, and 680 Brooktree Rd. plus the beautiful composition he designed as his own home in 1968 at 715 Brooktree.

Ten minutes after leaving the recreation center a second time, the house with the Streamline carport and distinctive stair railing on the right was designed in 1937 by architect Harwell H. Harris for designer John Entenza. Three wonderful stairways, one up and two down, take you the hard way out of the Rustic Canyon drainage and into Santa Monica Canyon.

Santuario San Lorenzo is the Pascual Marquez family cemetery. This is a remarkable presence at the back of a lot amidst multimillion-dollar homes. A native garden near the street has a plaque that explains the history. Two stairways separated by 800 feet climb out of Santa Monica Canyon to Adelaide Drive. These might be the most famous outdoor public stairs in Southern California. Climb the wood stairs and leave the vicinity for

The woodsy setting of Brooktree Road where architect Ray Kappe built this house for himself in 1968

Palisades Park. Then you will come back later to go down the concrete stairs. The John Byers Adobe is at 404 Georgina Ave., just where you turn right. Architect John Byers, a specialist in the genre, built this in 1920.

After the break in Palisades Park comes the grandeur of Adelaide Drive. The wonderful circa 1910 Craftsman houses have an interloper. The modern glass and metal house was designed by architect Frank Gehry as his own family home. These all look out over the canyon and the Santa Monica Bay.

Just before the 5-mile mark, you cross Entrada near the confluence of the two canyons. Rustic Creek is straight ahead of you coming out of the Santa Monica Mountains. On the other side of Sunset Boulevard, Rustic runs down poison oak thickets past the Will Rogers Ranch and Murphy Ranch. Santa Monica Creek comes from the right trickling out of the legendary Riviera Country Club. Ahead of you before the finish is West Rustic Road, the most tranquil spot on this hike.

MILES AND DIRECTIONS

0.0 START at Rustic Canyon Recreation Center. From the recreation center building, exit to Latimer Road and turn left. Veer right on Haldeman Road. Bear left at a Y and turn left on a connecting road (probably unsigned) to where Haldeman and Latimer reconnect.

0.2 Turn right on Latimer, which will be signed as a dead end.

0.7 At a cul-de-sac, cross the Rustic Creek footbridge and pass through a gate to continue straight on an access road leading to Rustic Creek Lane.

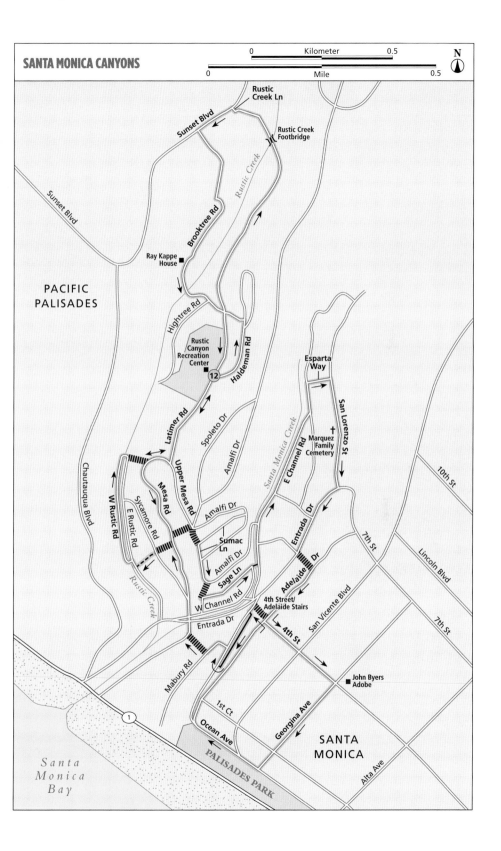

The popular wood stairway connecting Entrada and Adelaide Drives—166 steps up

0.8 Turn left on Sunset Boulevard. Turn left on Brooktree Road.

1.2 Ray Kappe House, 715 Brooktree Road.

1.4 Turn right on Latimer Road.

1.5 Rustic Canyon Recreation Center (second time after loop). Continue on Latimer Road.

1.7 Turn right on Mesa Road.

2.0 Near 404 Mesa Road, turn left up a long stairway. At the top, go down another stairway that begins just 70 feet to the right of the top of the stairway that you just came up. Go straight at the bottom on Sumac Lane, which becomes Amalfi Drive.

2.2 Near 271 Amalfi go down a stairway that is concealed behind a hedge. Bear left at the stairway split near the bottom.

2.4 Turn left on Sage Lane at the bottom of the stairs. Where Sage Lane ends at West Channel Road, take a footbridge over Santa Monica Creek and then turn left in front of the school onto East Channel Road. Pass Amalfi Drive and walk through two automobile barriers.

2.8 Turn right from East Channel to Esparta Way. Turn right on San Lorenzo Street. Pass Marquez Family Cemetery on the right.

3.1 Turn right on Entrada Drive. With the school on your right, take the crosswalk left and ascend the wood steps. Turn right on top onto Adelaide Drive.

3.5 Turn left on 4th Street.

3.7 John Byers Adobe at 404 Georgina Avenue. Turn right on Georgina Avenue. Cross Ocean Avenue to Palisades Park. Turn right to follow the park pathway to restrooms and a picnic area.

4.0 Palisades Park restrooms. Leaving the restrooms, first go back the direction (southeast) that you just came from, walking only so far as the crosswalk across Ocean Avenue. Cross and turn left. Turn right on Adelaide Drive.

4.4 Across from 4th Street, turn left down a long stairway. Turn left into the sidewalk at the bottom, walking on the left side of Ocean Avenue. Immediately go up a less obvious stairway along the red brick. This will climb to a path high on the slope. After 500 feet from the start of this stair/path, ignore how the path appears to keep going and turn right down the stairs to Ocean Avenue.

4.6 Cross Ocean Avenue carefully and turn right. Quickly turn left on Mabury Road.

4.7 Turn right down an inconspicuous stairway near 249 Mabury. At the bottom, cross Entrada Drive and continue north through the traffic signal and the double crosswalk to the northwest corner of Mesa Road and West Channel Drive. Follow Mesa straight, avoiding Sycamore Road on the left.

5.0 Near 401 Mesa turn left down a stairway. At the bottom, cross Sycamore Road and go straight ahead in a dirt pedestrian alley across from the steps.

5.3 Arrive out at the junction of East and West Rustic Roads. Go straight over the auto bridge to West Rustic. Follow West Rustic Road with the creek on the right. When it ends, cross right over another auto bridge. From the bridge, walk straight across East Rustic Road to enter a hard to discern public pathway. A painted arrow for address 544 is your route. After the pathway bends, go up the steps.

5.5 Turn left on Mesa Road. Turn left on Latimer Road.

5.8 End of hike at Rustic Canyon Recreation Center.

13 **TORRANCE**

Come for the six craft breweries on this hike; stay for the wonderful townscape of Old Town. Torrance has a fascinating early 1900s town center that is dwarfed by the city that grew around it. It is a picturesque place for a stroll, and connecting by foot six working breweries with public taprooms will turn that stroll into a fun 5-mile urban hike.

Start: Smog City Brewery and Taproom, 1901 Del Amo Blvd., Torrance 90501
Elevation gain: 50 feet
Distance: 5.0-mile loop
Hiking time: 2.5 to 4 hours
Difficulty: Moderate because of length
Best season: Year-round
Best days and times: Thurs–Sun; start midafternoon.
Trail surface: Sidewalks

Other trail users: Shoppers and diners
Restroom availability: Throughout
Canine compatibility: Dogs must remain on leash.
Parking status: Free lot parking as well as curb parking at the start point
Rail transit accessibility: N/A
Trailhead GPS: N33° 50.83' W118° 18.80'

FINDING THE TRAILHEAD

From I-405 just west of the 110 Freeway, take exit 38B for Western Avenue. Northbound, turn left on Western Avenue. Southbound, turn left on 190th Street, then turn right on Western Avenue. Turn right on Del Amo Boulevard. The destination is on the right-hand side.

WHAT TO SEE

The small-scale craft breweries on this counterclockwise loop hike are nothing like what is often associated with bars. Most of the breweries on this hike understand the value of providing an environment that is comfortable for adults who want a place to go with their children and for adults who want a place to go with their dog. Craft breweries are receptive to selling economical small tastes of their beer. That is very helpful for a hiking crawl.

Throughout this hike, you see rail lines, active and dormant, that indicate how Torrance was invented as an industrial city. Torrance was historically known for its steel mills into the 1970s. When the mills left, this area was blessed with some clean industry, including the white-collar regional offices for Honda that you pass on the left.

Between Strand Brewing and Yorkshire Square Brewery is your longest hiking interval between breweries and the best opportunity to get some appreciation for Torrance Old Town. Notice the cute 1918-built workers cottages at 2203-2207 Maricopa St. Some devotees of pub crawls insist that at least one dive bar with local patrons should be included. The Branch Office, a convivial place at 2320 Torrance Blvd., would fit that requirement. Beginning at Cota Avenue, the walking is along a diagonal street layout that generates a different light on the buildings than what you expect from the conventional north-south grid. There are also intriguing junctions. Torrance engaged the Olmsted firm to do the street and park planning and Lloyd Wright to do the landscaping.

In the taproom of Smog City Brewery

The Olmsted name is famous for the design of New York's Central Park. Lloyd Wright had studied under his father and was building his own reputation when he worked for Torrance. The high school anchors the southwest side of linear El Prado Park and the greenery points toward the northeast and Mount San Antonio, colloquially known as Mount Baldy. El Prado Avenue has a wonderful old town feel, and Chado Tea Room and Torrance Bakery are good brewery alternatives. The diagonal parking on El Prado

Ironwood eucalyptus
trees along Bow Avenue

and on Sartori Avenue and the signage on the Fox Drug building are urban artifacts that can't be taken for granted. Red Car Brewery is not one of the scheduled stops, but the handsome 1928 Mission Revival–style building it occupies is worth a glance. The Tree Arch at Sartori and Torrance is a bit more of old town charm.

Want to cut some breweries from this hike? Don't skip Yorkshire Square. It is the only one of the six with its own regular kitchen, open from late afternoon. The British-style beers and beer cocktails here are unique. Leaving Yorkshire Square, you go past the old streetcar depot building that has been turned into a restaurant. Torrance is justly proud of their Pacific Electric Railway El Prado Bridge designed by architect Irving Gill and built in 1913. Originally the center arch of the underpass served the streetcar while a freight line that served a steel mill passed overhead. The three remaining breweries come in quick succession. The Dudes' Brewing has sort of a Hawaiian surfer mood, while Cosmic Brewery and Taproom has an eye cast toward the stars. Monkish Brewing Company specializes in wood-aged Saisons, and they will always be busy, particularly with Millennials.

MILES AND DIRECTIONS

0.0 START at Smog City Brewery and Taproom. Leaving the parking lot, turn right (west) on Del Amo Boulevard. Turn left on Van Ness Avenue. Turn right on Dominguez Street.

0.8 Strand Brewing Company, 2201 Dominguez St. Cross Dominguez Way and Dominguez Street in front of Strand brewery. Walk to the right of the grassy median. Turn right on Dominguez Street. Turn left on Sartori Avenue. Turn right on Portola Avenue. Turn right on Maricopa Street.

1.2 Turn left on Cota Avenue.

1.5 Cross to the south side of Torrance Boulevard and turn right. Turn left on divided Madrid Avenue to walk down the right side of the railway line. Across from El Dorado Street, take the unusual ten-step pedestrian crossing over the tracks and then turn right to continue south on Madrid. Turn left on Sonoma Street.

1.9 Make a diagonal left turn on Engracia Avenue. Turn right on Manuel Avenue.

2.1 El Prado Park. Turn left into this linear park and walk 2 long blocks across the grass or on the sidewalk.

2.5 Cross Sartori Avenue and turn left.

2.6 At the Tree Arch feature, cross Torrance Boulevard and continue on Sartori Avenue. Turn right on Engracia Avenue.

2.7 Yorkshire Square Brewery, 1109 Van Ness Ave. Turn right on Van Ness Avenue. Cross twice to reach the southeast corner of Torrance Boulevard and Cabrillo Avenue. Head south on Cabrillo.

2.9 Turn left on 213th Street. Turn left diagonally onto Bow Avenue.

3.2 Turn right on Torrance Boulevard. Walk under El Prado Bridge.

3.3 Turn left on Western Avenue. Turn left on 208th Street.

3.7 The Dudes' Brewing Company, 1840 West 208th St. From the front of the brewery, go north on Manhattan Place. Turn left on 205th Street. Turn right on Gramercy Place. Turn down alley on the right side just before you would reach Del Amo Boulevard.

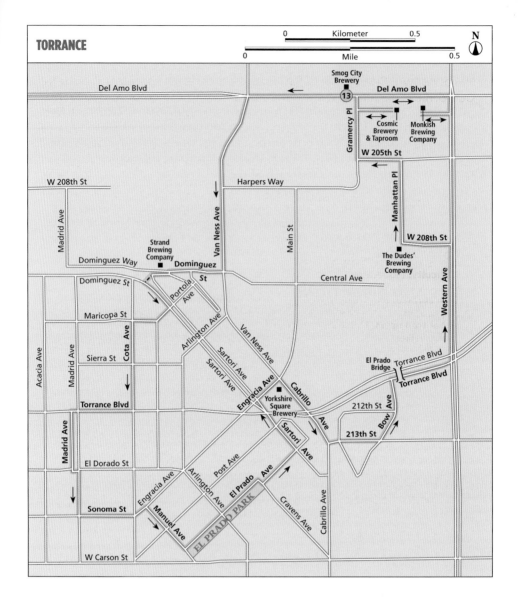

TORRANCE

Smog City Brewery

Del Amo Blvd

Del Amo Blvd

13

Gramercy Pl

Cosmic Brewery & Taproom

Monkish Brewing Company

W 205th St

Manhattan Pl

W 208th St

Harpers Way

Madrid Ave

Van Ness Ave

Main St

W 208th St

The Dudes' Brewing Company

Western Ave

Strand Brewing Company

Dominguez Way

Dominguez St

Central Ave

Dominguez St

Portola Ave

Maricopa St

Arlington Ave

Cota Ave

Sierra St

Sartori Ave

Van Ness Ave

El Prado Bridge

Torrance Blvd

Acacia Ave

Madrid Ave

Sartori Ave

Engracia Ave

Cabrillo Ave

Torrance Blvd

Torrance Blvd

Yorkshire Square Brewery

212th St

Bow Ave

Torrance Blvd

Sartori Ave

213th St

Madrid Ave

El Dorado St

Post Ave

Engracia Ave

Arlington Ave

El Prado Ave

Cabrillo Ave

Sonoma St

Manuel Ave

EL PRADO PARK

Cravens Ave

W Carson St

4.2 Cosmic Brewery and Taproom, 20316 Gramercy Place. Return through the alley back to Gramercy Place and turn right. Turn right on Del Amo Boulevard. Turn right on Western Avenue. Turn right into an alley signed as Del Amo Business Park.

4.7 Monkish Brewing Company, 20311 South Western Ave. Return through the alley to Western Avenue and turn left. Cross to the north side of Del Amo Boulevard and turn left.

5.0 End of hike at Smog City Brewery.

14 **SAN PEDRO**

Harbor town! San Pedro is magic and completely unique in Southern California. This hike is a sequence of enjoying the color and local history around Cabrillo Beach, feasting on the views around Point Fermin Park, visiting the lively patients at a marine animal care facility, exploring an old army base that has transitioned to a neighborhood resource, and checking out an amazing new mosaic mural.

Start: Cabrillo Marine Aquarium, 3800 Stephen M. White Dr., San Pedro 90731
Elevation gain: 450 feet
Distance: 6.1-mile loop
Hiking time: 3 to 4 hours
Difficulty: Moderate
Best season: Year-round
Trail surface: Sidewalks, paved paths, stairs
Other trail users: None aside from other walkers

Restroom availability: Miles 0.9, 2.1
Canine compatibility: Dogs must remain on leash.
Contact: Marine Mammal Care Center, (310) 548-5677
Parking status: Pay parking in beach parking lot
Rail transit accessibility: N/A
Trailhead GPS: N33° 42.68' W118° 17.12'

FINDING THE TRAILHEAD

Take the 110 Freeway south toward San Pedro. Take exit 1A for CA 47 toward Vincent Thomas Bridge/Terminal Island/Long Beach. Before crossing the Thomas Bridge, take the Harbor Boulevard exit. Turn right on Harbor Boulevard. Turn right on Miner Street. Turn right on 22nd Street. Turn left on Via Cabrillo Marina. Veer right onto Shoshonean Road at the signs for Cabrillo Marine Aquarium. The hike starts in front of the aquarium building.

WHAT TO SEE

In the mid-1920s, a move was afoot to build a safe new sandy beach here inside the breakwater. When it opened, the sandy east-facing Cabrillo Beach was second in size only to Coney Island among the artificial beaches in the United States. Angelenos came in droves in their Fords or on the streetcar to escape the city. The beautiful new Spanish-style bathhouse went up during the 1932 Olympics year. It offered enclosed outdoor changing areas and showers and provided rental bathing suits and towels. The bathhouse also began to assemble marine artifacts in a second-floor museum. When they were ready to translate that informal collection into a stand-alone marine aquarium, Los Angeles turned in 1980 to a relatively unknown local architect named Frank Gehry. Gehry got everyone scratching their heads with his bold but controversial reliance on a pipe framework and chain-link fencing. The expressionistic use of wooden piers, angled as if they have been beaten back by the waves, is part of an aquarium addition done by architect Barton Phelps. Today Cabrillo Beach seems somewhat forgotten.

Start this clockwise loop hike by climbing out of Cabrillo Beach and walking to the left of the statue of Stephen M. White, the man who waged the Free Harbor campaign to bring the new local harbor to here in San Pedro Bay instead of on the Santa Monica Bay.

A detail from the amazing 200-foot-long 25th Street Mosaic Wall, artist Julie Bender

You pass a nice public stairway near Bluff Place; this is the rare case where walking up the vehicular street is better than taking the steps. There is a fantastic harbor view on the left where 40th Street dead-ends. The Port of Los Angeles is the busiest port in the Western Hemisphere measured by overseas containers handled. Adjacent Long Beach is second. Yet it may come as a surprise how little impact that frenetic commerce has on most of San Pedro. The port becomes a picturesque backdrop, and watching a huge container or cruise ship come or go is thrilling. Up the hill, at the end of Pacific Avenue, there will hopefully be a clear view of Santa Catalina Island. Also look through the fence to study the remnants of the Sunken City in the foreground. A geologic slump in 1929 caused earth movement of as much as a foot per day. Several blocks of city streets were lost, but most of the wood bungalows on them were moved in time.

Point Fermin Park is a shady green space where you might see whales pass during their migrations. Monarch butterflies migrate to here and stick around during the winter. Tiny Walker's Café has a pleasant biker vibe. This location has been used a lot for filming; the scene in the movie *Chinatown* where Jake Gittes tails Hollis Mulwray was shot here. The unusual Victorian-era lighthouse is just that, a house with a light tower. The light was darkened for security reasons during World War II, and it has never been lit again. Just uphill, the Korean Friendship Bell was a gift from Korea for the 1976 Bicentennial. It is 17 tons of copper and tin modeled after a 7th-century original. Five days a year, the bell is ceremoniously rung by a log rather than a clapper. You also see a solitary basketball court; with a backdrop of sea and sky, this spot has been popular for filming commercials.

After 94 years as an army installation, Fort MacArthur was turned over to the city in 1982. You hike past bunkers and gun positions. Chief among these is the Battery Osgood-Farley, a monument of World War I–era technology that was obsolete by the 1920s. Disappearing carriage guns could project a 1,500-pound shell 14 miles. The new acreage gave the city room for many new or enhanced resources, but most of the base land remains undeveloped. One such resource is the Marine Mammal Care Center. At this hospital for ill, injured, and orphaned marine mammals, the primary work is the treatment and release of rescued seals and sea lions. The center is both instructive and fun as you view recovering animals in their pools behind fences. Use the restroom here; it is the last scheduled stop on the hike. You'll need to wait with your dog at the picnic table outside the animal recovery area. Angels Gate Park has a certain ambience as you walk through the eucalyptus trees and barracks buildings that have been repurposed for municipal arts and crafts uses. Hey Rookie Pool is a remnant of the old base that has been beautifully enhanced to become a civic resource. There are informational signs about the history, and the view is sensational. The gate to Gaffey Street from the pool gives you the opportunity to move on without backtracking.

Hiking 1.3 miles from Angels Gate takes you to the incomparable 25th Street Mosaic Wall by artist Julie Bender. Completed in 2019, this is a portrait of a special community. The realization of Ms. Bender's vision was assisted by many hours of local contributions. Starting back downhill, Busy Bee Market has an amazing sandwich-making tradition. It is the unique sort of business that can flourish in a place like San Pedro. The way back presents a few steep streets with good harbor views, a wonderful stairway under a graceful Peruvian pepper tree, and blocks of interesting houses, including some built on super-narrow lots on Carolina Street.

The dead end of 40th Street overlooks the breakwater, Angels Gate Lighthouse, and southern end of the Port of Los Angeles.

MILES AND DIRECTIONS

0.0 START in front of Cabrillo Marine Aquarium. You will be walking out the southwest vehicle entrance to Cabrillo Beach. The driving directions were through the north entrance. With your back to the aquarium facing the parking lot, turn right (south). Walk past several picnic tables in the grass. Head toward the entrance driveway, cross in the crosswalk, and turn right to leave the Cabrillo Beach complex. Turn left at the top of the slope, pass to the left of the statue, and cross to the other side of Stephen White Drive.

0.3 Stephen White Drive at Bluff Place. Steeply climb Bluff Place. Walk past an old blue shingled house on this one-way street.

0.5 Bluff Place and Pacific Avenue each dead-end at an overlook park. Make a clockwise half-circle to enjoy the views of this park. Turn left on Shepard Street.

0.8 Turn left at Gaffey Street.

0.9 Point Fermin Lighthouse. A walking circuit to see Walker's Café and to look over the ramparts could easily consume 0.4 mile.

1.2 Leave Point Fermin Park the way that you entered. Walk north on the right-hand side of Gaffey Street.

1.5 Cross to the west side of Gaffey Street across from 37th Street and enter the gate. If that gate is locked, walk another 250 feet and turn left through the Leavenworth Drive gate. Walk around the Korean Friendship Bell pagoda. Exit the Korean Friendship Bell area through a vehicle gate that is near the basketball court and the restroom building.

1.9 Turn left on Leavenworth Drive. Walk past the vehicle barriers.

SAN PEDRO

25th Street mosaic mural wall
Patton Ave
24th St
Busy Bee Market
25th St
26th St
Walker Ave
27th St
Hamilton Ave
29th St
Cabrillo St
25th St
26th St
27th St
Gaffey St
Peck St
30th St
Baywater Ave
Carolina St
Pacific Ave
Patton Ave
Alma St
36th St
Marine Mammal Care Center
Osgood Farley Rd
Hey Rookie Pool
37th St
Paseo Del Mar
Roxbury St
Leavenworth Dr
Leary Merriam Dr
34th St
Shoshonean Rd
Cabrillo Marine Aquarium
Cabrillo Beach
Bluff Pl
ANGELS GATE PARK
38th St
Stephen White Dr
San Pedro Bay
Gaffey St
Bluff Pl
Shepard St
Point Fermin Lighthouse
POINT FERMIN PARK

2.0 Junction of Leavenworth Drive and Osgood Farley Road. The route will return to this point after an out-and-back to the Marine Mammal Care Center. You may not enter Marine Mammal with a dog, so if you are with a canine companion perhaps just skip this out-and-back. The full hike route continues straight on Leavenworth Drive. Pass the high school and turn right in the parking lot to locate Marine Mammal in the far-right corner.

2.2 Marine Mammal Care Center. Return to the junction of Leavenworth Drive and Osgood Farley Road. Turn left on Osgood Farley.

2.5 Make the first right turn into narrow NCO Road; there is no sign. Look for Building H on the left and turn into the pathway directly in front of it. This path comes out to ORC Road, again unsigned. Turn right on this road; Building G will be on your right.

2.6 Come to a bend in the road on the left side with a flagpole in a half-circle field in front of Building D. On the right there is an unidentified two-story building. Just beyond that, turn right into the new reddish-colored path to the pool.

2.7 Hey Rookie Pool. Walk to the information displays with the great harbor view behind them. With the pool on your left, go down eighty-six steps to the gate. Push

In Angels Gate Park, old Fort MacArthur barracks have been repurposed as arts and crafts activity centers.

the bar, open the gate, and cross to the other side of Gaffey Street in the crosswalk. Turn left on Gaffey Street.

2.8 Use the signals at 32nd Street to cross back to the west side of Gaffey. Turn right on Gaffey. Turn left on 30th Street.

3.0 Turn right on Baywater Avenue. Turn left on 29th Street.

3.3 Turn right at an unsigned Y to remain on 29th Street. Turn left on Hamilton Avenue. Veer slight left onto 27th Street.

3.6 Turn left on Leland Street, which will soon bend to the right and become Walker Avenue. Turn left on 26th Street.

3.9 Turn right on Patton Avenue. Cross 25th and turn left.

4.0 25th Street mosaic mural wall. Walk to the end of the artwork on the north side of 25th Street. Turn around, return to Patton Avenue. Turn left on Patton. Turn right on 24th Street.

4.2 Busy Bee Market, 2413 S. Walker Ave. Continue east on 24th Street.

4.7 Turn right on Cabrillo Street. Carefully cross 25th Street, then turn left on 25th.

4.9 Cross to the east side of Gaffey Street then turn right.

5.0 Turn left on 27th Street. Cross Peck Avenue, then go down a stairway that is a continuation of 27th.

5.1 Turn right on Carolina Street.

5.6 Turn hard left into a stairway path that comes immediately after passing Point Fermin Elementary School. The path connects to 34th Street. Continue east on 34th.

5.7 Turn right on Pacific Avenue.

5.8 Turn left on Stephen M. White Drive following signs for Cabrillo Beach and Marine Aquarium. Turn left in the driveway for Cabrillo Beach. Turn left at the first picnic tables.

6.1 End of hike at Cabrillo Marine Aquarium.

15 LONG BEACH

Long Beach is a fantastic city for a discovery hike because there is a great variety of parkland, culture, and architecture that can be appreciated in a relatively small area. This loop hike features a fascinating downtown, a coastal blufftop, long quiet avenues of lovely homes, and vibrant boulevards full of cafes and culture.

Start: Metro A (Blue) Line 1st Street Station, 108 North Long Beach Blvd. at Broadway, Long Beach 90802
Elevation gain: 100 feet
Distance: 6.4-mile loop
Hiking time: 3 to 3.5 hours
Difficulty: Moderate
Best season: Year-round
Trail surface: Sidewalks, paved paths, stairs
Other trail users: Tourists, shoppers and diners, scooters

Restroom availability: Miles 3.8, 4.9
Canine compatibility: Dogs must remain on leash.
Parking status: Pay lot parking near the start point
Rail transit accessibility: Metro A (Blue) Line, 1st Street Station is the start point.
Trailhead GPS: N33° 46.17' W118° 11.38'

FINDING THE TRAILHEAD
Take I-710 south toward Long Beach. Take exit 1C on the left toward Downtown Long Beach/Convention Center/Aquarium. Continue onto West Shoreline Drive. Take the 6th Street ramp and continue on 6th Street. Turn right onto Long Beach Boulevard. The Metro station is between Broadway and 1st Street.

WHAT TO SEE
Two minutes into this counterclockwise loop hike, you turn into the pedestrian mall built during an urban renewal craze in 1982. Appreciate some of the children-themed ornamentation on the building that houses Congregation Ale; this was originally a boy's clothing shop. At the head of the mall, tiny Harvey Milk Park includes a WPA-era, Long Beach–themed mosaic. Peer through the doors at the period furnishings of Farmers & Merchants Bank. Another lovely mosaic of Long Beach scenes is at 4th and Pine.

The landmarked Dolly Varden sign is the start of a short incursion into the West Village where there are Craftsman homes, duplexes, and fourplexes from the early 20th century. This culminates in three landmarks which personified luxury living in 1920s Long Beach, the Crest on Chestnut and the Californian and the Wilmore on 3rd. Consider 3 essential years in Long Beach history. In 1897 a federal commission of maritime engineers decreed that the port for the region should be on San Pedro Bay, where Long Beach and San Pedro are situated, and not Santa Monica Bay. In 1902, the Pacific Electric Railway Red Cars connected Long Beach to Los Angeles. In 1934, a massive offshore earthquake resulted in 115 fatalities and massive property damage.

On lively Pine Street is the 1930 Art Deco masterpiece Rowan Building (now Shannon's) at Broadway. Here Long Beach motifs are expressed in terra-cotta. Pine hits Ocean and the turn to the east takes you a bit along the Gold Coast. Two iconic residential towers of the 1920s are here, the Ocean Center Building at Pine and The Breakers at

The history of Long Beach imagined on this mosaic mural by artist Millard Sheets

Locust. Each is crowned with a lighthouse-like feature and each saw restoration in 2020. Another recent restoration to be celebrated is the Millard Sheets Studios mosaic mural on the bank building at the northwest corner of Ocean and Long Beach Boulevards. The mosaic depicts oil rigs, ships, and images of rancho life on this 1979 work that is one of the best remaining examples of the partnership between Sheets and Home Savings.

Turning from Elm Street to 1st Street, you enter the East Village Arts District. The best intersection of this area is Broadway and Linden with the chic Broadlind Hotel. Your right turn from Linden to Broadway presents you with a veritable glossary of architectural style: first Churrigueresque, then Art Deco, then across the street, Art Deco going into Streamline, and then International Style around the corner. Back on Ocean the walking visuals are titillated by another sequence of buildings. International Tower is a cylinder of balconies; pure 1966 Mid-Century Modern, it reminds some viewers of a beer can. Châteauesque-style Villa Riviera is one of the great landmarks of Long Beach. When it opened in 1928, it was the second tallest building in the county, with only the Los Angeles city hall taller. A hexagonal pinnacle-tower adds four stories to the building height. At 1st Place is a 1904 house that has been quite altered but is the work of Charles and Henry Greene. At 2nd Place, the 1928 Saint Regis embodies elegant living.

Five blocks of 1st Street from Orange Street to Bixby Park are wonderfully walkable with some cool apartments along a narrow, one-way street. On Saturdays, Bixby Park has a farmers' market offering many tasty treats. After leaving the park, just before the stairs, you might encounter people enjoying the Long Beach tradition of Yoga on the Bluff. Near the sand, there is a pretty mural painted over where an old pedestrian tunnel had been capped. There is also the historic WPA-built Lifeguard Headquarters. After

Palm species are all around in this part of lovely East 1st Street in the Bluff Park neighborhood.

some beach path, the route climbs stairs back to the bluff. At the 3.8-mile mark, the art museum grounds include an outdoor cafe outside the original 1912 Craftsman-style house. This is a good place to pause even if you don't intend to visit the museum or sit down in the cafe.

Now in the Bluff Park neighborhood, 2 long blocks of 1st Street are lined with gracious houses displaying Craftsman and other styles. The curved streets and oval parklets of Carroll Park are a welcome departure from the conventional street grid. 4th Street brings the Art Theatre district, where you start walking west through Retro Row, named for the antiques shops. Two things to watch for near the end of the hike: On the right side of 4th Street, west of Bonita Avenue, the coffee pot top mounted on a small shop carries on the great Southern California tradition of programmatic (novelty) architecture, as expressed by other regional buildings that are shaped like doughnuts or hot dogs. Next, an Art Deco facade on a building on the east side of Alamitos Avenue indicates the former Long Beach skating palace from the 1930s.

MILES AND DIRECTIONS

0.0 START at the north end of the Metro 1st Street Station platform at the southwest corner of Long Beach Boulevard and Broadway. Cross to the north side of Broadway, then turn left. In the middle of the block, turn right into the Promenade. At 3rd Street, cross to the north side of the street and turn left.

0.3 Turn right on Pine Avenue. Turn left on 4th Street. Turn left on Chestnut Avenue.

0.7 Turn left on 3rd Street. Turn right on Pine Avenue.

The Art Theatre is a hub in the Long Beach 4th Street–Retro Row District.

A QUIET PASSION 130   6
ROCKY HORROR! SAT

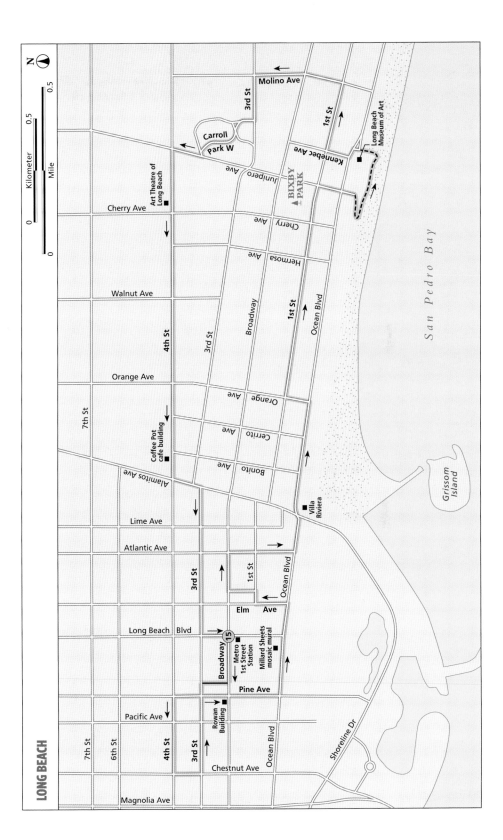

1.0 Rowan Building (now Shannon's). Pine Avenue at Broadway.

1.2 Turn left on Ocean Boulevard.

1.5 Millard Sheets mosaic mural at Ocean and Elm Avenue. Turn left on Elm Avenue. Turn right on 1st Street. Turn left on Linden Avenue.

1.7 Turn right on Broadway. Turn right on Atlantic Avenue.

2.0 Cross to the south side of Ocean Boulevard and turn left.

2.1 Villa Riviera, Ocean at Shoreline Drive.

2.5 Turn left on Orange Avenue. Turn right on 1st Street. Cross Cherry Avenue when safe.

3.2 Enter Bixby Park. Leave the southeast corner of the park at Ocean Boulevard and Junipero Avenue. Cross Ocean and go down the stairway toward the bay. Angle right using the stairs and ramps. At the tunnel mural, enter the Shoreline Way pedestrian/bike path headed (east) down the coast. After passing below the yellow umbrellas of the art museum complex, turn left up the steps leading to Ocean Boulevard. Turn left on Ocean.

3.7 Long Beach Museum of Art. Turn right on Kennebec Avenue. Turn right on 1st Street.

4.1 Turn left on Molino Avenue.

4.4 Turn left on 3rd Street.

4.6 Turn right on Carroll Park East. Veer to the left of a planted island for Carroll Park South, then stay to the right of a parklet so that you are now on Carroll Park West. Turn right on Junipero Avenue.

4.9 Turn left on 4th Street.

5.0 Art Theatre of Long Beach.

5.8 Coffee Pot cafe building.

5.9 Turn left on Alamitos Avenue. Turn right on 3rd Street.

6.3 Turn left on Long Beach Boulevard.

6.4 End of hike at the Metro 1st Street Station.

METRO LOS ANGELES

This section has the most hikes in this guidebook, which is fitting because this is the most urban place in Southern California. This is also the subregion where the author has lived for more than 60 years. Los Angeles covers a vast area, but these eleven hikes are concentrated in an area no larger than San Francisco. A key to enjoyable urban hiking in central Los Angeles is to head for the hills; only three of these hikes are flat. Of course, this section contains the most places that match the low expectations of some people who will assume the very worst of American cities. They might find it inconceivable that people happily come to walk these neighborhoods for good, clean, healthy fun.

Characterizing the hikes in this section is difficult because there is such a variety of singular moments. The University Park and USC hike has rows of houses that date to when Queen Victoria was alive. The Downtown Markets hike goes inside a floral mart. The Boyle Heights hike checks out a sequence of top-notch taco vendors. The Little Tokyo–Bunker Hill hike gets up close and personal with buildings created by four different international Pritzker Architecture Prize awardees. The Elysian Park–Elysian Heights hike follows a serene and shady hiking trail to an impressive overlook.

On the way out of Griffith Park and into the Los Feliz neighborhood

The Downtown Los Angeles skyline from Flat Top hill in Montecito Heights on the Northeast Los Angeles Hilltops hike

There are some aspects that these hikes share. These hikes occur at places where the infrastructure and upkeep are not always the best; watch out for irregular steps, uneven curbs, potholes, patchwork sidewalk repair, and other hazards that could trip you up. On the plus side, these hikes have the most mature shady street trees, the most semi-secret nooks and crannies, and the best street food. The hikes in this section provide the most opportunities to exclaim, "I had no idea that this was here." Favorite hike in this section? Tough choice! The Downtown Markets hike is purely in-your-face urban. Traipsing through the historic core and the markets is a great time, both artful and exhilarating.

16 WEST ADAMS

This short hike is full of history with block after block of fine old buildings. The residences range from one-story bungalows to grand Beaux-Arts mansions. Before wealthy Angelenos went farther west, they built their homes in West Adams. The neighborhood later played a key role in the African-American history of Los Angeles. The streets are oozing with old stories and fascinating people.

Start: Clark Memorial Library, 2520 Cimarron St., Los Angeles 90018
Elevation gain: 50 feet
Distance: 3.5-mile loop
Hiking time: 1.5 to 3 hours
Difficulty: Easy
Best season: Year-round
Best days and times: Weekdays are advantageous but not essential.
Trail surface: Sidewalks
Other trail users: None aside from other walkers
Restroom availability: Mile 0.3

Canine compatibility: Dogs must remain on leash.
Contacts: Clark Memorial Library, (310) 794-5155; Peace Awareness Labyrinth and Gardens, (323) 737-4055
Parking status: Free curb parking available on Cimarron Street outside the Clark Library
Rail transit accessibility: N/A
Trailhead GPS: N34° 02.00' W118° 18.93'

FINDING THE TRAILHEAD

From the east or west, take I-10 Freeway and take exit 10 for Arlington Avenue. If coming from the west, turn right on Arlington Avenue; if coming from the east, turn left. Then from either direction turn left on 25th Street. Turn right on Cimarron Street. The destination is on the left.

WHAT TO SEE

It is best to do this counterclockwise loop hike on a weekday so you can enjoy the grounds of the Clark Memorial Library. The grounds and library were a bequest to UCLA, and on days that the Westwood campus is open for classes, the grounds of the library will be open as well. The library is dedicated to the memory of William Andrews Clark, a Montana senator and copper king and a man who Mark Twain wrote was "as rotten a human being as can be found anywhere under the flag." It was the more erudite son, William Andrews Clark Jr., who assembled the estate here and acquired musical scores and rare books, including what is supposed to be the largest Oscar Wilde collection in the world. The brick wall was already part of the property when Clark purchased it in 1910. He kept extending that wall as he added neighboring lots to his parcel. Other buildings have come and gone here. The centerpiece that you observe today was built specifically in 1926 to house the library and is like a jewel box of brick in a field of green.

The beginning and ending of this hike, west of Saint Andrews and north of Adams Boulevard, is within a preservation zone identified as West Adams Terrace. *West Adams* is in most cases a regional classification, similar to saying the Wilshire District. The hike today takes place across three neighborhoods that are part of that broad West Adams classification including West Adams Terrace, Jefferson Park, and West Adams Heights.

UCLA's William Andrews Clark Memorial Library

At 24th and Arlington Avenue, the South Seas House has been lovingly characterized as Tahitian Tudor style. Built in 1902, it serves as a precursor to the exotic eclecticism in Los Angeles building styles that took off in the 1920s. Potter Park is a nice shady place with restrooms and would be a good stand-in if you are doing this hike on a day that the Clark Library is closed. When you turn right up dead-end 4th Avenue, you can see how West Adams was savaged by the building of the Santa Monica Freeway in 1963. Imagine the seemingly endless field of historic houses that was here before then. Notice on this street the Alice Lynch House at 2414 4th Ave. Built in 1923, it is a sublime local interpretation of the Andalusian farmhouses of southern Spain. The house at the northeast corner of 5th Avenue and Adams Boulevard was built for Percy Clark, the developer of Beverly Hills. Since the 1940s, this building has been the clubhouse for the Wilfandel Club, the oldest African-American women's club in Los Angeles.

Walking west on Adams merely to gain a crosswalk, a sad reality of this great boulevard begins to sink in. People did leave this neighborhood in droves as Windsor Square, Fremont Place, and Beverly Hills became the fashion. Few of these great houses were resold as single-family residences. The few houses that were not torn down for apartments were taken over by institutions and places of worship. Massive parking lots were paved over the stately setbacks. That is relevant to the next destination, the Guasti Villa at 3500 West Adams. This grand house was built in 1910 for Secundo Guasti, an itinerant farm worker and cook from Italy who eventually would create the largest winery in California. In the 1930s, the next owner was the famous stage and movie choreographer and director Busby Berkeley. Today the house and gardens are open for visits as sanctuary and place of meditation by the Peace Awareness Labyrinth and Gardens. Securing a reservation for a free tour in advance of this hike would enhance your day.

Behind the Polish church is the 1908 Lycurgus Lindsay House. The house is notable for having been built with the use of hollow terra-cotta building blocks. East of 2nd Avenue on the north side of the street is the Fitzgerald House. It looks straight from the Addams Family. The 1903 architect Joseph Cather Newsom declared that the style was Italian Gothic.

26th Place and 27th Street are in Jefferson Park, a neighborhood of single-story, early-20th-century bungalows. On Hobart Boulevard there is a wonderful 1904 firehouse that was built in a day when horses pulled the firewagon. Pass to the right of First African Methodist Episcopal Church (FAME). It was designed by master architect Paul Revere Williams; you will see the other side of it in a few minutes. Now you are entering West Adams Heights. After the initial wave of white elite left for points west, an African-American community began moving into this neighborhood around 1940. They called their new community Sugar Hill, a name inspired by Harlem's fabulous Sugar Hill. Residing at 2203 South Harvard, Oscar-winning actor Hattie McDaniel was one of the codefendants in a lawsuit that sought to use existing racial covenants to force her out of the neighborhood. The suit against her was lost in 1948 when the court ruled that racially restrictive covenants could not be enforced. Reaching a traffic circle, take a closer look at FAME on the left side. On the right side, the fabulous mansion with the fat corner towers was the town home of the Rindge family. They owned all of Malibu well into the 1920s.

At the northeast corner of Adams and Western Avenue is another important work from architect Paul R. Williams. Williams was the first African-American member of the American Institute of Architects. He was an architect for the stars, building homes for clients such as Frank Sinatra, Lucille Ball, and Desi Arnaz. But he also had a long résumé of work done for African-American organizations and businesses such as here for Golden State Mutual Life Insurance Company. The Neoclassical Britt House, at the northeast corner of Adams and Gramercy, today is LA84. This is a collection of sports memorabilia for the Amateur Athletic Foundation. Across Adams from here, a screen conceals a still-active oil and gas extraction operation. A few more blocks of lovely houses and street trees brings you back to the Clark Library.

MILES AND DIRECTIONS

0.0 START at the William Andrews Clark Memorial Library. Facing Cimarron Street with your back to the gate, turn right on Cimarron. Turn left on 24th Street. Cross Arlington Avenue carefully in the crosswalk and continue west on 24th.

0.3 Potter Park. Turn left on 2nd Avenue. Turn right on 25th Street. Turn right on 4th Avenue walking at least as far as address 2414. Turn around and return. Turn right on 25th Street. Turn left on 5th Avenue.

0.7 Turn right on Adams Boulevard. Cross to the south side of Adams using the crosswalk at 6th Avenue then turn left on Adams.

0.9 Peace Awareness Labyrinth and Gardens, 3500 W. Adams Blvd.

1.2 Cross to the east side of Arlington Avenue then turn right. Watch on the left for 26th Place, which is below the grade of Arlington. Turn left down a short set of steps into 26th Place. Turn right on Cimarron Street.

1.4 Turn left on 27th Street. Pass Western Avenue.

1.8 Turn left on Hobart Boulevard.

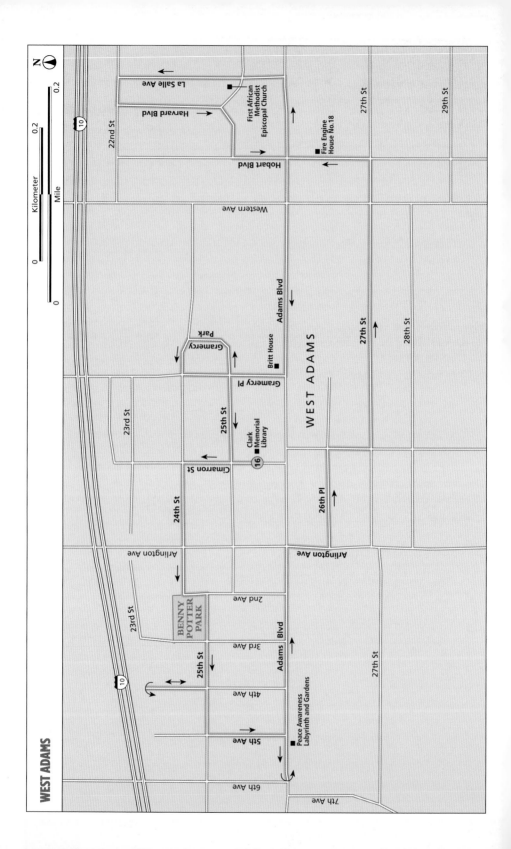

Murals frame the side entrance to the First African Methodist Episcopal Church, designed by architect Paul R. Williams.

1.9 Fire Engine House No. 18. Turn right on Adams Boulevard. Turn left on La Salle Avenue.

2.2 First African Methodist Episcopal Church.

2.3 Turn left on 22nd Street. Turn left on Harvard Boulevard.

2.5 Turn right at a traffic circle on 25th Street. Turn left on Hobart Boulevard.

2.7 Turn right on Adams Boulevard.

3.0 Turn right on Gramercy Place. Turn right on Gramercy Park.

3.2 Turn left on 24th Street. Turn left on Gramercy Place.

3.3 Turn right on 25th Street. Turn left on Cimarron Street.

3.5 End of hike at the William Andrews Clark Memorial Library.

17 UNIVERSITY PARK AND USC

When the population of late-19th-century Los Angeles burst out of the confines of the original four-square Spanish leagues, it came here. A great university was founded, and a fashionable new residential district followed. The area that this hike covers is exciting as well as old, with the vitality of student life and the nearness to transit and downtown. Short blocks and mature street trees make this a great place for walking.

Start: Metro LATTC/Ortho Institute Station, 2460 S. Flower St., Los Angeles 90007
Elevation gain: 50 feet
Distance: 4.0-mile lollipop
Hiking time: 2 to 2.5 hours
Difficulty: Easy
Best season: Year-round
Trail surface: Sidewalks, paved path
Other trail users: Students, scooters, cyclists

Restroom availability: Mile 1.9
Canine compatibility: Not a good hike for the dog
Parking status: Curb parking, either free or metered, has to be sought out. Try 23rd Street.
Rail transit accessibility: Metro E (Expo) Line, LATTC/Ortho Institute Station is the start point.
Trailhead GPS: N34° 01.72′ W118° 16.45′

FINDING THE TRAILHEAD

From the south, take 110 Freeway north and take exit 20C for Adams Boulevard. Turn left on Adams Boulevard. Turn right on Figueroa Street. Turn right on 23rd Street. Turn right on Flower Street. From the north, take 110 Freeway south and take exit 20C for Adams Boulevard. Turn left immediately from the exit onto 23rd Street. Turn right on Flower Street. The Metro platform is on the left.

WHAT TO SEE

The first and final 2 blocks of this counterclockwise lollipop hike are ragged; it will get a lot better. Saint Vincent was built in 1925 at a vital Los Angeles intersection by architect Albert C. Martin. It is considered one of the best ecclesiastical examples of Spanish Colonial Revival architecture in the United States. Along the first mile of this hike, Angels Walk LA has placed five informative stanchions that provide more background than this guidebook has space to include. In 1900, Chester Place was one of the most prestigious addresses in the city. The centerpiece is the house that belonged to oil magnate Edward L. Doheny. Going west on Adams, the classical Beaux-Arts domed church was founded as the Second Church of Christ, Scientist. Today it enjoys life as a yoga and meditation center. Before crossing Hoover Street, walk a few feet south to the stanchion to learn about the complex history of the Casa de Rosa.

This neighborhood of University Park commingles with the University of Southern California. This neighborhood is the historical linchpin to the vast area that is referred to broadly as West Adams. Development happened here first and then spread west, which explains why you see such a large inventory of 19th-century residential structures. Maps from the 1880s described where you are hiking today as West Los Angeles. The area around 27th Street and Magnolia Avenue displays a wonderful variety of buildings that

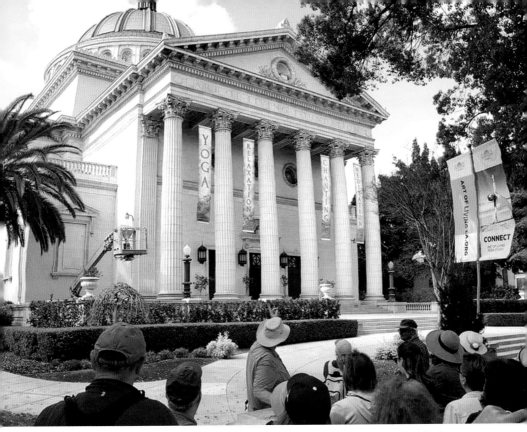

The author points out the historic Second Church of Christ, Scientist, on a group hike in University Park. *Gilbert Garcia*

are more than a century old. The corner of 27th Street and Hoover Street is framed by two excellent Queen Anne Victorians with great curved wraparound veranda.

USC Village is a recent development with residence halls and a retail base that serves both the campus and the local community. The statue of Hecuba from Homer's *Iliad* is a counterpoint to Tommy Trojan and is the center of a captivating plaza. The university was established in 1880. What you see today is a campus with a strong axial plan as laid out in 1919 with Trousdale Parkway as the center axis. The 1919 plan cultivated thirteen still-standing buildings built between 1921 and 1932. They are all clad in brick and express the Northern Italian Romanesque style. This hike is meant to be brisk recreation, not a studious stroll, so we'll try to cover just enough to reveal a variety of the building personality of the campus.

On 34th Street, if it is open and not in use, you should go inside what they like to call the Fishbowl Chapel. This post-and-beam work was done by architects Killingsworth, Brady and Associates. The Cinematic Arts school buildings include soundstages, and the whole package is dressed up as an Italian villa. The first of the historic core campus buildings that you pass is Physical Education; a look inside reveals an interior courtyard as well as a charming swimming arena. Still going southwest on Watt Way, the passage on the right signed as Viterbi School of Engineering is the start of a cluster of Mid-Century Modern engineering- and science-related buildings. They were designed over a 14-year

The dome of Saint Vincent Catholic Church

period by architect William Pereira. Pereira taught at USC, and he has many devotees 50 years later. Notice his use of concrete curved window hoods on Ahmanson and Stauffer; these remind some of cheese graters as you walk on Bloom Walk.

When you turn left from Bloom Walk into Trousdale Parkway, you are standing at the south end of the main artery of the university. First, look behind you at Mudd Hall of Philosophy. Designed by architect Ralph Carlin Flewelling, this is one of the great USC buildings. The chapel-like Hoose Library on the second floor begs for a few minutes' visit. Many of these other core buildings, as well as the 1919 master plan, were the work of architect John Parkinson. On the right, just past Downey Way, a campus favorite is the Allan Hancock Foundation building featuring large, cast reliefs of the Pleistocene-era mammals carved by sculptor Merrell Gage. On the left, the Wilson student union building displays some excellent cast stone detailing, including a monkey thumbing his nose at the university president of that time. The symbolic campus center comes with the Tommy Trojan sculpture in front of Bovard, where Childs Way meets Trousdale Parkway. Across the square of Alumni Park from Bovard, Doheny Memorial Library is one of the premier campus buildings. It is heavily decorated inside and out. A visit into the main reading room to see the elaborate ceiling is highly recommended. Beyond that, on the right, there is an enclave of three buildings, including a tower topped by a globe. Completed in 1968, architect Edward Durell Stone employed the then-popular New Formalist style. Across from this group and back on the left side of Trousdale Parkway is a peaceful green area of grassy mounds. To the rear of that, and probably strung with banners, is the lovely Annenberg School building from architect A. Quincy Jones.

We exit campus near USC Village again and walk up a lively student pedestrian corridor. Back at Adams and Figueroa, you might enjoy walking a few feet south to view the entryway and read the stanchion describing the Automobile Club Building. Even with the other grand church structures nearby, some would say this building best symbolizes the true religion of Southern California.

MILES AND DIRECTIONS

0.0 START at the Metro LATTC/Ortho Institute Station. Exit the platform to the south, which would be the Santa Monica direction if you were riding the train. Continue south on Flower Street. Turn right on Adams Boulevard.

0.2 Saint Vincent Catholic Church, Adams Boulevard at Figueroa Street. Continue west on Adams. Across from the next painted crosswalk on the left, turn right into the pedestrian entrance gate for the Doheny Campus of Mount Saint Mary's College. Walk beyond the T intersection and into the curved driveway in front of the Doheny House on the right.

0.4 Doheny Mansion, Chester Place. Turn back to the T intersection and turn right.

0.5 Exit the campus and Chester Place, passing a guard kiosk. Proceed straight on Saint James Park. Turn left on Scarff Street. Turn right at Adams Boulevard.

0.8 Turn left in the crosswalk at Portland Street. Turn right on Adams Boulevard.

1.1 Turn left on Magnolia Avenue.

1.3 Turn left on 27th Street. Turn right on Hoover Street.

1.6 Cross 30th Street and turn right. Follow the curve left so that you are on McClintock Avenue.

1.8 At the end of a sports field, turn left into USC Village. Walk toward Cowlings Residential College, then veer right into the central square of the village. Pass to the left of the umbrellas and the fountain, and locate the statue in the center of the square.

1.9 Hecuba statue. With your back to the statue, take the pedestrian path that diagonals to the left, passing to the right of a Starbucks. At Jefferson Boulevard, select the crosswalk going diagonally across Jefferson into Gavin Herbert Plaza.

2.1 Turn right on 34th Street. Pass Watt Way.

2.3 Turn left into the gate for USC School for Cinematic Arts. Walk directly through an enclosed square with a statue of Douglas Fairbanks. Exit this square through an archway and proceed in the same direction to leave the Cinematic Arts School out to the 35th Street service road. Turn left on 35th Street.

2.4 Turn right on Watt Way. A visit into the ground floor interior of the Physical Education building on the left is recommended.

2.6 Turn left on Bloom Walk, which appears just after the Loker Hydrocarbon Research Institute. Bloom Walk ends at Trousdale Parkway.

2.7 Mudd Hall of Philosophy. Turn left into Trousdale Parkway.

3.1 Gavin Herbert Plaza and campus exit at Jefferson Boulevard. Cross Jefferson from the Trousdale Parkway path.

3.2 Go straight into the Hoover Pedestrian Mall as vehicular Hoover Street veers left. Keep going straight passing 32nd, 30th, and 28th Streets, now on University Avenue.

3.5 27th Street at University Avenue. University Avenue ends at a parking lot. Walk across this lot, aiming for the far-right corner. Leave the lot for a paved pathway

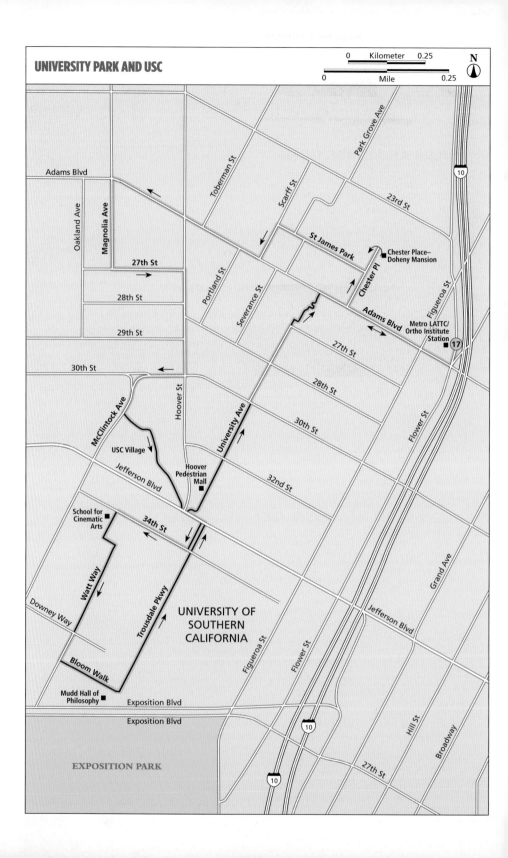

0   Kilometer   0.25
0   Mile   0.25

N

Adams Blvd

Oakland Ave

Magnolia Ave

Toberman St

Scarff St

Park Grove Ave

23rd St

St James Park

Chester Place–
Doheny Mansion

Chester Pl

Figueroa St

27th St

28th St

29th St

Portland St

Severance St

Adams Blvd

Metro LATTC/
Ortho Institute
Station

17

30th St

Hoover St

27th St

28th St

University Ave

30th St

Flower St

McClintock Ave

USC Village

Jefferson Blvd

Hoover
Pedestrian
Mall

32nd St

School for
Cinematic
Arts

34th St

Grand Ave

Watt Way

Jefferson Blvd

Downey Way

Trousdale Pkwy

UNIVERSITY OF
SOUTHERN
CALIFORNIA

Figueroa St

Flower St

Bloom Walk

Mudd Hall of
Philosophy

Exposition Blvd

Exposition Blvd

10

Hill St

Broadway

EXPOSITION PARK

10

27th St

10

In USC Village, the statue of Hecuba from Homer's *Iliad* is a counterpoint to Tommy Trojan.

that jogs right toward the half-timbered USC Kerckhoff Hall. Take a connecting path directly out to Adams Boulevard.

3.6   Turn right on Adams Boulevard.

3.9   Turn left to cross Adams at Flower Street. Turn right into a short crosswalk over Figueroa Way and a longer one over Flower Street. Cross the tracks and turn left on Flower.

4.0   End of hike at the Metro LATTC/Ortho Institute Station.

18 DOWNTOWN MARKETS

This hike explores a variety of retail and wholesale marketplaces in downtown Los Angeles. The fashion, textile, floral, piñata, produce, and toy districts appear one after another along the route. Add walking through the historic core of Broadway and a bit of the Arts District and you have a half-day along a route unlike any other in this guidebook.

Start: Spring Arcade Building, 539 S. Spring St., Los Angeles 90013
Elevation gain: 50 feet
Distance: 6.4-mile loop
Hiking time: 3.5 to 5 hours
Difficulty: Moderate
Best season: Year-round
Best days and times: Mon–Sat; start 10 a.m. or earlier.
Trail surface: Sidewalks
Other trail users: Shoppers and diners

Restroom availability: Miles 1.9, 3.5, 5.6
Canine compatibility: Not a good hike to bring the dog
Parking status: Paid parking lots and garages adjacent to the start point
Rail transit accessibility: Metro B (Red) or D (Purple) Lines, Pershing Square Station. Walk 0.2 mile on 5th Street to reach the start point.
Trailhead GPS: N34° 02.79′ W118° 15.04′

FINDING THE TRAILHEAD

Access the 110 Freeway between the 101 Freeway to the north and I-10 to the south. From the south, take the 6th/9th Street exit toward Downtown/Convention Center/Figueroa. Keep left to merge into 4th Street. Turn right on Spring Street. From the north and the northwest, take the exit toward 6th Street/Wilshire Blvd/4th Street. Keep right to continue on exit 23B; follow signs for Downtown and merge into 4th Street. Turn right onto Spring Street. From any direction, the Arcade Building is on the right side between 5th and 6th Streets.

WHAT TO SEE

This counterclockwise loop hike is designed to be done slowly. It would be both pointless and impossible to run through some of the congested space on this route. An early start by 10 a.m. ensures that you will catch the floral market open and see some activity in the produce market before they lock things up. Begin by walking through the open, skylighted shopping arcade that links Spring to Broadway. The upper floors of this were built for offices, but it has seen adaptive reuse mostly for residential living. Clifton's Cabinet of Curiosities is iconic Los Angeles, even if there are no longer enough customers to support a cafeteria. Look inside if you can, but they mainly operate now as an evening-nighttime bar. From 8th to 9th Streets nearly every building on Broadway is a designated monument. The best of these is the 1929 Eastern Columbia Building designed by architect Claud Beelman. After Olympic, the United Artists Theatre Building (now the Ace Hotel) is another favorite. The 1912 Los Angeles Herald-Examiner Building on Broadway south of 11th is a landmark from William Randolph Hearst's favorite architect, Julia Morgan.

The Los Angeles fashion or garment district is a huge economic engine that envelops parts of 100 downtown blocks, and your stroll up Santee Alley won't begin to reveal the

Santee Alley does not even hint at the size or importance of the Los Angeles fashion and garment industry.

importance of this industry. The textile district is affiliated with the fashion district, and it is similarly widespread. You see many small shops with bolts of fabric standing on end and with millinery items to sell, particularly on 9th and 8th Streets.

Although much smaller, the floral district has similarities to the produce district, which you will pass 1 mile later. For each, refrigerated semitrucks arrive early in the morning to deliver to jobbers the fresh harvest of the previous day. The items are received, sold, and distributed, and the jobbers lock up and go home by midday. At 1.9 miles, the Original Los Angeles Flower Market is well worth the negligible entry fee. It is well set up to be enjoyed by nonprofessionals, and they have good restrooms. Perfect for hikers, you go in the west door and exit the east where a smaller indoor floral mart awaits you. Exiting to San Pedro, notice the landmarked 1903 building across San Pedro that culminates with a corner bay tower at 7th and Agatha. Then there is an almost miraculous floss-silk tree in the traffic island at 8th and San Pedro. The piñata district might be the surprise of the day for the unsuspecting hiker. Purveyors of piñatas and party supplies occupy more than a quarter-mile of the south side of Olympic Boulevard. It is especially active on weekends when the south side of Olympic west of Central is a gauntlet for the urban hiker of color, noise, and freshly prepared food.

Walking north on Central from Olympic, this is a good view of the core of the produce district. The greater produce market extends several miles east and south. The newer warehouse buildings compose the Los Angeles Wholesale Produce Market, sometimes called the New Market, built in the 1980s to accommodate larger trucks, palletization, and improved food safety. Next you walk on the left side of the old 7th Street Market, which still has some holdout occupants. The old market is part of a century-old

The work of London-based Irish muralist Fin DAC on display above the intersection of Winston and Los Angeles Streets

complex of six concrete buildings designed by architect John Parkinson and built as the railroads' Union Terminal Market. At the 3.5-mile mark, the hike reaches the center of this facility, which is undergoing adaptive reuse under the name ROW DTLA. There are food choices, restrooms, and a terrific city view from the top of the parking garage.

Industrial (east of Mill), Mateo, Palmetto, and Colyton Streets are each good examples of the renaissance of this area as part of the Downtown Los Angeles Arts District. You then walk along the southern edge of Little Tokyo and the northern edge of Skid Row. Mumford Brewing opened in 2015, but it is a family business that grew out of home brewing in the 1970s. After 3rd and San Pedro, your next 6 blocks are within the Toy District. Just 3 curving blocks, long, narrow Winston Street reads as an open-air market where they forgot to install barricades to keep the cars out. Behind the street life, great signage, street murals, and distant office towers create a stage-set backdrop. Just past the gallery at 118 Winston St., the gate will be closed, but stop and look through it to the mural work of Indian Alley. Across the street is a charming mural of Audrey Hepburn and two outsized portraits of women done by Irish muralist Fin DAC. The end of the hike is in the old financial district. At 5th and Spring, The Last Bookstore occupies a former bank building and has a retail culture meant to inspire treasure hunts. 618 Spring Street was home to the Los Angeles Stock Exchange for 55 years before it was adapted for use as a nightclub in the 1980s. Back at the Arcade Building, gelato from Gelateria Uli or tacos from Guisados might be good bets.

MILES AND DIRECTIONS

0.0 START at the Spring Arcade Building next to Guisados. Walk through the arcade. Turn left on Broadway.

1.0 Turn left on 12th Street.

1.3 Santee Alley. Turn left into the street market just beyond Santee Street. Cross unsigned 11th Street to continue up Santee Alley. Turn right on Olympic Boulevard.

1.5 Cross to the east side of Wall Street and turn left. Proceed northeast to 754 S. Wall St.

1.9 Original Los Angeles Flower Market, $1–$2 admission required. Walk through the floral market and exit on San Julian Street. Cross San Julian carefully, turn left, and turn right into the LA Flower Mall at 720 San Julian; there is no admission. Walk through and exit through the east doors. Turn right on San Pedro Street.

2.3 Turn left on 8th Street. Turn right on Stanford Avenue.

2.6 At the signal, cross to the south side of 9th Street, which immediately changes names to Olympic Boulevard. Turn left.

2.8 Piñata District. Keep to the sidewalk as you thread the narrow passage of vendors.

2.9 Exit the Piñata District at Central Avenue. Cross twice to reach the diagonal northeast corner of Olympic and Central. Head north on Central.

3.3 Turn right on 7th Street. In 500 feet, turn right through the pedestrian-only entrance of what maps will call Industrial Place. If the pedestrian gate is locked, the route is 0.3 mile longer as follows: Continue east on 7th, turn right on Alameda Street, turn right into the parking gateway for ROW from Alameda.

3.5 ROW DTLA. When leaving the shop and food area, walk north on Industrial Place. The gate is designed to push open if it is closed.

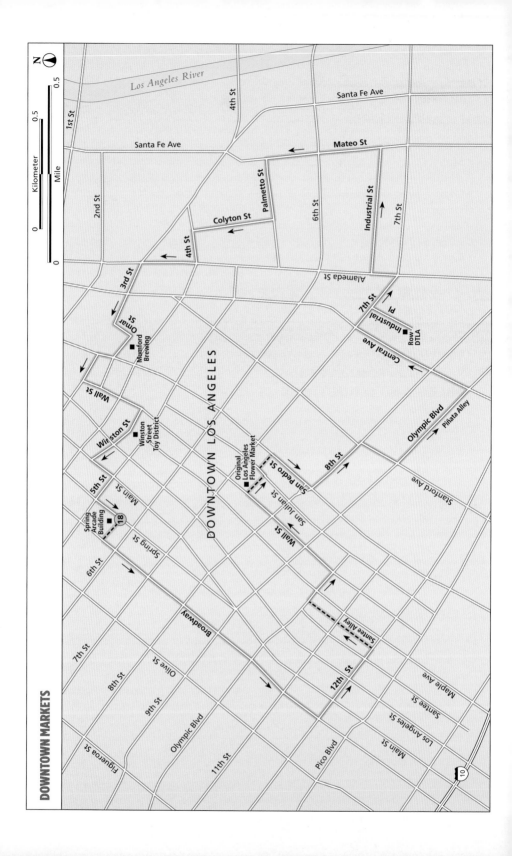

DOWNTOWN MARKETS

The Original Los Angeles Flower Market is well set up to be enjoyed by nonprofessionals. Come early.

3.7 Industrial Place at 7th Street. Turn right on 7th. At Alameda Street, cross twice to reach the diagonal corner by McDonald's. Turn left on Alameda. Turn right on Industrial Street.

4.3 Turn left on Mateo Street. Turn left on Palmetto Street.

4.8 Turn right on Colyton Street.

5.0 Turn left on 4th Street. Turn right on Alameda Street.

5.2 Turn left on 3rd Street.

5.5 Turn left on Omar Street. Turn right on Boyd Street.

5.6 Mumford Brewing, 416 Boyd St. Leaving the brewery, turn left to continue west on Boyd Street. Turn right on San Pedro Street. Turn left on 3rd Street. Turn left on Wall Street.

5.9 Turn right on Winston Street.

6.0 Winston Street sidewalk markets between Wall and Los Angeles Streets.

6.2 Turn left on Main Street. Turn right on 5th Street. Turn left on Spring Street.

6.4 End of hike at Spring Arcade Building.

19 LITTLE TOKYO-BUNKER HILL

This short hike through the civic and cultural core of downtown Los Angeles is designed for out of town visitors as well as "been there-done that" locals. This zone is always changing, and this hike route passes iconic century-and-older landmarks as well as dynamic 21st-century additions.

Start: Japanese American National Museum (JANM), 100 N. Central Ave., Los Angeles 90012
Elevation gain: 100 feet
Distance: 3.2-mile loop
Hiking time: 1.5 to 3 hours
Difficulty: Easy
Best season: Year-round
Trail surface: Sidewalks, park paths
Other trail users: Shoppers and diners, tourists, scooters
Restroom availability: Miles 1.6, 1.9

Canine compatibility: Not a good hike for dogs
Parking status: Pay parking is available in nearby commercial garages.
Rail transit accessibility: Metro E Line, Little Tokyo / Arts District Station will be directly downstairs from the start point when it reopens in 2022.
Trailhead GPS: N34° 02.96' W118° 14.35'

FINDING THE TRAILHEAD

Take the 101 Freeway. From the north, take exit 2B for Los Angeles Street. Turn right onto Los Angeles Street. Turn left onto Temple Street. Turn right on Alameda Street. Turn right on 1st Street. From the south, take exit 2B toward Alameda Street/Union Station. Turn left on Alameda. Turn right on 1st Street.

WHAT TO SEE

Weekends will add more color and buzz to this clockwise loop; workdays are less likely to have events that could disrupt the flow of the hike. Begin in a plaza around JANM that includes a 1920s theater building that served for decades as a Buddhist temple. Farther back in this plaza is the Go for Broke Monument, a tribute to the Japanese-American soldiers of World War II. The hike passes a replica of a Japanese fire lookout tower and enters Japanese Village Plaza. Turning out of the plaza onto 2nd Street, there are other businesses and symbols related to Little Tokyo, including the *Friendship Knot* fiberglass sculpture by artist Shinkichi Tajiri.

On the right at 2nd and Los Angeles Streets is the Caltrans Building, a 2004 work by Morphosis Architects. On the left is Saint Vibiana, which was built in 1876. This building is now decommissioned as a church in favor of the new cathedral that you will visit later on this hike. At Main Street, the handsome Higgins Building was built in 1910, intended for architects and engineers. In the basement, the Higgins Building had the first privately owned power plant in Los Angeles. This space is now occupied by The Edison, a swanky nightclub. On 3rd between Spring and Broadway is the Victor Clothing Company mural *The Pope of Broadway*, painted by artist Eloy Torrez in 1984. The character of course is Mexican-born actor Anthony Quinn, who grew up in East Los Angeles. Across the street is the doorway into the 1893 Bradbury Building, the most beloved interior space in the city. An Angels Walk stanchion outside the Broadway doorway describes the building history in detail. Cross Broadway and there is another informative Angels Walk stanchion

The Victor Clothing Co. building painted by artist Eloy Torrez with Anthony Quinn as the model

for the 1918 Million Dollar Theatre building and Grand Central Market. The Market remains an engaging place full of delights, even as the culture of the place has changed to accommodate eat-on-the-spot customers instead of the historic customer base that would shop for provisions to take to their nearby flats.

Angels Flight was built one-half block north of the current location. It served a vital role for mobility for 60 years after its 1901 opening. The historic residential community atop Bunker Hill was lost to redevelopment. There is another stanchion here with more of the story. Stepping off the funicular at California Plaza, the top of the Bunker Hill of today is as much as 30 feet lower now than before; the crown of the hill was scraped away for the office buildings. The plaza takes you to MOCA Grand Avenue, a fascinating building designed by Pritzker Architecture Prize awardee Arata Isozaki.

The Broad is named for the benefactors of the building and for their collection of modern art in this free gallery. The architects, Diller Scofidio + Renfro, speak of the building as the veil and the vault. The lacy concrete and steel lattice is the veil; the vault is the core bunker where art not on display is stored. The art and the building interior are worth even a short look. Before your hike begins, you might check ahead about reserving an entry slot. The Frank Gehry–designed Walt Disney Concert Hall opened in 2003 and is easily one of the most significant and written about buildings in Los Angeles. Your visit to the Disney Hall goes up steps to the garden level, where there is a lovely sculpture dedicated to Lillian Disney that is made of fragments of Royal Delft Blue porcelain. The climb up through the steel folds of the building is a must. However, it is closed at night

Angels Flight is an opportunity to ride instead of hike.

and anytime that there are performances. East of Disney Hall, The Grand is another Frank Gehry design in early construction as this guide is published.

The Music Center opened in the 1960s as a key early piece in the Bunker Hill redevelopment. There are three performance halls around a plaza. Looking toward City Hall, you can see how planners worked to create a strong axial plan of civic buildings around Grand Park with Grand Avenue as a cross axis of cultural and financial buildings. At this point, the hike is a bit over halfway complete, and there are restrooms and coffee places both at the Music Center and at the top of Grand Park. Leaving Grand Park to go north on Hill Street, the Hall of Records across the street was designed by architect Richard Neutra. The Cathedral of Our Lady of the Angels dates to 2002 and was designed by Spanish architect José Rafael Moneo. The interior is exquisite with soft light filtered through sheets of alabaster.

Returning to Grand Park, note how the 2012 reinvention of this space strove for rich and varied landscaping. The City Hall is a 1920s skyscraper that is an international symbol for the city thanks to a variety of appearances in TV and movies. On weekdays, consider a free visit to the 27th floor observation deck. Entry is from the opposite side of City Hall, so detour from the hike route at 1st and Main Streets. The end of the walk along 1st Street displays how much this area is a cultural hub for Japanese-American institutions and entertainment. You just might be inspired to join the line of customers for ramen at Daikokuya.

MILES AND DIRECTIONS

0.0 START at Japanese American National Museum. Cross 1st Street and enter the Japanese Village Plaza. Follow the main concourse in this outdoor pedestrian mall. The path shifts right by a pavilion then veers left by Café Dulce.

0.1 Turn right on 2nd Street.

0.4 Turn left on Main Street. Cross to the south side of 3rd Street and turn right.

0.7 Turn left into the doorway of the Bradbury Building directly across from the Victor Clothing mural. Follow the short L-shaped lobby path to turn right and exit the Bradbury Building through the Broadway door. Turn right. Cross Broadway at 3rd Street and turn left.

0.8 Turn right into the Grand Central Market, 317 S. Broadway. Walk westerly through the market court and exit to Hill Street. Turn left and immediately right into the crosswalk toward Angels Flight.

0.9 Angels Flight Railway. Board the funicular and ride to the top, where you will pay a fare. Turn right from the ticket office. Veer left and walk to the left of the Omni Hotel and Noe Restaurant. Continue ahead, aiming for the right side of the glass rooftop pyramid of the Museum of Contemporary Art (MOCA). With a reflecting pool on your right, turn left to walk through the MOCA entry plaza.

1.2 Turn right on Grand Avenue. At 2nd Street, cross Grand Avenue toward The Broad. Then turn right, crossing 2nd Street, and walk toward the Disney Concert Hall.

1.3 Walt Disney Concert Hall. On the near side of the structure, walk up a wide stairway. If it is closed, proceed to the corner of 1st and Grand. From the top of the stairs, walk clockwise around the building facade past an amphitheater and into the Blue Ribbon Garden. Walk to the right of the rose sculpture. Look for a doorway and an exterior stairway going up. Climb fifty-nine steps, then follow the path through the steel folds of the building facade as far as you can. Descend 124 steps to reach the front of the concert hall at Grand Avenue. Turn left and cross to the northwest corner of 1st and Grand Streets.

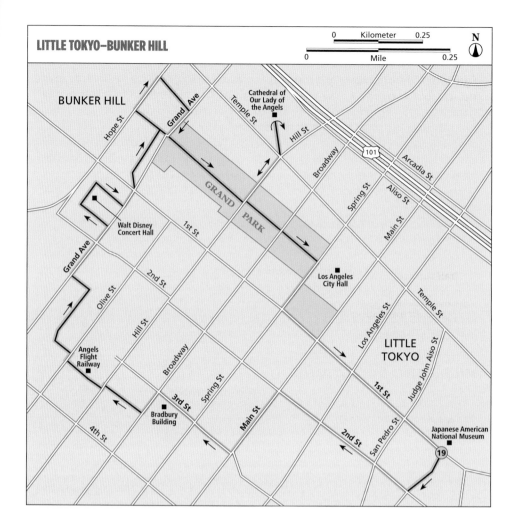

1.6   Los Angeles Music Center. Climb the steps near the corner of 1st and Grand to the plaza level. Pass to the right of the Chandler Pavilion then walk to the left and clockwise around the circular Mark Taper Forum. Return to the center of the complex and turn left (east) to go down some steps. Cross to the other side of Grand Avenue. Continue down more steps on either side of the fountain to enter Grand Park.

1.9   Grand Park. Head downhill in this linear park by any combination of park stairs, path, or ramp. Turn left on Hill Street, which is the next street bisecting the park. Cross Temple Street and turn left. Enter the plaza of the cathedral on the right.

2.3   Cathedral of Our Lady of the Angels plaza. Leave the plaza by the same route and return to the corner of Temple and Hill Streets. Cross twice to reach the diagonal southeast corner and continue on Hill Street. Turn back into Grand Park, walking past the subway entry plaza. Again, head downhill in this linear park by any combination of park stairs, path, or ramp. Cross Broadway, which is the next street to bisect the park. Continue downslope until the park ends at Spring Street. Cross Spring in front of city hall.

2.7   Los Angeles City Hall. Turn right on Spring Street. Turn left on 1st Street.

3.2   End of hike at Japanese American National Museum.

20 BOYLE HEIGHTS

Come for a wide variety of tacos delivered fresh from the grill to your hands. Stay for the history and culture of a neighborhood sometimes referred to as the Ellis Island of Los Angeles. .

Start: Metro Indiana Station, 210 S. Indiana St., Los Angeles 90063
Elevation gain: 200 feet
Distance: 4.0-mile point-to-point
Hiking time: 2 to 3.5 hours
Difficulty: Easy
Best season: October–June
Best days and times: Daily; start late morning to ensure the food vendors are open.
Trail surface: Sidewalks, stairs
Other trail users: Shoppers and diners
Restroom availability: Miles 0.2, 1.6, 2.6

Canine compatibility: Not a good hike to bring the dog
Parking status: Free parking in transit lot; street parking can be located nearby to the east when transit lot is at capacity.
Rail transit accessibility: Metro E (Expo) Line, Indiana Station is the start point. Until Metro reorganization is complete, this station is served by the Gold Line.
Trailhead GPS: N34° 02.10' W118° 11.53'

FINDING THE TRAILHEAD

Take the 60 Freeway and from the east, use exit 2 for Indiana Street. Turn right on Indiana Street. Turn right on 1st Street. Turn right on Alma Avenue. From the west, use exit 1B for Lorena Street. Turn left on Lorena Street and keep left. Turn right on 1st Street. Turn right on Alma Avenue. The station entrance is at the dead end of Alma.

WHAT TO SEE

A note before you begin this point-to-point hike. Perhaps no other Los Angeles neighborhood has as much anxiety about gentrification and cultural appropriation as Boyle Heights. Come here to walk as a polite guest. Keep your group size and noise down, be judicious with your camera, and don't bring your dog. The author has enjoyed well over 100 miles of walking the streets of Boyle Heights solo or with groups and has always encountered people who are happy that I am there. Also note that many of the food vendors that are suggested on this hike do not have restrooms.

El Mercado is a blend of swap meet, food court, and mariachi music hall. There are restrooms upstairs and a great place to choose a refreshing agua fresca downstairs. Crossing Lorena Street, a corner of Evergreen Cemetery has a plaque that tells the story of more than 150 unmarked graves that were encountered with the transit excavation in 2005. The soft-surfaced path around the cemetery is well used in this park-poor neighborhood. Los Cinco Puntos is a historic location, and Los 5 Puntos restaurant has been here 55 years serving sensational carnitas on handmade tortillas. Parked near the El Super store are several taco trucks that get great reviews. A stairway takes you up to a ridge where a bunya pine is beloved to the community and referred to simply as *El Pino*.

Open 65 years, El Tepeyac Café is famously old school and maybe too much to include on a multi-stop taco tasting hike. Legendary food critic Jonathan Gold described

A chicken shawarma taco with an agua fresca made with cucumber and mint from X'tiosu Kitchen

their Hollenbeck burrito as "an old-line Mexican restaurant's entire menu wrapped into a bedsheet-size tortilla." Stop at X'tiosu Kitchen, a window vendor that offers an unusual Oaxacan-Lebanese fusion. Try something tasty like the chicken shawarma taco. Across the street there is a distinctive branch library. Records from 1923 illustrate the historic cultural diversity of Boyle Heights; books were being read then from this branch in Armenian, French, German, Hungarian, Italian, Russian, Serbo-Croatian, Spanish, and Yiddish, as well as English. Just off Soto, Carnitas el Momo is the real deal. It is just a few taco preparation tables along the sidewalk where enthusiasts gather from miles away for a carnitas mixta taco.

Historic Brooklyn Avenue was renamed for César Chávez in the 1990s, and here you will quickly find Milpa Grille. They have an inventive menu that strives to pay "homage to our ancestors and the practice of milpa by featuring the three core ingredients—corn, squash, and beans." Before crossing Soto, look at the *Greatest Love* mural by East Los Angeles artist Paul Botello on the west side of the 70-year-old Farmacia Ramirez.

A few feet south of César Chávez, the imposing Breed Street Shul was built in 1924 and was the largest Orthodox synagogue west of Chicago until 1950. Guisados has expanded around Los Angeles, but they refer to this original Boyle Heights location as their "OG." There are many choices, including several that are vegetarian, on handmade tortillas. Perhaps try a quesadilla made with pan-fried tortillas and melted Cotija cheese. On Chicago Street, an imposing Gothic-Romanesque church building is hanging on, a relic built in 1884.

On 1st Street, Al & Bea's Mexican Food has been cooking in this little stand since 1966, and they will always have a line. Their burritos are famous, but stuffed jalapeños

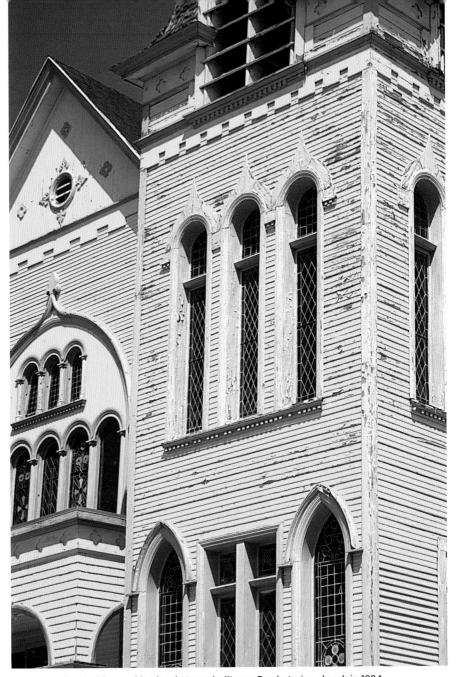
Iglesia Bautista Unida worships in what was built as a Presbyterian church in 1884.

that they call Jalitos are another good choice. 1st Street takes you to Mariachi Plaza. Birri-
ería Don Boni is an indoor spot across the street specializing in *birria*, spicy stewed goat,
Jalisco style. The plaza was built in 1998. There is a 90-year tradition for hiring Mariachi
bands near this spot. There is a traditional *cantera* or gazebo that was made by a Guadala-
jaran craftsman. Across from the plaza is an 1889 building with a corner belvedere. Here,

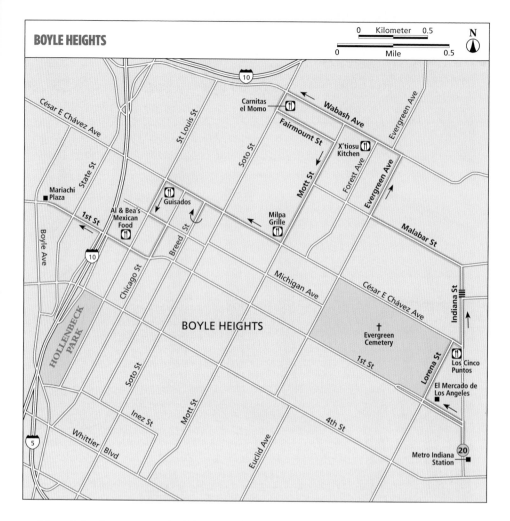

Libros Schmibros serves as both lending library and cultural icon. Next door, La Monarca is a perfect place to finish the hike with something like a Café Oaxaca.

MILES AND DIRECTIONS

0.0 START at Metro Indiana Station. Leave the platform, exit on the west side of the tracks at Indiana Street and Gleason Avenue. Cross to the west side of Indiana and turn right. At 1st Street, cross to the north side of the street and turn left. Walk to address 3425.

0.2 El Mercado de Los Angeles. Exit to 1st Street and turn right. Cross to the west side of Lorena Street and turn right. At César E Chávez Avenue, cross back to the east side of Lorena.

0.5 Los Cinco Puntos. From the front of the restaurant, cross to the traffic island and walk past the memorial with the spire. Use crosswalks twice to reach the northeast corner of César E Chávez Avenue and Indiana Street near El Super. Turn left on Indiana Street. Cross Floral Drive and ascend a long stairway where Indiana Street ends. At the top of the stairs, resume on Indiana, walking downhill.

Guisados does business in a 1928 commercial building on historic Brooklyn Avenue, which is now César E Chávez Avenue.

0.8 At the base of the hill turn left on Malabar Street, which is not signed.

1.2 Turn right on Evergreen Avenue. Walk to address 812.

1.3 El Tepeyac Café. Continue walking north on Evergreen Avenue.

1.4 Turn left on Wabash Avenue. Walk to the corner of Wabash and Forest Avenues.

1.6 X'tiosu Kitchen (closed Mondays). Resume west on Wabash. Turn left on Soto Street. Turn left on Fairmount Street. Walk to address 2411. Look up the alley if their tables are not visible on Fairmount.

2.0 Carnitas el Momo. Continue east on Fairmount. Turn right on Mott Avenue. Turn right on César E Chávez Avenue and locate address 2633 near the corner.

2.6 Milpa Grille (closed Sundays). Resume west on César Chávez.

3.0 Turn left in the crosswalk over César E Chávez Avenue at Breed Street and continue another 200 feet south to the Breed Street Shul. Turn around, return to César Chávez, and turn left. Walk to address 2100.

3.2 Guisados. From the front of the restaurant, turn left on St. Louis Street. Turn left on Michigan Avenue. Turn right on Chicago Street.

3.6 Turn right on 1st Street. Walk to address 2025.

3.7 Al & Bea's Mexican Food. Continue west on 1st, walking under the freeway to address 1845.

3.9 Birrieria Don Boni.

4.0 End of hike at Mariachi Plaza. The light rail runs underground here. Take the escalator to the ticketing area. Swipe your TAP card or purchase fare at the machine. Catch any train in the East Los Angeles direction and ride two stops to the Indiana Station. The shortest hiking distance back to the trailhead is 1.8 miles going entirely on 1st Street until the right turn at Indiana Street.

21 ELYSIAN PARK-ELYSIAN HEIGHTS

Elysian Park and Heights are joined at the hip. Elysian Park is the oldest Los Angeles park, and it is one of the largest. There is green space and pleasant paved paths and dirt trails. Elysian Heights is a residential neighborhood of dramatic contours that is full of beauty and eclectic charm. This loop combines the best of both, adding hilltop views in all directions and a mid-hike visit to a hip part of Sunset Boulevard.

Start: Grace E. Simons Lodge, 1025 Elysian Park Dr., Los Angeles 90012
Elevation gain: 400 feet
Distance: 4.3-mile loop
Hiking time: 2 to 3 hours
Difficulty: Moderate
Best season: Year-round
Trail surface: Sidewalks, pavement without sidewalks, park paths, dirt, stairs

Other trail users: None aside from other walkers
Restroom availability: Mile 3.1
Canine compatibility: Dogs must remain on leash.
Parking status: Free parking in the lot at the park
Rail transit accessibility: N/A
Trailhead GPS: N34° 05.15' W118° 14.77'

FINDING THE TRAILHEAD

From I-5, Golden State Freeway between the 110 and the 134 Freeways, southbound or northbound, take exit 138 for Stadium Way. Traveling south, turn left from the exit onto Stadium Way. Traveling north, turn left from the exit onto Riverside Drive. Pass under the freeway and turn left on Stadium Way. From either direction, drive uphill into Elysian Park and turn right on Elysian Park Drive, which comes well before Dodger Stadium. The lodge is on the right but is merely a landmark for this trailhead.

WHAT TO SEE

This counterclockwise loop hike begins and ends with the pathways of Elysian Park. Given the nearness to both downtown and Dodger Stadium, many of the paths in this park can be ratty and marred with vandalism. The paths that you are hiking today are in good to excellent condition. They are frequently used, but you can also find solitude. The premise of the lodge has been controversial. It is a beautifully maintained oasis that is available for event rental. Outside the gates, the amenities available to everyday folks are meager by comparison. The lodge is named for a woman who was a journalist, a progressive activist, and a nonstop battler who worked to keep the 550 acres of Elysian Park out of the hands of those who would have allowed oil fields, an airport, a convention center, condominiums, and other encroachments.

At the outset, the walking turns from tarmac to dirt along a beautiful loop. There is an illusion of climbing because the parkland below drops away into Elysian Valley. As you curve into the ridgetop, consider how Elysian Park is the east end of the Santa Monica Mountains; the west end occurs at the Pacific beyond Malibu. Up to the Marian Harlow Memorial Grove, the views are to the north. Below are the Los Angeles River

The Elysian Park Hiking Trail on a winter day

neighborhoods. Elysian Valley (Frogtown) is on this side of the river; Cypress Park is on the other side. Then there are the hills of Glendale, Glassell Park, and Mount Washington. Beyond those are the Verdugo Mountains on the left and the San Rafael Hills on the right. Behind them all are the San Gabriel Mountains.

Back among houses along Park Drive, you are now in the Elysian Heights district of greater Echo Park. This is a neighborhood of great character with houses old and new tucked densely in the impossibly steep contours. There are many public stairways, including a dozen with more than one hundred steps each, that are semi-hidden in an area of just over one-half square mile. Linger for the view of the Hollywood Hills before going down Baxter Stairs. Echo Park Avenue is at the bottom of one of the two valleys that compose this neighborhood. The cat graphics on the elementary school refer to Room 8, a real-life feline who inhabited the school and who inspired a best-selling children's story as well as a three-column obituary in the *Los Angeles Times* when he died in 1968. A stairway climbs to Lemoyne Street, the center ridge of Elysian Heights. Randyland is an artistic reimagination of a front yard. The project is an ever-changing mosaic created by strings of glass lenses. The artist calls his assembly *Phantasma Gloria*. You drop out of the Heights and enter the vibrant Echo Park commercial district on Sunset Boulevard. There are good choices just west and east of the single block that this hike covers of Sunset. One choice for good food with a restroom for customers would be Señor Fish at 1701 Sunset.

The Laveta Stairs were built in 1910 and are a beautiful segue into a residential avenue lined with palms. Headed back toward Elysian Park, the lovely domes of the Ukrainian Orthodox Church are not as old as they look. For 1 mile you follow the path of an old road that was mostly taken out of service to vehicles. The greenery, dominated by eucalyptus, is luxuriant.

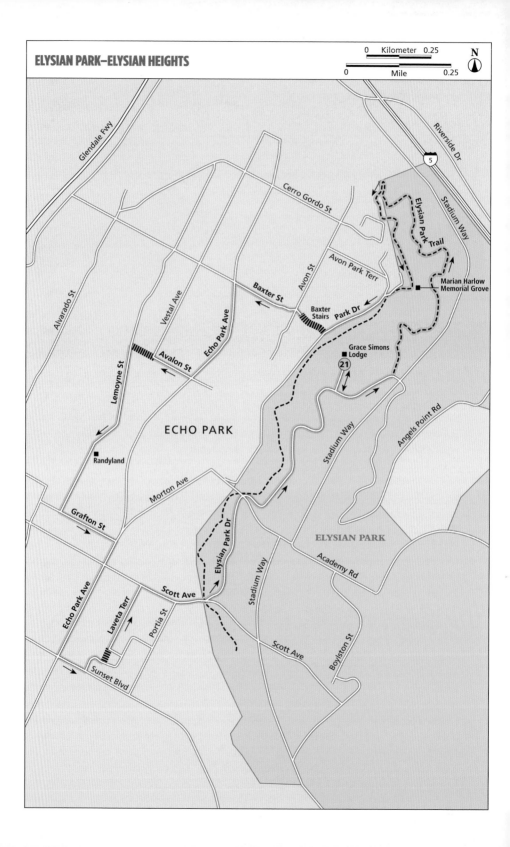

0 Kilometer 0.25

0 Mile 0.25

N

Glendale Fwy

Riverside Dr

5

Cerro Gordo St

Stadium Way

Elysian Park Trail

Avon Park Terr

Avon St

Baxter St

Marian Harlow
Memorial Grove

Baxter
Stairs

Park Dr

Alvarado St

Vestal Ave

Echo Park Ave

Avalon St

Grace Simons
Lodge

21

Lemoyne St

ECHO PARK

Angels Point Rd

Randyland

Stadium Way

Morton Ave

Grafton St

Elysian Park Dr

ELYSIAN PARK

Echo Park Ave

Stadium Way

Academy Rd

Scott Ave

Laveta Terr

Portia St

Scott Ave

Boylston St

Sunset Blvd

View of Elysian Valley from the Baxter Stairs

MILES AND DIRECTIONS

0.0 START outside the gate to Grace Simons Lodge. Walk in the direction that you drove in from (northeast). Just before you might connect to wide Stadium Way, turn left on a bare dirt path in the grass going off toward a barrier.

0.2 Enter Elysian Park Hiking Trail. Follow the wide pathway through a long loop to the left as smaller use-trails split off.

1.2 Marian Harlow Memorial Grove viewpoint. Continue on the same wide path, which is now headed south. One hundred yards from the viewpoint, turn right at a brief transition path that connects to where Park Drive meets Avon Park Terrace. Follow Park Drive south.

1.4 Baxter Stairs, behind 2101 Park Dr. Go down the stairs. At the bottom, jog right and continue straight on Baxter Street.

1.7 Turn left on Echo Park Avenue.

2.0 Turn right on Avalon Street. When the street curves right, proceed up the Avalon Stairway. Turn left on top onto Lemoyne Street.

2.4 Randyland, 1646 Lemoyne St. Continue on Lemoyne. Turn left on Grafton Street.

2.7 Turn right on Echo Park Avenue.

3.0 Turn left on Sunset Boulevard. Good food choices are to the right.

3.1 Turn left from Sunset to Laveta Terrace. Turn left up the wide Laveta Stairs and go straight on Laveta. Turn right on Scott Avenue. Enter Elysian Park soon after passing the Orthodox church. Pass a dirt trail on the left.

3.6 Veer left onto Elysian Park Drive, which is paved but closed to automobiles. Cross Academy Road. Select the level paved walking path that is right of a steeper dirt trail.

4.3 End of hike at the parking lot for Grace E. Simons Lodge.

22 SILVER LAKE

Silver Lake is a storied Los Angeles neighborhood built over a cluster of steep hills with narrow streets of imaginative houses. This hike improves upon the popular 2-mile path around the lake by utilizing half of that path while visiting many great locations that are high above it. The narrative provides a brief spotters' guide to the rich assembly of Modernist domestic architecture built here beginning in the 1930s.

Start: Silver Lake Branch Library, 2411 Glendale Blvd., Los Angeles 90039
Elevation gain: 700 feet
Distance: 5.0-mile loop
Hiking time: 2 to 3 hours
Difficulty: Moderate
Best season: Year-round
Trail surface: Sidewalks, pavement without sidewalks, paved path, dirt, stairs
Other trail users: None aside from other walkers

Restroom availability: Miles 2.2, 3.0
Canine compatibility: Dogs must remain on leash.
Parking status: Free curb parking 1,000 feet east of the start point, after hours parking in bank parking lots
Rail transit accessibility: N/A
Trailhead GPS: N34° 06.03' W118° 15.57'

FINDING THE TRAILHEAD

Navigate to I-5 between the 2 and the 134 Freeways. From the north, take exit 140A for Fletcher Drive. Turn right on Fletcher, which will blend into Glendale Boulevard. From the south, take exit 138 for Stadium Way. Turn left on Riverside Drive. Turn left on Fletcher, which will blend into Glendale Boulevard. The library is on the right, at the intersection of Glendale and Silver Lake Boulevards.

WHAT TO SEE

Silver Lake on this counterclockwise loop hike is the name for both the neighborhood and the 140-acre reservoir complex that you begin walking around. Modern regulations have moved drinking water storage away from open air facilities, so there is now an ongoing reassessment to modify this outdated infrastructure into a place with greater recreational use. Along Tesla Street, approaching West Silver Lake Drive, great blue herons might be present in seasonal nests high in the conifers. Just after the 1-mile mark, consider the houses on either side of the right turn you make from Moreno to Kenilworth. As much as enthusiasts focus on the work of the famous Modernist architects in Silver Lake, it is the dreamy Spanish Colonial Revival homes like these, with tile roofs and white stucco walls, that embody the Mediterranean theme of the area. Each of these was built around 1927.

Kenilworth Drive, between Moreno and Balmer Drives, provides several examples of the work of architect Rudolph Schindler. Schindler emigrated from Vienna, arriving in Los Angeles in 1920. His three decades of Los Angeles work are largely characterized by austere, sculpted volumes of stucco. He was a master with windows and with light. You can see the lake-facing, rear side of Schindler's 1939 Wilson House on the right just

The Swan Stairs go up 288 steps in three segments. The mural was done by artist Evelyn Leigh.

after passing 2127 Kenilworth. Next is his 1936 Walker House at 2100 Kenilworth. The third in this Schindler group is the 1940 Droste House at 2025 Kenilworth. Just before the 2-mile mark, you hike across the dam. After that comes the recreation center, a good restroom option.

After the mighty Swan Stairs, there is an eclectic minaret and dome on your way to the Lipetz House at 1843 Dillon St. Here, architect Raphael S. Soriano's 1936 design features an oval-shaped projection overlooking the lake. Dillon Street delivers nice views, and the view straight ahead is of office towers located near Wilshire and Vermont. Soon, Century City is in view to the right. Turning left onto Effie Street provides a great view of downtown. When you pass the 7-11 store, there are some coffee and food choices on the boulevard farther to the right.

Climbing the hill east of Silver Lake Boulevard, 1530 and 1536 Easterly Terrace are a pair of houses designed by architect William Kesling in the 1930s. His style blended the International Style with Streamline Moderne. Another example of his work is on the other side of the street at 1519 Easterly. After another stairway, Angelus Avenue has a wonderfully quiet ridgetop feel and some great houses, including another 1939 example by Soriano at 1607 Angelus. After that, 1816–1818 Silverwood Terrace is the Koblick House, a duplex built in 1937. It features dramatic cantilevers and is the first example on this hike of the work of architect Richard Neutra.

Silver Lake and meadow as viewed from Richard Neutra's VDL House

Back on the Silver Lake path, pause across from where Cove Street comes down on the right. At the dead end of Cove Street, you can see the Mattachine Steps. They are named to honor a society that was an early force in the gay rights movement. Harry Hay was instrumental in founding the group while living on this street. Look left across the lake and notice a structure with a bold arching canopy roof. This is known as Silvertop, and it was designed in 1964 by architect John Lautner. Approaching the meadow via the Silver Lake path, you are now well into Neutra country. Richard Neutra came from Vienna to Los Angeles in 1925 at the urging of his friend Rudolph Schindler. He became the most important figure in Los Angeles Modernism in a career that extended through the 1960s. Neutra lived in Silver Lake, as did his architect son Dion, who partnered on some of the work that you will pass. Across from the meadow is the VDL House. Next is a colony of ten homes located 1 block south near the corner of Silver Lake Boulevard and Earl Street. Neutra's work exhibits structure of almost ethereal framing sitting softly in the landscape, with creative use of windows, louvers, and geometry. Neutra worked out of an office that he designed on Glendale Boulevard, and you pass it just before the return to the Silver Lake Library.

MILES AND DIRECTIONS

0.0 START at Silver Lake Branch Library. Cross to northwest corner of Glendale and Silver Lake Boulevards and turn left (west).

0.1 Turn right into the Silver Lake path at Armstrong Avenue.

0.6 Exit the Silver Lake path at the corner of Tesla Avenue and West Silver Lake Drive. Continue straight and Tesla Avenue becomes a stairway to climb after crossing Kenilworth Avenue. On top of the stairs, turn left onto Moreno Drive.

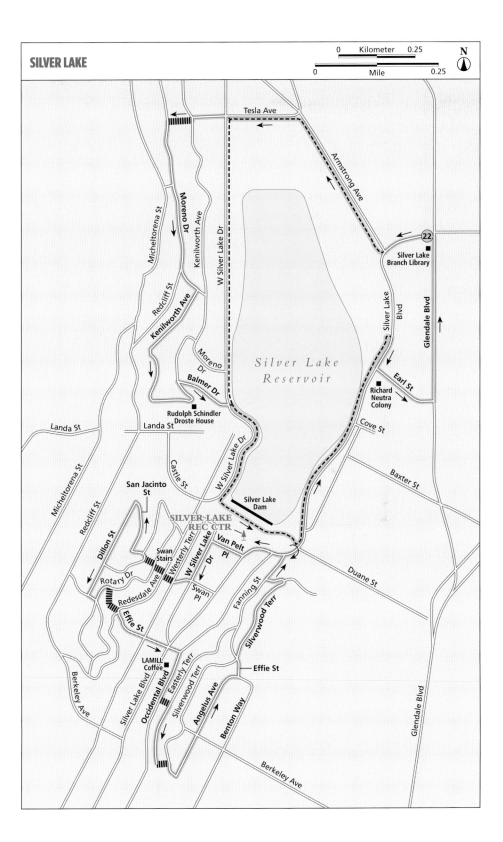

SILVER LAKE

Silver Lake Reservoir

Silver Lake Dam

SILVER LAKE REC CTR

Rudolph Schindler Droste House

Richard Neutra Colony

Silver Lake Branch Library

22

LAMILL Coffee

Swan Stairs

San Jacinto St

Streets and features:
Tesla Ave, Armstrong Ave, Glendale Blvd, Silver Lake Blvd, Earl St, Cove St, Baxter St, Duane St, Moreno Dr, Micheltorena St, Kenilworth Ave, Kenilworth St, Redcliff St, W Silver Lake Dr, Moreno Dr, Balmer Dr, Landa St, Castle St, Dillon St, Rotary Dr, Redesdale Ave, Westerly Terr, W Silver Lake Dr, Swan Pl, Van Pelt Pl, Fanning St, Silverwood Terr, Effie St, Berkeley Ave, Silver Lake Blvd, Occidental Blvd, Easterly Terr, Silverwood Terr, Angelus Ave, Benton Way, Berkeley Ave, Glendale Blvd

Scale: Kilometer 0 — 0.25, Mile 0 — 0.25

N

1.0 Veer left to avoid Redcliff Street and stay on Moreno Drive. Turn right on Kenilworth Avenue.

1.4 Rudolph Schindler's Droste House, 2025 Kenilworth Dr. Take the next right turn (perhaps unsigned) onto Balmer Drive. Cross West Silver Lake Drive.

1.6 Turn right into the Silver Lake path.

1.8 Turn left into the pathway across the Silver Lake dam. At the other side of the dam, turn right on the path by the dog park. Turn right on Van Pelt Place. If a locked gate prohibits access to the top of the dam, skip it and continue downhill and across the grass to Silver Lake Recreation Center.

2.2 Silver Lake Recreation Center at 1850 West Silver Lake Dr. The center is fully or partially closed Sunday mornings. Turn left on West Silver Lake Drive. Turn right on Swan Place.

2.3 Where Swan ends at Westerly Terrace, go up the three flights of the Swan Stairs. Turn right at the top on Webster Avenue. Turn left on Swan Place. Turn right on San Jacinto Street. Turn left on Dillon Street.

2.6 Lipetz House, 1843 Dillon St. Go downhill on Dillon Street. Turn left on Effie Street. Turn left on Rotary Drive. After 1718 Rotary, turn right down a stairway. At the bottom, jog right and then walk straight down Effie Street.

3.0 Cross Silver Lake Boulevard. Beverage and food places, including LAMILL Coffee, are located to the right. Continue on Effie Street. Turn right on Occidental Boulevard.

3.1 Across from 1603 Occidental, turn left up a stairway. At the top is Easterly Terrace. Don't continue up the next set of stairs; instead, turn right on Easterly.

3.3 At the road "End" sign, turn left up a stairway. Turn right at the top on Silverwood Terrace. Turn sharp left to take Angelus Avenue north where Silverwood Terrace ends.

3.6 Turn left on Effie Street. Turn right on Silverwood Terrace. Follow Silverwood through a hairpin left turn. Turn right on Fanning Street. Veer right at Silver Lake Boulevard.

3.9 At the traffic signal, cross left in the direction of the dog park. Turn right to reenter the Silver Lake path.

4.2 Cove Street, across from Silver Lake path. Stay on the path. As you approach the meadow, choose the path that goes outside of it toward the right. Take the access path toward the traffic signal on the right. Cross to the other side of Silver Lake Boulevard.

4.4 Neutra VDL House, 2300 Silver Lake Blvd. Turn right (south) on Silver Lake Boulevard.

4.5 Neutra Colony, centered on 2242 Silver Lake Blvd. Turn left on Earl Street.

4.7 Turn left on Glendale Boulevard.

5.0 End of hike at Silver Lake Library.

23 GRIFFITH PARK–LOS FELIZ

This energetic trek is a loop that begins and ends in Griffith Park before exploring the hilly parts of Los Feliz that nestle against the park. Highlights include the views from the Griffith Park trails, a Frank Lloyd Wright design and other notable residential architecture, a few nice public stairways, the vibrant Los Feliz Village area, and movie-making history associated with Walt Disney.

Start: Griffith Park and Southern Railroad and Pony Ride, 4400 Crystal Springs Dr., Los Angeles 90027
Elevation gain: 950 feet
Distance: 8.0-mile loop
Hiking time: 3.5 to 5 hours
Difficulty: Difficult
Best season: October–June
Trail surface: Sidewalks, pavement without sidewalks, dirt, stairs

Other trail users: Shoppers and diners
Restroom availability: Miles 3.1, 5.3, 6.8
Canine compatibility: Dogs must remain on leash.
Parking status: Free parking in the park lot
Rail transit accessibility: N/A
Trailhead GPS: N34° 07.31' W118° 16.42'

FINDING THE TRAILHEAD

From the Wilshire or Hollywood areas: Take Western Avenue north to Los Feliz Boulevard. Turn left at Riverside Drive to enter the park. Otherwise, take I-5 to exit 141 for Los Feliz Boulevard. Going southbound, follow signs for Los Feliz west and merge into it. Going northbound, turn left from the ramp onto Los Feliz. Turn right at Riverside Drive to enter the park. The train and pony ride are on the right side of Crystal Springs Road, which is a continuation of Riverside Drive.

WHAT TO SEE

This counterclockwise loop hike begins with a stiff climb to a five-point trail junction near Beacon Hill. Looking back the way that you came, the standout physical features are the Glendale Narrows of the Los Angeles River running to the southeast. Left of the river are the heights of Glassell Park and Mount Washington. Leaving dirt trail, paved Vista del Valle Drive is thankfully a motor-free zone. Eight miles of secondary park roads were closed to cars because of fire concerns in 1992; then they were damaged in a heavy rainfall year. Lovely Cedar Grove provides an exquisite unique forest cover compared to the rest of the park. Climbing back up from Vermont Canyon, another trail saddle provides a great view of the Los Angeles basin from downtown to (hopefully) the ocean. A semi-secret pedestrian gate gives passage out of Griffith Park and into the Los Feliz neighborhood.

Designed by Frank Lloyd Wright, the Ennis House was built in 1924. The massive residential structure is an example of the knit-block construction that Wright was employing at this phase of his career. Glendower Avenue curves around the Ennis House for a good look at the other side. From Bryn Mawr Road a curving stairway includes a neighborhood-themed mosaic. Next, the landmarked Berendo Stairs are one of the best in Los Angeles.

Cedar Grove in Griffith Park includes an invasive palm tree.

Los Feliz Boulevard is notable for its signature wide setbacks and deodar cedar trees. At New Hampshire Avenue, take a discreet glance through the grate on the gate of the house at the northwest corner to see a delicious Moorish-style residence built in 1925 and called Villa Fez. A few blocks compose a fascinating pedestrian zone centered on the 1934 Los Feliz Theatre. There is the historic, independent Skylight Books and a variety of places for food and drink.

Walking through the Franklin Hills, 4230 Franklin is an excellent example of a Streamline Moderne apartment building from the late 1930s. Next, look left at Myra Avenue just before the bridge to view the sculpted angles in stucco on a 1952 Rudolph Schindler house. The Shakespeare Bridge was built in 1926 to cross over the Arroyo Sacatella. That seasonal creek has long since been channeled into an underground storm drain. Look right when crossing over the bridge to observe the smaller circle-roofed structures that were built in 1960 as part of a school campus designed by architect John Lautner.

Just to the right of St. George Street, 2495 Lyric Ave. is one of two similar small houses side by side. Here in 1926, Walt and Roy Disney bought adjacent lots for about $1,000 each and then had these precut, ready-to-assemble homes shipped to here and erected by contractors. At the corner of Tracy Street, the 1931 Collegiate Gothic–style John Marshall High School is arguably the most beautiful campus in the Los Angeles school district. On the left side of Griffith Park Boulevard, there is a beloved 1931 courtyard of storybook cottages. Something bad happened here in David Lynch's film *Mulholland Drive*. At Hyperion Avenue, the Gelson's store indicates the location of the first Walt Disney studio. *Snow White and the Seven Dwarfs* was made during the 1925–1939 period that Disney was here. The Mulholland Fountain at the edge of Griffith Park is a 1940 monument to honor William Mulholland. He was the chief engineer of the aqueduct

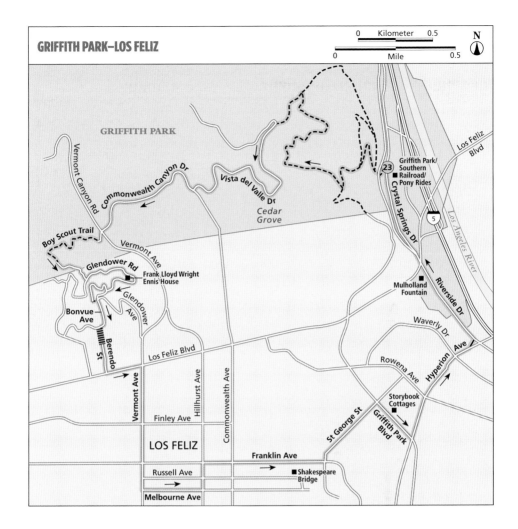

that, when it opened in 1913, reinvented Los Angeles. This sometimes-dancing fountain is a famous location that people typically just drive by; this is a good time for you to enjoy it up close before the final half-mile back to the trailhead.

MILES AND DIRECTIONS

0.0 START at Griffith Park and Southern Railroad and Pony Ride. Facing out from the ticket office, head right toward the end of the paved parking lot. Across the street from the lot exit, walk up a bridal path with a rail fence to the upper part of Crystal Springs Road. Use the crosswalk and enter a wide fire road named Cadman Trail. At the top of two switchbacks, ignore a smaller trail. Continue to the right side of a golf driving range.

0.5 Turn right on Coolidge Trail as Cadman Trail keeps going straight. Follow this fire road as it makes a long arcing climb to a saddle.

1.4 Five-point junction. Leave the saddle, taking the first trail to the left of the one you arrived on.

1.6   Turn left on Vista del Valle Drive.

2.0   Cedar Grove. Leave the pavement and walk a hundred yards or so to the left to explore. Return to the road and resume going downhill.

2.5   Turn right on Commonwealth Canyon Drive.

3.1   Cross to the other side of Vermont Canyon Road and turn left. Turn right at the triangular traffic island for Vista de Valle Drive. Locate and ascend the Boy Scout Trail across from the restrooms.

3.5   Turn left at a junction. Where the dirt trail and most of the walkers go to the right, follow the narrow, paved road to the left. Leave Griffith Park through a gate to Glendower Road.

3.7   Turn left on Glendower Avenue and walk to address 2607 for the Ennis House.

4.0   Ennis House. Continue down Glendower Avenue. Turn right on Bryn Mawr Road. Do not take the major stairway on the right. At the cul-de-sac, take a shorter stairway curving down to the left.

4.3   Turn right on Bonvue Avenue. Turn left down the long Los Feliz Steps near 4796 Bonvue Ave. At the bottom of the stairs, continue down Berendo Street.

4.7   Turn left on Los Feliz Boulevard. Turn right on Vermont Avenue. Walk downhill on Vermont.

5.4   Los Feliz Village. Turn left on Melbourne Avenue, which is past the theater. Turn left on Hillhurst Avenue.

5.8   Turn right on Franklin Avenue.

6.4   Turn left on St. George Street. Turn right on Griffith Park Boulevard.

6.7   Storybook cottages, 2906–2912 Griffith Park Blvd.

6.8   Turn left on Hyperion Avenue. Walk on the left side of Hyperion. Approaching Hyperion Bridge at Ettrick Street, stay to the far left to follow one-way pavement to Waverly Drive above the bridge. Continue straight ahead on a walkway that goes down to the bridge traffic level. The walkway connects to a stairway that you take down to Riverside Drive.

7.2   Turn left on Riverside Drive.

7.5   Mulholland Fountain. At Los Feliz Boulevard and Riverside Drive, cross twice to reach the northwest corner. Keep going northwest as Riverside has changed names to Crystal Springs Drive.

8.0   End of hike at Griffith Park and Southern Railroad and Pony Ride.

24 NORTHEAST LOS ANGELES HILLTOPS

Three miles from Los Angeles City Hall there are several undeveloped ridgetops that are each 500 feet higher than the city center. Brilliantly green in winter, gold in spring and summer, and brown in fall, they contribute to the iconic look of the city. This frisky hike gains 1,000 feet as it climbs three of those ridges, mostly by means of trails and narrow, sometimes primitive streets.

Start: Rose Hill Park, 3606 Boundary Ave., Los Angeles 90032
Elevation gain: 1,000 feet
Distance: 6.7-mile loop
Hiking time: 3 to 3.5 hours
Difficulty: Difficult
Best season: October–June
Trail surface: Sidewalks, pavement without sidewalks, dirt

Other trail users: Students
Restroom availability: Miles 2.1, 4.8
Canine compatibility: Dogs on leash OK (see note below)
Parking status: Free parking in the park lot
Rail transit accessibility: N/A
Trailhead GPS: N34° 05.26′ W118° 11.57′

FINDING THE TRAILHEAD

Take the 110 Freeway north or south. From the north, take exit 29 for Avenue 60. Go straight from the short ramp and turn right on Benner Street. Turn right on Avenue 60. Turn right on Monterey Road. From the south, take exit 28B for Via Mirasol. Turn right on Via Mirasol. Turn right on Monterey Road. Then the directions are the same: Where Monterey Road curves left, go straight on Armour Avenue. Veer slightly left at the top of the hill. Armour becomes Florizel Street. Go straight (with a little wrinkle) on Florizel. Turn right where Florizel ends at Boundary Avenue.

WHAT TO SEE

Before you begin this counterclockwise loop hike, consider that your dog on a leash would love this hike, but he/she would incite a chorus of barking through much of the route. The hike begins by climbing both path and road to reach the ridgeline of Montecito Drive. Here some of the homes on the left extend dramatically over the chasm on pillars. The route breaks out into a two-legged peninsula of undeveloped green space known as Flat Top. The open space was obtained by the city for parkland in 2016. The views sweep across downtown, Dodger Stadium and Elysian Park, and up toward Griffith Park.

A steep descent puts you on North Broadway, the lifeline of Lincoln Heights. Lincoln High School and predecessor schools have been located here or nearby for more than 140 years. The campus buildings were a WPA project. Lincoln High School played an important historical role in the Latino civil rights movement in the late 1960s. From the high school, you walk up Happy Valley anticipating the climb to your second ridgetop. The top of Rose Hill is reached by an almost comically steep and rutted dirt road the city identifies as Telluride Street. In just over 800 linear feet, you gain more than 200 feet of elevation. Amethyst Street reads like an island in the sky because it seems so inaccessible.

On Radio Road in Montecito Heights with snow on Mount Baldy

Amethyst, Topaz, Turquoise, Onyx, Tourmaline, Sardonyx, and others—these are the Gem Streets of Los Angeles. The open space at the end of Amethyst is private property. Maybe it will get developed; perhaps, like Flat Top, the city will find the means to save it as open space. Forest Park Drive is well named with an odd mix of Peruvian pepper trees, Southern California black walnut trees, and ponderosa pine.

The bottom of the next valley is Huntington Drive. Here there is still some influence of Henry Huntington's Pacific Electric Railway, even through the last trolley came through in 1951. A new parklet at Huntington and Soto was designed and planted by Northeast Trees. There is a plaque commemorating the recent removal of an old railway overpass and the reclamation for green space. Ascot Hills Park is a delight. Here there is open space that has been reclaimed, not for manicured fields and structured games, but for hiking and nature appreciation. Park trails take you to the third and final ridgetop. Exit into an eclectic neighborhood of rustic streets. Then you go back across Huntington and through more of the Gem Streets. Just before the end of the hike, consider walking up the short stairway into the Native American Gardens. The highlight in late spring is the bloom of the Matilija poppies.

MILES AND DIRECTIONS

0.0 START at the Rose Hill Park restroom building. Take Boundary Avenue out of the park the way that you drove in. Across from Victorine Street, turn right up a park stairway. Turn right into a dirt path at the top of the steps. The path goes through a white vehicle barricade and arrives at the edge of an open, level park area. Immediately look for an asphalt path on the left leading to a distinctive square patch of asphalt.

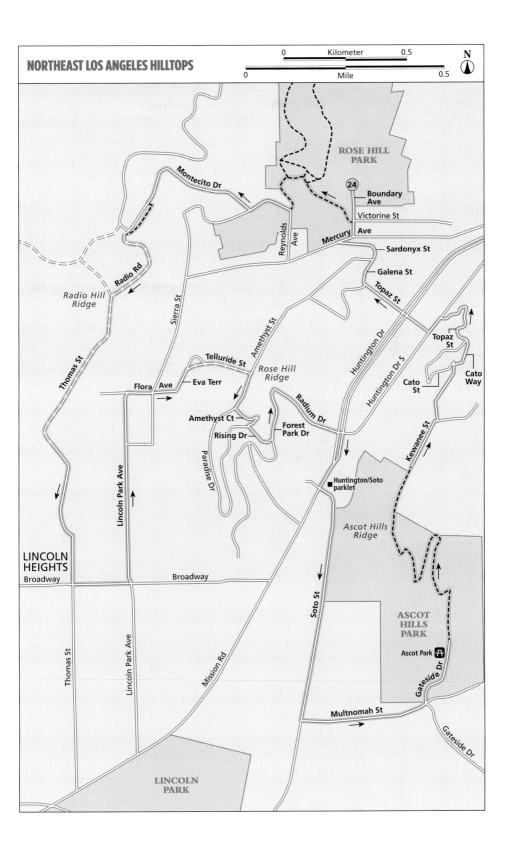

0   Kilometer   0.5

0   Mile   0.5

N

ROSE HILL PARK

Montecito Dr

24

Boundary Ave

Victorine St

Reynolds Ave

Mercury Ave

Sardonyx St

Radio Rd

Galena St

Topaz St

Radio Hill Ridge

Sierra St

Amethyst St

Huntington Dr

Topaz St

Thomas St

Telluride St

Rose Hill Ridge

Huntington Dr S

Cato Way

Flora Ave

Eva Terr

Cato St

Amethyst Ct

Radium Dr

Rising Dr

Forest Park Dr

Paradise Dr

Kewanee St

Huntington/Soto parklet

Lincoln Park Ave

Ascot Hills Ridge

LINCOLN HEIGHTS
Broadway

Broadway

Soto St

ASCOT HILLS PARK

Thomas St

Lincoln Park Ave

Ascot Park

Mission Rd

Gateside Dr

Multnomah St

Gateside Dr

LINCOLN PARK

0.2 Turn left and walk across that asphalt square into a dirt path that is less distinct than the one you started on. This climbs steeply at times. At a T turn left. The path climbs farther and goes to the right through a gap in the fence to arrive at a street junction with Reynolds Avenue going downhill and Roberta Street heading slightly uphill to the right. These streets are not signed.

0.4 Exit the path and turn right onto Roberta Street. At the first stop sign, ignore Montecito Drive on the right and go straight. At the second stop sign, turn right on Montecito Drive. Just beyond 1070 Montecito, a chain-link fence begins on the left. Walk to the left of the first fence post and turn right into an obvious trail.

0.9 Enter the Flat Top–Radio Hill trail. Follow this singletrack pointed toward the radio tower. It becomes doubletrack as it curves left around that tower. Maps identify this as Radio Road. Ignore the first road that skirts off to the left.

1.2 Radio Hill ridge. At a cairn, turn left on (unsigned) Thomas Street. Choose the right-hand of two parallel dirt tracks separated by an ungraded median. Thomas Street holds to the top of the ridge as it passes several driveways and houses on the left. This ridge walk dips before ascending a low knoll.

1.6 From the knoll, turn left on Thomas Street (now paved) and descend very steeply.

2.0 Broadway in Lincoln Heights. The route turns left, staying on the left side of the street. Ponder here that your next restrooms on the route are more than an hour away. Consider generic fast food 0.1 mile to the right on Broadway or several small restaurants across the street and to the left on Broadway.

2.1 Turn left on Lincoln Park Avenue.

2.6 Turn right on Flora Avenue. Turn left on Eva Terrace.

2.8 Just beyond 3100 Eva Terrace, turn right into a dirt drive that immediately splits. On the left is a parking circle and a driveway. On the right is the beginning of Telluride Street. Turn right here and climb very steeply on the 850-foot length of this street.

3.0 Rose Hill Ridge. Turn right on Amethyst Street. Turn left on Amethyst Court. Turn right on Paradise Drive. Turn left on Rising Drive. Rising Drive ends almost immediately at a T intersection with Forest Park Drive, which is not signed.

3.3 Turn left on Forest Park Drive. Forest Park becomes Radium Drive.

3.6 Cross to the east side of Huntington Drive. Turn right, walking southbound on the left side of the Huntington Drive inner lanes, and not on Huntington Drive South.

3.8 Huntington/Soto parklet. Cross Soto Street and turn left to walk on the right-hand side of Soto.

4.4 Turn left at Multnomah Street.

4.7 Turn left into Ascot Hills Park. After a parking lot on the left, the park road quickly comes to a Y. Select the pavement to the right, even as hikers are observed taking the trail to the left.

4.8 Ascot Park picnic area and restrooms. Shaded picnic areas are found just beyond and above the restrooms. Follow this road beyond the restrooms. There is a vehicle barrier where the road becomes a dirt walking path; 700 feet from the restrooms there is a trail junction with a park map on a signpost. Turn into the trail immediately to the left. Turn right 200 feet later on what the park refers to as the West Valley Trail.

5.1 As this trail is about to run into the fence line, follow a sharp left turn onto the West Hillside trail. Begin a moderate climb. Make a sharp right turn onto the path that heads directly to the top of the ridge. Climb more steeply and arrive at the West Ridge Road.

5.4 Ascot Hills Ridge. Turn right on the West Ridge Road. When you are parallel with the reservoir tank, a pedestrian gate takes you from Ascot Hills Park to Kewanee Street.

Chicanx culture is celebrated on this mural at Lincoln High School in Happy Valley.

5.6 Park exit. Bear left to remain on Kewanee. Turn right at a 4509 address marker onto unsigned Cato Street. Immediately veer left for Cato Way.

6.0 Turn right at a Y junction where a paved street, Dudley Drive, goes left and a dirt street, Topaz Street, goes right. Again, these streets are not signed. Turn right on Topaz Street as it curves downhill until it ends at a paved street.

6.1 Turn left on Huntington Drive South. Carefully cross Huntington Drive South to turn right on Topaz Street.

6.3 From Topaz Street, cross the main line of Huntington Drive at a signal. Continue northwest on Topaz. Turn right on Galena Street. After passing Amethyst Street on the left, veer left onto Sardonyx Street.

6.5 Turn right on Mercury Avenue. Turn left on Boundary Avenue.

6.7 End of hike at Rose Hill Park.

25 HIGHLAND PARK

This hike mixes quiet historic neighborhoods with a thriving boulevard commercial zone. There are great views, great old houses, and some intimate passages. A creative vibe throughout the route connects back to the Arts and Crafts tradition of the Arroyo Seco.

Start: Metro Southwest Museum Station, 4600 Marmion Way, Los Angeles 90065
Elevation gain: 300 feet
Distance: 4.0-mile point-to-point
Hiking time: 2 to 2.5 hours
Difficulty: Easy
Best season: October–June
Best days and times: Weekends, starting 9:30 a.m. to 2 p.m.
Trail surface: Sidewalks, pavement without sidewalks, paved path, stairs
Other trail users: Shoppers and diners

Restroom availability: Miles 3.1 to 3.5
Canine compatibility: OK for dogs, but you would need to walk back to the start.
Parking status: Street parking is available on either side of Figueroa Street adjacent to Sycamore Grove Park.
Rail transit accessibility: Metro L (Gold) Line, Southwest Museum Station is the start point.
Trailhead GPS: N34° 05.92' W118° 12.36'

FINDING THE TRAILHEAD

From the 110 Freeway between downtown Los Angeles and Pasadena, take exit 27 for Avenue 43. From the north, turn right from the exit to Avenue 43; from the south, turn left from the exit to Avenue 43. Then from either direction, turn right on Figueroa Street. The platform is reached by going up a ramp or stairs from Woodside Drive, just east of Figueroa Street. The hike begins by coming down these steps.

WHAT TO SEE

This point-to-point hike is designed for a Metro rail ride back to the starting point, but it is also an easy walk back. The hike begins by walking southwest to the Lummis Home. The city has been looking for a private entity to manage the property; for now, it is only open Saturday and Sunday. When the grounds are open, take a look inside the home. Beginning in 1897, Charles Fletcher Lummis spent 15 years to build this rambling house using stones that he pulled from the neighboring Arroyo Seco. He named his home *El Alisal*, Place of the Sycamore Trees. This house is perhaps the boldest physical representation of the Craftsman movement, active 1895–1925 all along the Arroyo Seco in Highland Park and the western edge of Pasadena. Lummis was a journalist, a regional booster, an advocate for the American Indian, and a scholar of the culture of the Spanish and Mexican eras of the Southwest. In his years here, he held court for an amazing list of guests.

The bike path offers a glimpse of the Arroyo Seco in an environment of oak and western sycamore trees on the Montecito Heights side. You return to Highland Park via a pedestrian bridge over the Arroyo Seco and the freeway. The San Gabriel Mountains, with the antennae of Mount Wilson, dominate the view. The headwaters of the Arroyo Seco is at Red Box Saddle, not too far from Mount Wilson. The stream runs through

The Mary Field House, built in 1904, is among the landmark homes on Professors' Row.

wilderness for 12 miles before breaking out near Jet Propulsion Lab, 9 miles upstream from here. The Arroyo Seco ends at its confluence with the Los Angeles River 2 miles downstream from here.

Sycamore Grove Park has a great social history, which is described on an Angels Walk stanchion. Sycamore Terrace presents a dozen sensational historic homes built between 1898 and 1912 along what has been called Professors' Row. Turning from Sycamore Terrace to Avenue 50, an Angels Walk stanchion describes how Occidental College was located here between 1898 and 1914. Near the tracks, Avenue 50 Studio is a cornerstone of the Northeast Los Angeles arts community. The Metro Gold Line follows a right-of-way that was once the Santa Fe main line; the legendary *Super Chief* from Chicago to Union Station would pass here.

Hiking on Avenue 50, Mount Washington towers above you on the left. The hillside is mostly too steep for building and is largely undeveloped and dotted by Southern California black walnut trees. Before the school, look left up Eldred Street. After dipping from Avenue 50, the street accelerates into a 33 percent grade. Where the pavement ends, there is a long wooden stairway. Save that for another hike. The stairs of Salient Place climb to a ridgeline in the highlands of Highland Park. After you turn right on Avenue 53, pause your short climb up and look behind you. The area below is the York Valley region of Highland Park. Visible beyond that is a solar array behind the Occidental College campus and the ridge that separates Highland Park from the Eagle Rock neighborhood to the north. The next range would be the San Rafael Hills, and you can see the antennae on Flint Peak in that range with an elevation of 1,892 feet. Beyond that are the San Gabriel Mountains.

The fiberglass Chicken Boy statue was relocated to Highland Park from Downtown by artist Amy Inouye.

Figueroa Street from Avenue 55 to Avenue 60 is the heart of Highland Park. The first interurban railway in Southern California was built in this corridor in 1895. This was the seminal event that sparked the development of Highland Park as a suburb with strong links to both Los Angeles and Pasadena. Figueroa Street was known as Pasadena Avenue until 1937, and this was part of the original 1926 route of Route 66. The fiberglass Chicken Boy statue was relocated to Highland Park from Downtown by artist Amy Inouye. On the left side of Figueroa above Avenue 56, one spot that hikers should look inside is the restored wood interior of Highland Park Bowl. There are two other Angels Walk stanchions with Highland Park descriptions between Avenues 58 and 60. The final feature of this hike is the Echo-Hayes historic district, which begins soon after you have walked past CVS. This is a marvelous collection of houses built on a bluff, mostly in the 1910s.

MILES AND DIRECTIONS

0.0 START at Metro Southwest Museum Station. Trains running in either direction exit to the same stairway leading up to Marmion Way or down to Woodside Drive. Go down the stairs or ramp to Woodside Drive and continue to Figueroa Street. Turn right on Figueroa.

0.4 Turn left in the second crosswalk to go downhill on the right side of Avenue 43. Turn right on Carlota Boulevard.

0.5 Lummis Home—*El Alisal*, 200 East Avenue 43. Enter the gate from Carlotta when the grounds are open. Return to Avenue 43 and cross it at the stop sign. Turn right on Avenue 43. Pass over the freeway and the creek channel. Turn left on Mosher Avenue.

0.7 At the Montecito Heights Recreation Center, turn left at bike route sign into the parking lot and then enter the Arroyo Seco Bike Path. At a Y in the path, go right toward the bottom of a pedestrian bridge.

1.1 Pedestrian bridge. Pass over the Arroyo Seco creek and the freeway. Turn right down a stairway at the end of the bridge, then turn left through a short tunnel to reach Sycamore Grove Park. Walk to the right of the performance area and angle further right across the grass toward Figueroa Street and the far-right corner of the park.

1.3 Cross Figueroa Street at the signal and continue uphill on Sycamore Terrace.

1.5 Professors' Row. At Avenue 50, cross to the north side of the street.

1.6 Turn left on Avenue 50 and pass over the train tracks.

2.0 Turn right into the Salient Place stairway. It is marked by a street sign on the left-hand side of the street in front of Aldama School. Turn left at the top of the stairs on Montezuma Road (which is not signed) and follow Montezuma as it climbs a bit farther and then curves right.

2.2 Merge into Aldama Street, which intersects on the left.

2.4 Turn right on Avenue 53. Turn left on Granada Street.

2.7 Granada Stairs. Take the wide stairway. Turn right at the bottom on Avenue 54.

3.0 Turn left on Figueroa Street.

3.2 Highland Park Bowl. Cross to the southeast side of Figueroa Street toward Baskin-Robbins at Avenue 58. Turn left on Figueroa Street.

3.5 Turn right on Avenue 60.

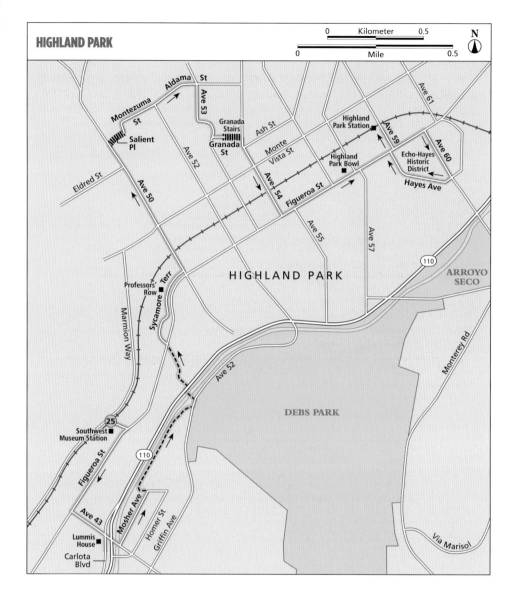

3.7 Echo-Hayes historic district. Turn right on Hayes Avenue. Walk to either side of the traffic circle where Hayes ends at Avenue 59.

3.9 Cross to the other side of Figueroa Street, walking toward the Dollar Store. Turn right on Figueroa. Turn left on Avenue 59.

4.0 End of hike at Metro Highland Park Station. Enter the platform on the left from Avenue 59. Scan your TAP card or purchase fare from the machine. Board any train in the Los Angeles Union Station direction and ride one stop to Southwest Museum Station. Or take the interesting 1.5-mile walk back. Take Avenue 59 a block farther; turn left on Monte Vista Street. Turn left on Marmion Way.

26 EAGLE ROCK

Eagle Rock has a distinct neighborhood character. There is at times a solitary trail-like feel when hiking on quiet, undulating residential lanes. You will get some great views, enjoy an intriguing district of shops and eateries, and explore a beautiful college campus.

Start: Target Store, 4211 Eagle Rock Blvd., Los Angeles 90065
Elevation gain: 300 feet
Distance: 5.8-mile loop
Hiking time: 3 to 3.5 hours
Difficulty: Moderate
Best season: October–June
Best days and times: Daily. The passage gate at the 3.7-mile mark closes at dusk. Some Sundays, it might not open until noon.

Trail surface: Sidewalks, pavement without sidewalks, stairs
Other trail users: Shoppers and diners, students
Restroom availability: Miles 2.5, 4.7
Canine compatibility: Dogs must remain on leash.
Parking status: Unmetered curb parking on Avenue 42
Rail transit accessibility: N/A
Trailhead GPS: N34° 07.35' W118° 13.53'

FINDING THE TRAILHEAD

From Route 2 Freeway south, take exit 15B for York Boulevard. Turn left on York. Turn right on Avenue 42. From Route 2 Freeway north, take exit 15 for Verdugo Road. Turn left onto Eagle Rock Boulevard. Turn left onto Avenue 42.

WHAT TO SEE

This clockwise loop quickly encounters a long, lonely stairway to gain the top of a north-south ridge. Views include Forest Lawn Glendale to the west, Griffith Park and the Santa Monica Mountains to the south, and a long look over Eagle Rock and far east to Mount Baldy. The narrow road walking on a ridge near where Castle Crest Drive meets Norwalk Avenue is a delight for urban hikers. This is the sort of roadway that drivers wisely avoid. The great view includes the sandstone mound of the Eagle Rock at the end of the valley. Turning left from Norwalk, a lovely flat, curving stroll begins on College View Avenue with the 1920s-era homes displaying a variety of styles.

Arrive at Colorado Boulevard at Ellenwood Drive. Across from you, there is a rare brick 1920s automobile service station. Now headed east, notice the beautiful 1927 former library building, today serving as the Center for the Arts. There are good choices for food and/or beverage on the hike along Colorado Boulevard between Eagle Rock Boulevard and Glen Iris Avenue. In these blocks is the old city hall. Eagle Rock was an independent town before its annexation in 1923. The Women's Twentieth Century Club of Eagle Rock has occupied this rustic, barnlike lodge since 1914. The National Register listing for the building notes how the club embodied the progressive goals of architecture and civic activity in the early 20th century.

Leaving Colorado, little roads take you over a low ridge to get to Yosemite Drive. The hill-climbing apartment courtyard at Hermosa and Chickasaw Avenues is a classic of this genre. To the rear of Yosemite Recreation Center, Sylvan Amphitheater was built by the WPA in 1938. The materials were concrete rubble and river rock. The transition

The view over Eagle Rock Valley and beyond from the top of Norwalk Avenue

between the recreation center and the college area is managed by using a handy gateway. The blend of narrow street, oak trees, great view, and intriguing houses makes remarkable Escarpa Drive a highpoint on this hike.

On the Occidental College campus, there is an option to add a great view with a walk up to Fiji Hill. This requires an additional half-mile of walking and 200 feet elevation gain. At the 4.5-mile mark, simply turn left instead of right to go up the steps to a parking structure with a solar rooftop. A well-used dirt extension of this road climbs to 360-degree views. Return to the hike route the same way. The path down to the campus quad goes past Haines Residence Hall. In 1979 the freshman class at this small independent college included a young man from Honolulu named Barack Obama. Haines was his freshman dorm, and there is a display of period photos in front. The college quad is a nice place to linger. The campus has been here since 1914, and much of its beauty comes from the tile-roofed buildings designed for the most part by architect Myron Hunt. For refreshment, try the Tiger Cooler to the right of the steps below Haines or the Green Bean Coffee House upstairs in the college union building.

Your path out of the campus goes by the bottom of the broad formal stairs between Fowler and Johnson Halls. Freshman Barack Obama's first political speeches ever may have been the ones he made from these steps. Alas, after 2 years of Occidental, Obama moved on to Columbia University. Near the end of the hike, the 1929 Sparkletts Water plant is a good example of the exoticism that is sometimes found in Los Angeles industrial buildings of that era. It had to give up its minarets after the 1971 earthquake.

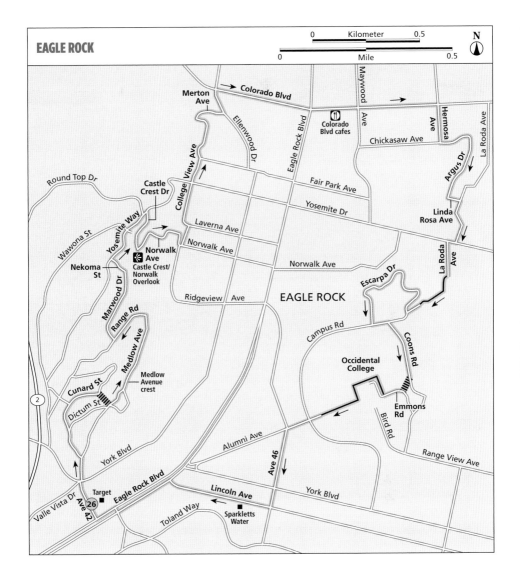

MILES AND DIRECTIONS

0.0 START at the Avenue 42 driveway for the Target Store. With your back to the store, turn right on Avenue 42. Cross York Boulevard and follow Avenue 42 as it goes left at the four-way stop and later as it veers left at a Y. Coming to a T intersection, go straight on Cunard Street as Avenue 42 goes left. Near 2686 Cunard, turn right up a long stairway.

0.5 Medlow Avenue crest. At the top of the stairs, turn left on Medlow Avenue.

0.8 Turn left on Range Road. Turn right on Marwood Drive. Turn left on Nekoma Street.

1.2 Turn right on Yosemite Way. Turn right on Castle Crest Drive. Castle Crest makes a hairpin turn left at the ridgetop to become Norwalk Avenue.

1.7 Castle Crest/Norwalk overlook. Head downhill steeply on Norwalk Avenue. Turn left on College View Avenue.

A long stairway comes early on the Eagle Rock hike.

2.1 Turn right on Merton Avenue. Turn left on Ellenwood Drive. Turn right on Colorado Boulevard.

2.5 Colorado and Eagle Rock Boulevards.

2.6 Colorado Boulevard cafes.

2.9 Turn right on Hermosa Avenue. Turn left on Chickasaw Avenue. Go straight from Chickasaw onto Argus Drive.

3.3 Turn left on Linda Rosa Avenue. Turn right on La Roda Avenue. Veer left to remain on La Roda. Cross Yosemite Drive in the crosswalk and turn right. Turn left to regain La Roda Avenue.

3.6 Turn right into a passage gate that comes after passing the ball field. Enter Yosemite Recreation Center. Turn left from the gate to enter a path that goes around the left side of the pool. Pass to the right of the stone bleachers of an outdoor theater.

3.7 Passage gate to Campus Road. Turn right on Escarpa Drive and walk the loop of this street.

4.2 Western junction of Campus Road and Escarpa Drive. Turn left on Campus Road. Turn right on Coons Road. Pass the yellow vehicle barriers. Stay on Coons Road as you pass to the right of both the Bird Hillside Theater and the Keck Theater.

4.5 Below the parking lot with the solar rooftop, consider the half-mile addition for Fiji Hill. Otherwise, turn right down a stairway that passes between the two wings of Norris Residence Hall. At a patio-like area, turn right to go down some more steps. Turn right into a quiet campus lane named Emmons Road. Leave this road on the right for a pathway that passes in front of Emmons Wellness Center. Continue down the steps to the front of Haines Residence Hall.

4.7 Turn left in front of Haines and walk across the access road and down a stairway to the campus quad.

4.8 Occidental College quad. From the front of the student union building, turn left in the quad and then turn right down some steps to walk past the leaflike metal sculpture and exit the college.

4.9 Campus Road at Alumni Avenue. Go straight on Campus. Turn left on Avenue 46 and cross York Boulevard.

5.3 Sparkletts Water. Turn right on Lincoln Avenue.

5.5 Turn left on Eagle Rock Boulevard.

5.7 At El Paso Drive, turn right into the crosswalk across Eagle Rock Boulevard. Turn left on Eagle Rock. Turn right on Avenue 42.

5.8 End of hike at Target Store.

SAN GABRIEL VALLEY

In the hikes of this section, the nearness of the San Gabriel Mountains introduces a notion of wilderness rusticity. Four hikes in this section share a narrative that is mostly fact with a bit of folklore. With connections via the Santa Fe Railway complete in the 1880s, a Garden of Eden was within reach of the Midwest. The area attracted wealthy snowbirds, who spent the winter here. By 1900, they were paying for marvelously crafted homes of wood that seemed to match the spirit of the place. They hired architects like Charles and Henry Greene, two brothers who were able to tap into this social upheaval and put their own artistic stamp on it. People with respiratory issues followed advice from doctors to go west to the dry air. In the early 1900s, common folk came and built more economical wood houses. In 1926, Route 66, the Main Street of America, was established, and it came through here. You still get a feel for that in Monrovia and on Pasadena's Colorado Boulevard.

Whether it is in the Arroyo Seco, Bungalow Heaven, Altadena, Monrovia, or even in upscale Madison Heights, there is a similarity in these hikes. The mountains are

A house designed by Greene and Greene overlooks the Arroyo Seco on the Pasadena–Arroyo Seco hike.

Greene and Greene's famous Gamble House with the San Gabriel Mountains in the background

represented by the use of polished stone that washed out of them. Street trees, particularly live oak, are soothing. The pleasing Craftsman homes are built to hug the landscape rather than tower above it. And they often have porches that help connect the homes to the street and connect the passing walker to the home.

Of course, on some streets on these hikes, you will also see Craftsman-flavored mansions that were built to be staffed by butlers and maids. This section includes a hike in Whittier, even though it lies south of the San Gabriel Valley. Whittier is difficult to pigeonhole, but it shares historical attributes with Pasadena, Altadena, and Monrovia and the weather is similar. Favorite hike in this section? Do the Altadena hike and see beautiful old houses and independent mountain spirit carry on in Altadena and North Pasadena.

27 PASADENA-ARROYO SECO

Mention Arroyo Seco in Pasadena and you are not just talking about a place; the words also suggest a woodsy rustic culture. This hike will travel above the canyon on Arroyo Terrace and Grand Avenue, enjoying the work of Greene and Greene and other great architects. You will go deep into the greenery along Arroyo Boulevard, where artists built more modest houses on the edge of the wild. And you will walk on dirt paths through the sycamores and along the creek itself.

Start: Rose Bowl Aquatics Center, 360 North Arroyo Blvd., Pasadena 91103
Elevation gain: 200 feet
Distance: 4.1-mile loop
Hiking time: 1.5 to 2.5 hours
Difficulty: Easy
Best season: October–June
Trail surface: Sidewalks, stairs, dirt
Other trail users: None aside from other walkers

Restroom availability: Mile 2.9 (0.2-mile detour to the left)
Canine compatibility: Dogs must remain on leash.
Parking status: Free parking in the park lot when there is no Rose Bowl event
Rail transit accessibility: N/A
Trailhead GPS: N34° 09.12′ W118° 09.91′

FINDING THE TRAILHEAD

From the south: Take the 110 Freeway toward Pasadena. Use exit 31A for Orange Grove Avenue. Turn left to follow Orange Grove Avenue through and north of Colorado Boulevard. From the east: Take I-210 to the 134 Freeway. Use exit 13A for Orange Grove Boulevard. From the exit ramp, turn right on Orange Grove Boulevard. From the west: Take the 134 Freeway toward Pasadena. Use exit 13A for Orange Grove Boulevard. Turn left on Orange Grove Boulevard. Then from all three directions, follow Orange Grove Boulevard north of Colorado and the 134 and turn left on Rosemont Avenue. Turn left on Seco Street in front of the Rose Bowl. Turn left on Arroyo Boulevard. Turn into the Rose Bowl parking lot at Gate I. The Aquatics Center is beyond the far side of the parking lot.

WHAT TO SEE

This steps and trail at the beginning of this clockwise loop will get the heart pounding. Suddenly, you level off onto Arroyo Terrace. This immediate area has the largest concentration of homes built by Charles and Henry Greene. The fame for these brother architects came from their infusion of the English countryside house with their own artistic sensibilities, including facets of Japanese design. Their wood interiors featured a fantastic level of fit and finish inspired by the Arts and Crafts aesthetic of that age. Typically, their exteriors have a dark wood sheathed appearance. Homes were built to connect to the outdoors with an abundance of doorways and with provisions for outdoor lounging, dining, and sleeping.

From these heights, you get a good idea of how the arroyo has broken out of the wilderness after its course within the folds of the San Gabriel Mountains. Here, the floodplain, including around the Rose Bowl, is very wide. It will get much narrower as you hike south. Directly across from the gateway into Arroyo Terrace, there is a cobblestone

This was the home of Craftsman tile maker Ernest Batchelder in the Arroyo Seco.

The Colorado Street Bridge has soared high above the Arroyo Seco since 1913.

wall framing the small garage of a home to the right. Built in 1901, this was Charles Greene's house. It is the first of six houses in a row from the Greene and Greene office. 424 Arroyo Terrace is an odd one because the owner here decided his 1908 woodsy house was out of style and it was converted in 1927 to Spanish. The Neighborhood Unitarian Church is a 1970s design by architect Whitney Smith that harmonizes in this environment. The next building is the Greene and Greene Scott House that has been adapted to serve church functions; walk up the courtyard to observe the massive chimney of boulders. Then arrive at Charles and Henry Greene's most famous work, the Gamble House. It was built in 1908 for a founder of the Procter and Gamble company. This is considered one of the most important works of American domestic architecture.

Across Orange Grove Boulevard, the Fenyes Mansion is a museum today. It was built at nearly the same time as the Gamble House, so it is interesting to see how different the styles are. This was the beginning of Millionaires Row, built along Orange Grove in the early 1900s. That avenue of mansions was built for a different market than the clients who sought these exquisitely detailed, rusticated houses nearer to the Arroyo Seco. At the corner on the right side, where Grand Avenue ends at Arroyo Terrace, is the Duncan-Irwin House. Built with a complex, multi-gabled roof, this is one of the best of the lesser-known works from Greene and Greene.

Every January 1, Colorado and Orange Grove is the most famous intersection in the world. Floats, bands, and equestrians turn left to go east here from Orange Grove. Starting down Grand Avenue, the buildings on the right, including the grand Court of Appeals building, were part of the Vista del Arroyo Hotel of the 1920s and 1930s. Like other great hotels of the day, this one offered lodging in detached cottages, and there are restored examples of these before reaching the main building. Grand Avenue is glorious hiking as it tilts gently downhill. There are few cars and many striking houses.

Crossing California Boulevard, you are no longer on the rim of the Arroyo Seco but are on a bench within it. The land parcels and the houses built on them are smaller. These houses were more likely the work of builder-craftsmen, not trained architects. This area hits its aesthetic stride on Arroyo Boulevard, where one side of the street is free of structures. A narrow band of trees gives way to a steep drop to the base of the arroyo. This is where the Pasadena Arts and Crafts movement flourished. 626 S. Arroyo Blvd. was the home and early workshop for Craftsman tile maker Ernest Batchelder. You can see examples of his decorative tiles on the house walls and walkway. The Batchelder House has also long been associated with famous Pasadena historian and architecture critic Robert Winter, who lived there 47 years before he passed away in 2019. A sign on 500 S. Arroyo Blvd. indicates that this was the home and studio for German-born plein air painter Jean Mannheim. Both Batchelder and Mannheim built their homes in 1909.

Lower Arroyo Park is a short detour but offers restrooms and a chance to see locals practice their fly casting. The hike route stays above the arroyo bottom just a bit farther. La Casita del Arroyo is a clubhouse that was built in 1933. A plaque by the door describes its interesting history. The dirt path along the bottom of the Arroyo Seco leads to the base of the Colorado Street Bridge. This 1913 viaduct is the most dramatic visual object in the area. Regrettably, a long list of incidents, the first in 1919, has linked this structure to another name: Suicide Bride. Below Colorado Street Bridge, you can make out its predecessor. Scoville Bridge, built in 1887, was the first structure in Pasadena to cross the arroyo. Then comes the more prosaic 1950s bridge built for the freeway. Upstream from Scoville Bridge, find a rare spot where the creek runs over a natural soft bottom and is not encased in concrete. There are western sycamore trees with their identifying broad leaves and their angled trunks. You pop out of the arroyo bottom to the side of the road and soon are back at the aquatics center.

MILES AND DIRECTIONS

0.0   START at Rose Bowl Aquatics Center. Facing the entrance door, walk away from the parking lot in a paved path between the aquatics center and the tennis courts. Turn right to walk under a pergola, then walk on the grass to the right side of the children's play equipment. Enter the bottom of an old stairway that is diagonally left after passing the play equipment. Turn right into a dirt path where the steps end. At the first trail junction, make a hard-left turn.

0.3   Exit these paths through a gate (that is locked at dark) to Arroyo Terrace next to a signpost cairn for Brookside Park. Turn left on Arroyo Terrace. Pass Scott Place. Turn left into a walkway after passing the gray shingled Neighborhood Church building. Stay to the left of the parking lot.

0.5   Gamble House, 4 Westmoreland Place. Follow the half-circle drive toward the front door and then back to the sidewalk of Westmoreland Place near the bookshop. Continue in the same direction then exit Westmoreland Place through a passage by the ornamental gates. Turn right on Rosemont Avenue.

0.6   Turn right on Orange Grove Boulevard.

0.9   Turn right on Live Oaks Avenue. Turn right on Grand Avenue.

1.0   Turn left on Arroyo Terrace. Turn right on Grand Avenue.

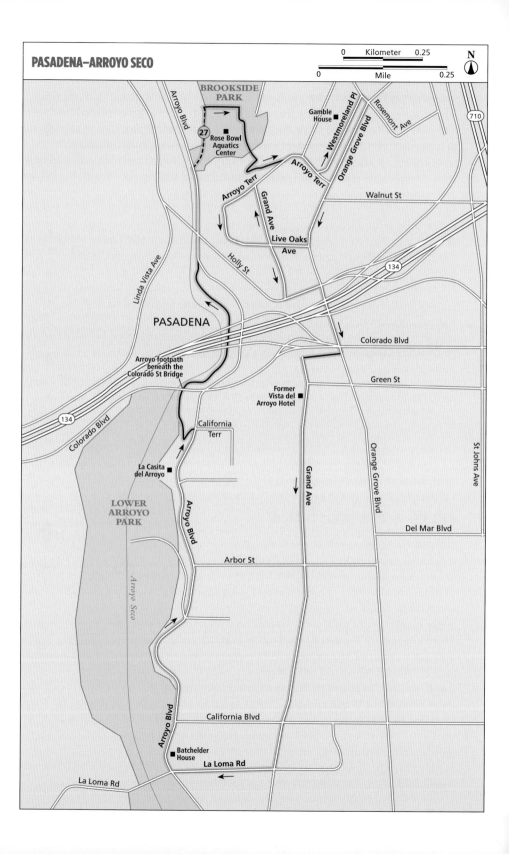

0   Kilometer   0.25

0   Mile   0.25

N

BROOKSIDE PARK

Gamble House

Rosemont Ave

710

Arroyo Blvd

27

Rose Bowl Aquatics Center

Arroyo Terr

Westmoreland Pl

Orange Grove Blvd

Arroyo Terr

Walnut St

Arroyo Terr

Grand Ave

Live Oaks Ave

Linda Vista Ave

Holly St

134

PASADENA

Colorado Blvd

Arroyo footpath beneath the Colorado St Bridge

Green St

Former Vista del Arroyo Hotel

134

Colorado Blvd

California Terr

La Casita del Arroyo

LOWER ARROYO PARK

Arroyo Blvd

Grand Ave

Orange Grove Blvd

St Johns Ave

Del Mar Blvd

Arroyo Seco

Arbor St

California Blvd

Arroyo Blvd

Batchelder House

La Loma Rd

La Loma Rd

1.3 Turn left on Holly Street. Turn right on Orange Grove Boulevard. Cross over the freeway and pass an off-ramp then turn right into a park pathway. Turn left at the cul-de-sac of Grand Avenue.

1.6 Former Vista del Arroyo Hotel. Continue south on Grand Avenue. Cross California Boulevard.

2.4 Turn right on La Loma Road. Turn right on Arroyo Boulevard.

2.6 Batchelder House.

2.9 Driveway on left side for Lower Arroyo Park. There are restrooms 0.2 mile down the driveway.

3.2 La Casita Del Arroyo, 131-199 South Arroyo Blvd. Veer left into the south gate and walk across the parking lot to see this feature up close. Exit through the north gate.

3.3 Across from California Terrace on the right, make a hard-left turn into a dirt access path that leads to the bottom of the arroyo. After one switchback this trail intersects the main arroyo path. Keep going in the same upstream direction (north) that the access path has pointed you.

3.4 Pass under the Colorado Street Bridge. The trail briefly turns quite steep here. Keep to the main trail; ignore options to turn right.

3.9 Leave the woods and meet paved Arroyo Boulevard. Walk on the dirt margin on the left side of Arroyo Boulevard. Cross Arroyo Boulevard when you are parallel with the "Gate I" sign. Walk across the parking lot.

4.1 End of hike at Rose Bowl Aquatics Center.

28 PASADENA-OAK KNOLL

Pasadena is famous for its tree-lined avenues filled with distinctive homes. This mostly flat hike winds through classy neighborhoods, particularly Oak Knoll, where the houses mostly date to the first three decades of the 1900s. This is a hike full of oak trees and a wide variety of great houses.

Start: Metro Fillmore Station, 753 South Arroyo Pkwy., Pasadena 91105
Elevation gain: 200 feet
Distance: 5.0-mile lollipop
Hiking time: 2 to 2.5 hours
Difficulty: Moderate
Best season: October–June
Trail surface: Sidewalks
Other trail users: None aside from other walkers
Restroom availability: Miles 2.0, 3.7

Canine compatibility: Dogs must remain on leash.
Parking status: Difficult to find near the station, but curb parking is available east of Marengo Street in the direction of the start of the hike.
Rail transit accessibility: Metro L (Gold) Line, Fillmore Station is the start point.
Trailhead GPS: N34° 07.98' W118° 08.89'

FINDING THE TRAILHEAD

From the south take the 110 Freeway north until it ends at Arroyo Parkway. The Metro Station is on the left side of Arroyo Parkway. From elsewhere, take exit 25C from the 134 Freeway or exit 25B from I-210. Turn south on Fair Oaks Avenue. Turn left on California Boulevard. Turn right on Arroyo Parkway. The Metro station is on the right side behind a Starbucks.

WHAT TO SEE

The end of this hike will overlap the initial 0.4 mile on this counterclockwise lollipop. Begin in the Madison Heights neighborhood, which was mostly developed between 1910 and 1917 as a neighborhood with quality homes for professional people. At the northwest corner of Los Robles Avenue and Wallis Street, an experimental bubble house was created in 1946 by applying the stucco skin over a pneumatically filled bladder. Architect Wallace Neff built this one and others around the country as experiments in low-cost housing construction. At the southwest corner of Allendale Road and Oakland Avenue is a lovely example of the Pueblo Revival style. Behind the guard house at 1288 Oakland Ave. is a massive 5-acre property with a fifteen-bedroom mansion. What you see of this are some charming carved lion heads at the other gates. The current mansion is a 1990 rebuilding of the 1913 Harry Charles mansion that was damaged in a fire. At 1315 Oakland, a sublime Craftsman is notable because designer/builder Guy S. Bliss was not a trained architect. This is a reminder that many unsung artistic hands created the zenith of the Pasadena Craftsman age, not just famous architects such as Greene and Greene.

At El Molino Avenue, the passage into Oak Knoll is apparent as the street plan departs from the rectilinear grid and becomes a curving flow drawn to adhere to valleys and ridgelines under a canopy of trees. Oak Knoll was anticipated to be a community of prosperity. By 1907 the first houses were built, the Wentworth Hotel opened, and a Pacific

The Ledyard House, built in Oak Knoll in 1909, has a distinctive log pergola.

Haskett Court is a nice example of the bungalow courts that Pasadena is famous for.

Electric trolley connected the area to the downtowns of Pasadena and Los Angeles. At 1361 Ridge Way, the Ledyard House from 1909 is covered with log-detailing, including a striking pergola across the front. The Langham, Huntington Hotel comes at the 2-mile mark. In 1914 Henry E. Huntington reopened the failed Wentworth Hotel and named it for himself. The Huntington became a fabled player in the great hotel era of Pasadena. Hikers who are "presentable" might enter the lobby to use the restrooms or even get a beverage in The Tap Room. Henry Huntington's San Marino Ranch was just east of the Oak Knoll tract, and that fiefdom would later become The Huntington Gardens and Library as well as the city of San Marino.

After turning left on Hillcrest Avenue from Oak Knoll Avenue, 1344 Hillcrest is the Spinks House that Greene and Greene built in 1909. You cannot see much of the house through the greenery, but you can study their wonderful mailbox, which mimics the house. In the next 3 blocks there are houses designed by the great residential architects of the region in the early 20th century: Roland Coate, Arthur and Alfred Heineman, Reginald Johnson, Myron Hunt, Joseph Blick, George Washington Smith. The crowning architectural achievement on today's route is at the southeast corner of Wentworth and Hillcrest Avenues. This is the Robert Blacker House built by Charles and Henry Greene in 1907. The image created by Greene and Greene is very different at 1188 Hillcrest on a house they built in 1911 for the three Culbertson sisters. Here, the design is Asian with a wavy green tile roof and gunite walls. 1290 Hillcrest was designed by Wallace Neff; this is the style you expect of this architect, nothing like the bubble house seen earlier. The knoll drops away dramatically as you leave it on Kewen Drive. In the canyon at the bottom, enough surface water would flow at one time to power El Molino Viejo. This was

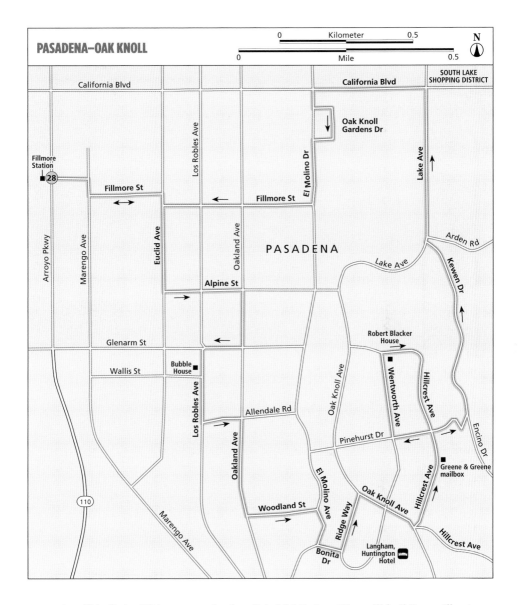

a gristmill built in 1816 to serve the San Gabriel Mission. The mill buildings still exist about 0.4 mile away but are not directly accessible from this location. San Marino begins on the other side of Kewen.

The intersection of California Boulevard and Lake Avenue is the south end of what has been a fashionable shopping district for 90 years. Just west of Lake, look carefully for a marvelous example of a bungalow court. This is Haskett Court, and it was built in 1926 with five buildings along both sides of a path sharing an English country cottage design. There are massive hipped roofs, and tall chimneys. After turning on El Molino Avenue, Oak Knoll Gardens is another delightful example of living small with a series of cute two-bedroom cottages.

MILES AND DIRECTIONS

0.0 START at the Metro Fillmore Station platform next to the Starbucks. Cross Arroyo Parkway and continue east on Fillmore Street. Cross Marengo Street in the crosswalk. Turn right then left to resume eastward on Fillmore.

0.3 Turn right on Euclid Avenue. Turn left on Alpine Street. Turn right on Oakland Avenue.

0.9 Turn right on Glenarm Street. Turn left on Los Robles Avenue.

1.0 Bubble House at Wallis Street. Continue on Los Robles. Turn left on Allendale Road. Turn right on Oakland Avenue.

1.4 Turn left on Woodland Road. Turn right on El Molino Avenue. Walk above the traffic island then proceed carefully on the right side of El Molino to a stop sign. Turn left on Bonita Drive. Turn left on Ridge Way. Turn right on Oak Knoll Avenue.

2.0 Langham, Huntington Hotel. Turn left in front of the hotel onto Hillcrest Avenue.

2.2 Greene and Greene mailbox. Turn left on Pinehurst Drive (opposite Kewen Drive). Turn right on Wentworth Avenue.

2.5 Robert Blacker House. Turn right on Hillcrest Avenue.

2.7 Turn left on Kewen Drive (opposite Pinehurst Drive). Follow Kewen where it bends right as it crosses Canon Drive.

3.3 Turn 90 degrees right on Oak Knoll Avenue, ignoring the smaller street that is a harder right. Oak Knoll Avenue becomes Lake Avenue.

3.7 South Lake shopping district. Turn left on California Boulevard.

4.0 Turn left on El Molino Avenue. Turn left into Oak Knoll Gardens Drive. Begin a circuit in the residential enclave. Turn right; walk to what seems to be a dead end but is not; turn right into an alley back to El Molino Avenue.

4.1 Turn left on El Molino Avenue. Turn right on Fillmore Street. Turn right on Euclid Avenue.

4.6 Turn left on Fillmore Street.

5.0 End of hike at Metro Fillmore Station.

29 ALTADENA

This is a tranquil urban hike with tons of residential charm. It starts in the Bungalow Heaven historic district of Pasadena and ascends more than 400 feet to the charming independent hamlet of Altadena. You will pass many distinctive old houses as you gaze upward into the San Gabriel Mountains. Learn a bit about the historic Mount Lowe Railway. Walk 6 long blocks under the canopy of the deodar cedar trees of Christmas Tree Lane. And you will go by a renowned gelateria.

Start: McDonald Park, 1000 East Mountain St., Pasadena 91104
Elevation gain: 450 feet
Distance: 5.2-mile loop
Hiking time: 2.5 to 3 hours
Difficulty: Moderate
Best season: November–June
Best days and times: Tues–Sun, start late enough so that you do not get to Bulgarini Gelato at mile 2.4 before they open at 1 p.m.

Trail surface: Sidewalks, pavement without sidewalks
Other trail users: None aside from other walkers
Restroom availability: Miles 2.4, 4.1
Canine compatibility: Dogs must remain on leash.
Parking status: Free curb parking around McDonald Park
Rail transit accessibility: N/A
Trailhead GPS: N34° 09.77' W118° 07.67'

FINDING THE TRAILHEAD

From the east or the west: Take I-210 to exit 27 for Hill Avenue. From the frontage road, turn north on Hill. Turn left onto Orange Grove Boulevard. Turn right onto Mar Vista Avenue.

WHAT TO SEE

If you cannot see the mountains clearly before beginning this counterclockwise loop, save this hike for another day. The beginning and end of this hike are different half-mile lengths of the Bungalow Heaven Historic District. This community contains more than 800 Craftsman bungalows built between 1900 and 1925. The Arts and Crafts movement that fostered the Craftsman bungalow was a rebellion against the industrial age and a spiritual dedication to dwellings that emphasized artisanal workmanship. The typical bungalow in this group displays a wood exterior, wide verandas, and sloping roofs.

North of Washington Boulevard, the hike spends more than a mile on fascinating Mar Vista Avenue. This is in the Pasadena Historic Highlands landmark district. A front yard at the southeast corner of Mar Vista Avenue and Elizabeth Street has a labyrinth. Unlike a maze, labyrinths are designed with a single path to the center and are associated with meditation. On the left at the corner of Woodbury Road, there is a striking Craftsman house built by architect Sylvanus Marston in 1912. The use of boulders gives the impression of a home that has grown out of the lot.

Altadena begins at New York Drive. This land was part of the massive Rancho el Rincon de San Pascual, which also included what is now South Pasadena, Pasadena, and part of San Marino. This unincorporated community remained more rustic with its gaze seemingly directed toward the San Gabriel Mountains above it rather than the

A bungalow built in 1917 off Mar Vista Street with a labyrinth in the front yard

metropolis below it. At the corner of Sonoma Drive, a Greene and Greene–designed house has a green tile roof and subtle Japanese-influence styling. Deep culverts appear north of Mendocino Street. These were part of an 1880s zanja (irrigation ditch) system devised by dairyman Francis Beckwith and built by Chinese laborers. Beckwith brought from his native Yorkshire a dry-stone technique where no grout or mortar was used. The massive gullies remain useful in heavy rainstorms, but they are no longer part of an irrigation scheme. At the southwest corner of Maiden Lane and Mariposa Street, a storybook home designed by architect Elmer Grey in 1911 is called *Thatch Cottage* for the weaved roof. This hike turns just short of where the first segment of the three-phase Mount Lowe Railway once ran. From 1893 to 1938, this popular attraction swept tourists up nearly 4,000 feet to the side of Mount Lowe. A trolley would start from the streetcar terminus on Lake Avenue and would turn from Lake to Palm Avenue, which is 2 blocks north of the turning point. The trolley finished its short run at Rubio Canyon where riders hopped off and climbed aboard an incline railway.

In the Altadena commercial town center, Bulgarini would be part of any debate about the best gelato in greater Los Angeles. It is great to find a purveyor of a product so identified with artisanal ingredients and expensive tastes in unpretentious Altadena. They open at 1 p.m. and are closed Mondays.

Santa Rosa Avenue at Mariposa Street is a key intersection for historic-cultural Altadena. At the northwest corner, a Girl Scout campground is the site of a house where Socialist activist Kate Crane Gartz would host Sunday salons. She welcomed left-wing political idealists like Gaylord Wilshire, George Bernard Shaw, H. G. Wells, Albert Einstein, and Upton Sinclair. On the northeast corner, the Theosophical Society has been here since the 1920s and hides mysteriously behind landscaping and gateposts. Near the

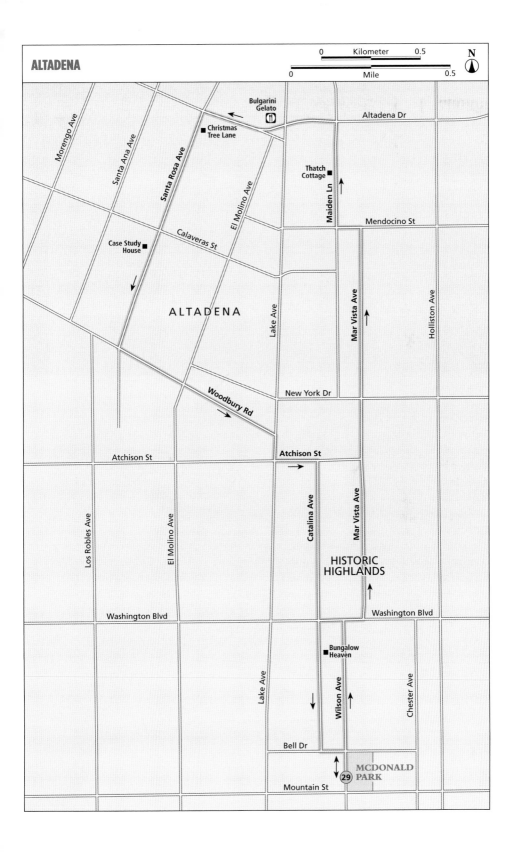

Mar Vista Street beckons you up the gentle slope.

southeast corner, Andrew McNally of the world of maps had a home built in 1887. The mansion has a distinctive bowler hat roof. A wing of the house houses the smoking room from the Turkish Pavilion of the 1893 Chicago World's Fair. Near the southwest corner, a striking cobblestone tower indicates a former carriage house built for a fleet of carriages and horses for the Colonel G. G. Green estate. The colonel's mansion itself is gone; a Mid-Century Modern library took its place.

Santa Rosa Avenue is Christmas Tree Lane where John Woodbury had 135 Himalayan deodar cedars imported and planted. The long line of trees has been decorated for the holidays since 1920. After passing Calaveras Street, a surprise in this bosky environment at 2275 Santa Rosa is the crisp Modern Case Study House #20 built in 1958 by the firm of Buff, Straub, and Hensman. Crossing Lake Avenue, you walk between a Spanish bell tower and a Gothic steeple. The hike has a big finish with a long series of quality houses on Atchison Street and Catalina Avenue.

MILES AND DIRECTIONS

0.0 START in McDonald Park at the restrooms. Turn out to the west edge of the park and proceed north on Wilson Avenue. Turn left on Washington Boulevard. At Catalina Avenue, cross to the north side of Washington and turn right.

0.6 Pasadena Historic Highlands district. Turn left on Mar Vista Avenue.

1.8 Turn left on Mendocino Street. Turn right on Maiden Lane.

2.1 Thatch Cottage. Maiden Lane and Mariposa Street.

2.2 Turn left on Altadena Drive.

2.4 Cross Lake Avenue, walking on Altadena Drive. Bulgarini Gelato is in the Rite Aid shopping center on the right. Patronize the Rite Aid for restrooms. After Bulgarini, turn right on Altadena Drive.

2.7 Turn left on Santa Rosa Avenue.

2.8 Christmas Tree Lane.

3.2 Case Study House.

3.5 Turn left on Woodbury Road.

4.0 Turn right on Lake Avenue.

4.1 Turn left on Atchison Street.

4.2 Turn right on Catalina Avenue.

4.7 Reenter Bungalow Heaven.

5.1 Turn left on Bell Drive.

5.2 End of hike at McDonald Park.

30 **MONROVIA**

Monrovia is a gem with a foothill setting and a rich architectural legacy built on streets lined with oak trees. In some places, you find block after unspoiled block of well-preserved homes from the 1880s to the 1920s. Many of the streets are very elegant, with wide and parklike pavement and stunning architecture. Monrovia has a vibrant commercial district, a Route 66 vibe, and an independent, ethnically diverse population that is justly proud of their delightful little city.

Start: Monrovia Historical Museum, 742 E. Lemon Ave., Monrovia 91016
Elevation gain: 300 feet
Distance: 5.4-mile loop
Hiking time: 2.5 to 3 hours
Difficulty: Moderate
Best season: November–June
Trail surface: Sidewalks, dirt
Other trail users: None aside from other walkers

Restroom availability: Miles 3.6 to 4.2
Canine compatibility: Dogs must remain on leash.
Parking status: There is free street parking at the start.
Rail transit accessibility: N/A
Trailhead GPS: N34° 08.81' W117° 59.33'

FINDING THE TRAILHEAD

From the east or the west: Take I-210 and take exit 35A toward Mountain Avenue. From the frontage road turn north on Mountain Avenue. Turn left on Lemon Avenue. The starting point is on the left side of the street.

WHAT TO SEE

If you cannot see the mountains clearly before beginning this counterclockwise loop, save this hike for another day. The hike begins with the path along Sawpit Wash. Cross exit points at Wildrose Avenue and Deodar Lane where the path goes up to the road surface and then back down along the right side of the channel. Curving left, you become more aware of the high wilderness of Monrovia. Monrovia is unique in that 1,400 acres of mountain area immediately north of the developed town is city owned and preserved as wilderness. That is different from the nearby communities, where Angeles National Forest generally begins immediately where developed towns end. Your view also takes in observatory buildings and towers of Mount Wilson, elevation 5,713 feet. After leaving Sawpit Wash, you find a nice garden of native plants at Norumbega Road. This garden was planted in a traffic island in front of an eclectic house full of storybook details. The house is *Le Château des Reves*, built in 1922 as a studio for artist Frederick Melville DuMond.

Grand Avenue Park is a nice place to sit, but it does not have restrooms. A painted bear figurine at the top of the park stairs is one of several Monrovia mascots that can be seen around town. It does remind hikers that bear incursions into the residential streets are common Monrovia events. West of here, vistas open looking south to the other side of the San Gabriel Valley, where the basin eventually gives way to the Hacienda Hills due south. Between Encinitas and Myrtle Avenues, the north side of Greystone Avenue is graced by an unusual low wall of upturned river-polished stones in front of

The Aztec Hotel, designed by architect Robert Stacy-Judd, is on old Route 66.

the Craftsman-style homes. Monroe Place is named for town founder William Monroe, and he is connected to two homes here. *The Oaks* is the 1887-built house with the mansard tower at Monroe Place and Primrose Avenue; the more modest 1884-built Monroe House is at 225 Monroe.

On Melrose Avenue, *Mills View* is an 1887 Eastlake Victorian mansion that has been a popular filming location. *Idlewild*, on Mayflower Avenue, is an 1887 Queen Anne designed by the famous California architect Joseph Cather Newsom for a former Civil War Union Army general. The *Idlewild* property has a wonderful side gate that you detour a few feet to enjoy.

The Aztec Hotel was built in 1925, a pinnacle year for regional exoticism. Today, this Pre-Columbian theme reads as delightful LA kitsch. However, England-born architect Robert Stacy-Judd was dead serious in his pursuit of an indigenous American architecture when he designed it. The hotel has long been in a restoration process, but it reopened to the public in 2020. Next comes the town center, where the beautiful library is open every day but Sunday and worth a long glance even if you don't go inside. Gonzalez Goodell Architects took some cues from Frank Lloyd Wright in this design. After the library comes an impressive array of old church buildings and a knockout New Deal–era school building. The Wild Rose Tract Historic District is a cluster of 1910–1922 Craftsman bungalows in a single block. Even in a town that has many other examples of this style, this block is notable. The hike ends at century-old Recreation Park, whose paths and driveways have a formal quality to them. The Boys and Girls Club building was originally an American Legion Post. The museum building at the end is Spanish Colonial style, built in 1925 to serve as a bathhouse.

MILES AND DIRECTIONS

0.0 START at Monrovia Historical Museum. Facing the street, turn right (east) on Lemon Avenue.

0.2 Turn left into the Sawpit Wash Trail.

0.9 Exit Sawpit Wash Trail at Greystone Avenue and turn left. Turn right on Norumbega Road.

1.4 Turn left on Valle Vista Avenue. Turn right just past 357 Valle Vista into the alley access to the park.

1.5 Grand Avenue Park. Walk across the grassy field and exit the park via the colorfully painted steps. At the top, go straight on Prospect Avenue.

1.9 Turn left on Canyon Boulevard. Turn right on Greystone Avenue.

2.3 Turn right on Myrtle Avenue. Turn left on Greystone Avenue. Turn left on Primrose Avenue. Turn right on Monroe Place.

2.5 Monroe House, 225 Monroe Pl. Turn right on Magnolia Avenue. Turn left on Hillcrest Boulevard. Turn right on Melrose Avenue.

2.8 *Mills View*, 329 Melrose Ave. Turnaround from *Mills View*. Return to Hillcrest Boulevard and turn right.

3.1 Cross twice to reach the southwest corner of Hillcrest Boulevard and Mayflower Avenue. Continue west on Hillcrest just 150 feet to check out the artful side gate that shows the image of the front of the house. Turn around. Return to Mayflower and turn right.

3.2 *Idlewild*, 255 N. Mayflower Ave. Keep going downhill on Mayflower.

A block of Greystone Avenue has an unusual low wall of upturned river-polished stones.

3.4 Turn left on Foothill Boulevard.

3.7 Aztec Hotel, 311 W. Foothill Blvd. Turn right on Magnolia Avenue. Turn left on Lime Avenue. Turn into Library Park to reach the front of the library. From the library entrance, walk diagonally left across the park to the corner of Palm and Myrtle Avenues.

4.2 Myrtle Avenue dining district. Continue east on Palm. Turn left on Canyon Boulevard. Turn right on Wildrose Avenue.

4.7 Wild Rose Tract Historic District. Turn right on California Avenue.

5.1 Turn left on Colorado Boulevard.

5.3 Enter the formal park paths of Recreation Park and go to the left of the Boys and Girls Club building. Angle through the park, keeping to the right of the play area. Turn right on Lemon Avenue.

5.4 End of hike at Monrovia Historical Museum.

31 **WHITTIER**

Founded by Quakers in 1887, Whittier is relatively isolated as it snuggles against the undeveloped Puente Hills. This hike tours historic and charming Uptown Whittier and then finishes with a mile along a nifty rails-to-trails pathway.

Start: Palm Park Aquatic Center, 5703 Palm Ave., Whittier 90601
Elevation gain: 100 feet
Distance: 5.0-mile loop
Hiking time: 2 to 3 hours
Difficulty: Moderate
Best season: October–July
Trail surface: Sidewalks, paved path
Other trail users: Shoppers and diners, bicyclists, scooters

Restroom availability: Miles 2.8 to 3.3
Canine compatibility: Dogs must remain on leash.
Parking status: Free parking in the park lot
Rail transit accessibility: N/A
Trailhead GPS: N33° 59.43' W118° 03.36'

FINDING THE TRAILHEAD

From the south: Exit I-605 on exit 15 for Whittier Boulevard toward Whittier. Turn right onto CA 72 E/Whittier Boulevard. Turn left onto Broadway. Turn left onto Palm Avenue. From the north: Exit I-605 on exit 16 for Beverly Boulevard East. Merge onto Beverly Boulevard. Turn right onto Palm Avenue.

WHAT TO SEE

The beginning of this clockwise loop hike is unremarkable but pleasant as it travels easterly on Floral and Orange Drives. As you get east of Pickering Avenue, the high Puente Hills become very apparent on your left. There are good fire roads to walk up there, and you might see hikers heading to or from the Hellman Park Trailhead. These hills make Whittier exceptional and hard to place regionally. The San Gabriel Valley is on the north side of the crest, but the undeveloped hills extend far to the east. Immediately southeast of Whittier is Orange County.

After 1.4 miles, Bright Avenue immediately displays how rich this part of Whittier is with well-maintained historic houses. A variety of styles of the period are represented. The Tudor Revival house at 5847 Bright has a wonderful eyebrow dormer. At the corner of Beverly Boulevard and Painter Avenue, there is a magnificent Queen Anne built in 1888. Lou Henry Hoover School was built in 1938 and is a marvelous example of both Streamline Moderne and the New Deal era. The frieze depicts a scene of the early Quakers and was done by WPA sculptor Bartolo Mako.

The Bailey House on Camilla Street is an important Whittier landmark. This ranch house was erected on a homestead in the 1860s. Twenty years later, a Chicago Quaker and financier selected this plot and other land nearby to be the home of a new Pacific Coast Quaker community. Jonathan and Rebecca Bailey were elderly Quakers already living in Los Angeles. Four days after moving into this house, they held the colony's first Quaker meeting on the porch. It was attended by about ten people, but it marked the birth of the community that incorporated in 1898, named for poet John Greenleaf Whittier. As with other outlying communities around Greater Los Angeles, Whittier

The hike ends with walking about one-third of the 4.5-mile-long Whittier Greenway Trail.

grew prosperous in the early 20th century with the development of the citrus and the petroleum industries. Its true growth as an identifiable community came when those industries gave way to housing after World War II. Many houses in this area were heavily damaged by the 1987 Whittier Narrows earthquake. Happily, the trend was to restore them rather than replace them.

Central Park is ringed by fine buildings and has public restrooms. Minutes after that comes the attractive Uptown commercial district of Greenleaf Avenue. Two blocks between Bailey and Wardman Streets are lively with shops and places to eat and drink. When it is open, consider a bowl of *fideo* at Colonia Publica. Two stellar buildings are on the left at the corner of Greenleaf Avenue and Philadelphia Street. The northeast corner is a 1932 Art Deco–Moderne beauty designed by Whittier's finest architect, William H. Harrison. The southeast corner is a Beaux-Arts masterpiece designed by John and Donald B. Parkinson. It was built for First National Bank in 1922 but is commonly known as Nixon Plaza. Whittier native Richard Nixon, the thirty-seventh president of the United States, had his law offices here in the 1930s. The ground floor of this building is now a food court. The Art Deco Whittier Village Cinemas opened as the Wardman Theatre in 1932. In the 1980s the theater already seemed to be at the end of its rope when it was shattered by the earthquake. Seeing how much the theater contributes to the street today is a feel-good story.

The hike ends with walking about one-third of the 4.5-mile-long Whittier Greenway Trail. This is an excellent rails–to–trails conversion of abandoned Union Pacific right-of-way. The trail has historic or natural interpretive displays that they call stations. Begin your part of the trail going north from Penn Street. Before starting, take a moment to look at the displays at the south side of Penn Street. You can learn some of Whittier's

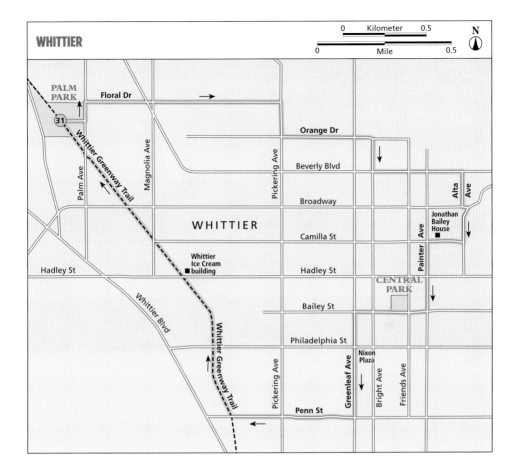

early agricultural history of citrus growing and shipping. Crates of oranges headed east with the *Quaker Girl* label. Where the greenway crosses Hadley Street, Art Deco enthusiasts will love the Whittier Ice Cream structure built in 1930. When the hike ends at Palms Park, look at the station displays that cover local architecture, including a series of birdhouses showing home styles in miniature.

MILES AND DIRECTIONS

0.0   START at Palm Park Aquatic Center. Exit the park to Palm Avenue and turn left.

0.2   Turn right on Floral Drive.

0.9   Turn right on Pickering Avenue.

1.0   Turn left on Orange Drive.

1.4   Turn right on Bright Avenue. Turn left on Beverly Boulevard.

1.8   Turn right on Alta Avenue. Turn left on Broadway. Turn right to resume south on Alta.

2.1   Turn right on Camilla Street.

2.2   Bailey House. Turn left on Painter Avenue.

Lou Henry Hoover School was built in 1938 and is a marvelous example of both Streamline Moderne and the New Deal era.

2.5 Turn right on Bailey Street.

2.6 Central Park.

2.8 Turn left on Greenleaf Avenue.

2.9 Nixon Plaza.

3.2 Turn right on Penn Street.

3.6 Turn right into the Whittier Greenway Trail immediately after Union Avenue.

4.2 Whittier Ice Cream building, Whittier Greenway Trail and Hadley Street.

5.0 End of hike at Palm Park Aquatic Center.

POMONA VALLEY AND THE INLAND EMPIRE

Look at a map of the urban area of Southern California and notice how in Santa Barbara, Ventura, Orange County, and San Diego, population density extends inland from the Pacific Ocean for only 5 to 20 miles then stops. Then look how population extends from Santa Monica Bay through central Los Angeles and inland. Population sprawl here finally slows down in Redlands, 80 miles inland. Pomona, Claremont, Riverside, and Redlands each had their own foundings before 1890. The arrival of railroads and the promise of an agricultural bounty brought each of these towns to life. Los Angeles then was just a place far in the distance with a population of 10,000. A century and a half later, all these places seem fused together.

But regardless of that sprawl, these four cities and the hikes through them are unique. All of these hikes are in college towns, and a youthful vitality and creative spirit will be found when walking through the right blocks. However, each of these hikes also has a certain time machine effect. Even in the context of a guidebook that generally assumes old stuff equals good stuff, that sentiment is heightened on the Pomona Valley and Inland Empire hikes. Pomona at first glance seems a tired place that has not been very well endowed. Get out and hike here and discover that the Lincoln Park Historic District is a fantastic, well-preserved residential area with a kaleidoscope of rich architectural detail in mostly modest homes. The Pomona Downtown Arts Colony is unpretentious but full of fascinating content. Everyone loves Claremont, and expectations are high here. Everything is beautifully kept up and the street trees are lovely. Hike here to see how well village life and college life can blend. Redlands has an astonishing display of upscale houses and mansions built more than 100 years ago. Favorite hike in this section? Riverside cannot be beat with its combination of hiking up to a popular and historic hilltop overlook and an incredible, dense assembly of public buildings.

32 POMONA

Pomona is one of California's oldest cities. The downtown is fascinating even at those spots where it reads as a tired product of the 1960s. The historic residential district of Lincoln Park exhibits block after block of unaltered and well-preserved homes from the late 1800s to early 1900s. This loop hike shows off the best of these features. A recurring theme of the hike is the many contributions made by Pomona native Millard Sheets to the visual fabric of downtown Pomona.

Start: Fox Theater Pomona, 301 S. Garey Ave., Pomona 91766
Elevation gain: 50 feet
Distance: 4.4-mile loop
Hiking time: 1.5 to 2.5 hours
Difficulty: Easy
Best season: December–May
Trail surface: Sidewalk
Other trail users: Shoppers and diners, students

Restroom availability: Miles 2.2, 2.7
Canine compatibility: Dogs must remain on leash.
Parking status: Pay parking lot recommended is 1 block east at the corner of 3rd and Locust Streets.
Rail transit accessibility: N/A
Trailhead GPS: N34° 03.41' W117° 45.03'

FINDING THE TRAILHEAD

Take I-10 to exit 45 for Garey Avenue. Going west, turn left on Orange Grove Avenue, then turn left onto Garey Avenue. Going east, turn right on Garey Avenue. Fox Theater will be on the right-hand side at the corner of 3rd Street.

WHAT TO SEE

The late–Art Deco Pomona Fox Theater opened in 1931. Its Wurlitzer was one of the largest and most advanced of its time, and the furniture in the lobby, mezzanine, and lounging rooms was made of solid mahogany. The theater has undergone a nice restoration within the past 15 years. Pomona tried closing 2nd Street in 1963, but the mall languished, and this part of it was eventually reopened to cars. The six-story Chase Bank building was the Home Savings Tower, and it was imagined as a cornerstone for the pedestrian mall. Artist Millard Sheets is best known today for his partnership with Home Savings. He designed the bank buildings and the mosaics that adorned them all over Southern California. Here, over the doorway facing Garey Avenue, is *Early Pomona Family*. Notice how the letters *H* and *S* (Home Savings) repeat in a vertical weave designed to shield the windows. Sheets was born in Pomona, and he taught for decades at nearby Scripps College.

The hiking pace quickens after you cross the elaborate pedestrian bridge over the tracks and leave the historic commercial district. The distinguished brick building across Garey opened as the YMCA in 1922. On the left, the American Museum of Ceramic Art (AMOCA) was founded in 2003 with a mission to champion the art, history, creation, and technology of ceramics. AMOCA is located within a former bank building designed by Millard Sheets, and the museum's permanent collection includes a 78-foot-long Sheets Studio mural depicting a century of Pomona Valley history. A right turn on Pasadena Street passes between a Mediterranean-style funeral home and a Gothic-style church.

The late–Art Deco Pomona Fox Theater opened in 1931.

Pasadena Street has many homes built between 1895 and 1905. East of Towne Avenue, the hike passes through a dreamy double row of palm trees on San Francisco Avenue.

West of Towne again, the route spends a mile in the Lincoln Park Historic District. The entire district of about 800 houses on 45 blocks takes the name of circular Lincoln Park, which was opened in 1908. A National Register application noted the assembly of late Victorian and National Folk houses, Craftsman and Craftsman-influenced houses, and a variety of late-19th- and early-20th-century revival buildings provide a contrasting range of styles and a kaleidoscope of rich architectural detail. Take your time through here; there is plenty to enjoy. Across Alvarado Street from the Starbucks on Garey, a 1903 firehouse looks forlorn as it sits hoping for restoration.

Wilton Heights Historic District on the west side of Garey gives you a further notion of what early-20th-century Pomona was like. Notice the ornamental gateposts at the corner of Alvarado and Park. The best thing here is a pair of boulder-lined apartment courts built in 1920 and named Boardwalk and Park Place. Pomona was founded as a railway/agricultural town in the 1880s. Before the freeways and the smog, it must have seemed like the Garden of Eden. The fertile ground was planted first with vineyards, but citrus and olive trees took over. In the mid-20th century, Pomona had a role in the region's aerospace industry. With the departure of General Dynamics, that also is just a fragment of local history.

Returning to downtown, you can see some artifacts of the Pomona Edison Historic District along 2nd Street from Parcels Street to just west of Park Street. The Mission Revival–style building at 637 2nd was built in 1904 as a National Guard armory. Pomona is named for the Roman goddess of fruit and fruit trees, and she is imagined on a mosaic and fountain designed by Millard Sheets at 2nd and Gordon Streets. The interesting

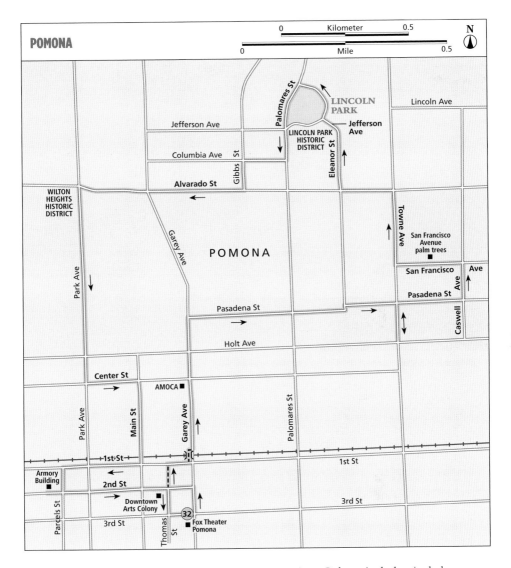

tenants in the old storefronts of this Downtown Arts Colony include vinyl shops, a multicultural bookshop and gallery named Cafe con Libros Press, the excellent Homage Brewing, and the Latino Art Museum.

MILES AND DIRECTIONS

0.0 START at Fox Theater Pomona. Facing away from the theater at the corner of 3rd Street and Garey Avenue, turn left (north) on Garey. Turn left on 2nd Street. Turn right in the pedestrian path that is a continuation of Thomas Street. Take this path to 1st Street. Find the shortest route through the parking lot to the base of the railroad pedestrian bridge on your right.

0.2 Railroad pedestrian bridge. Walk up and over the tracks. At street level on the north side, walk to the right of a traffic loop and aim for the pedestrian passage to Garey Avenue. Proceed north on Garey.

Pomona is named for the Roman goddess of fruit and fruit trees, and she is imagined here by artist Millard Sheets.

0.4 AMOCA (American Museum of Ceramic Art). At Garey and Holt Avenues, cross twice to reach the northeast corner and continue north on Garey.

0.6 Turn right on Pasadena Street.

1.1 Turn right on Towne Avenue. At Holt Avenue, cross at the signal to reach the east side of Towne, then turn left going north on Towne. Turn right on Pasadena Street.

1.4 Turn left on Caswell Avenue. Turn left on San Francisco Avenue.

1.6 San Francisco Avenue palm trees. Turn right on Towne Avenue.

1.8 Turn left on Alvarado Street. Turn right on Eleanor Street. Turn diagonally left on Jefferson Avenue.

2.2 Lincoln Park. Walk counterclockwise on the perimeter paths around most of Lincoln Park. At the southwest corner of the park where Como Drive, Jefferson Avenue, and Palomares Street all meet, exit the park and walk south on Palomares.

2.4 Turn right on Columbia Avenue. Turn left on Gibbs Street.

2.6 Turn right on Alvarado Street.

3.0 Wilton Heights Historic District. At Park Avenue, cross twice to reach the southwest corner of Park and Alvarado. Walk south on Park.

3.4 Turn left on Center Street. Turn right on Main Street.

3.8 Turn right on 1st Street. Turn left on Parcels Street. Turn right on 2nd Street.

4.1 Armory Building at 601 2nd Street. Turn around and go east on 2nd Street.

4.3 Downtown Arts Colony. Turn right on Thomas Street. Turn left on 3rd Street.

4.4 End of hike at Fox Theater Pomona.

33 CLAREMONT

Claremont styles itself as the City of Trees and PhDs. At the foot of a 10,000-foot mountain peak, here there is a mix of culture, colleges, tree-lined residential streets, architectural pedigree, and great places to choose from for food and beverage. Town and gown, this short hike introduces the best of beautiful Claremont.

Start: Claremont Station, 200 W. 1st St., Claremont 91711
Elevation gain: 200 feet
Distance: 4.9-mile loop
Hiking time: 2.5 to 3 hours
Difficulty: Moderate
Best season: November–June
Trail surface: Sidewalks, paved pathways
Other trail users: Shoppers and diners, students
Restroom availability: Miles 1.8, 3.1

Canine compatibility: Not a good hike for the dog
Parking status: Free street parking is normally available along 1st Street east of College Avenue. Read signs carefully. Walk about 1,000 feet west to the starting point.
Rail transit accessibility: Metrolink Claremont Station is the starting point.
Trailhead GPS: N34° 05.66' W117° 43.01'

FINDING THE TRAILHEAD

Take I-10 from the west or the east. Take exit 47 for Indian Hill Boulevard. Turn north onto Indian Hill Boulevard. Turn right onto 1st Street. The station is on the right across from Harvard Avenue on the left.

WHAT TO SEE

If you cannot see the mountains clearly before beginning this counterclockwise loop, save this hike for another day. Built in 1927, the station's doorways are covered with Churrigueresque decoration, and the Santa Fe Railroad's logo appears in glass on the door panels. When founded in 1887, Claremont was already a leader in Southern California citrus production. The Queen Anne Victorian at 1st and College Avenue is the oldest house in Claremont, but like Claremont's oldest college, it came here from Pomona. After a year in Pomona, the college found a temporary home in Claremont that turned out to be permanent. Built for the college founder, this house was rolled on timbers from Pomona to this location in 1901.

This 1.7-mile hiking route through the campuses is mostly linear, designed to give the user a brief, fun taste of the physical character of each campus. Campus features are not signed as clearly as city streets, and the college circuit is a sequence of turns. When in doubt, make use of campus maps and ask the students. You might stray from the recommended route, but it should be easy to reorient yourself. On the campuses, consider yourself a guest among a community of people whose activities are on a different pace than your hike.

Pomona College chose in the 1920s to initiate a consortium of colleges, using Cambridge and Oxford as a model. Scripps, Claremont McKenna, Harvey Mudd, and Pitzer were founded as part of that consortium between 1926 and 1963. Begin in the southwest quadrant of the group with Pomona College. Across from the Neoclassical-style

Scripps College's Balch Auditorium across Elm Tree Lawn

Carnegie Hall, you turn into the greenery of Marston Quad, walking to Bridges Auditorium. An intriguing doorway takes you to the fountain and steps of Bixby Plaza. Take a few minutes to detour to the right from here into Frary Dining Hall to see a famous mural that was executed by Mexican artist José Clemente Orozco in 1930.

Claremont McKenna (CMC) was founded as a men's college in 1946. Of the five colleges, it is the one that has seemed most willing to supplement its architectural legacy with some dynamic new buildings, including the Living Room element of the Kravis Center. It was designed by Uruguayan-American architect Rafael Viñoly. Your walking segue from the eastern edge of CMC to the southern edge of Pitzer is two late 1960s Mid-Century Modern buildings, circular Bauer Center to McConnell Center. Founded in 1963, two facets of the Pitzer campus personality enhance your walking experience. The landscape employs a theme of desert and native California plants and, secondly, many of the buildings display large-scale mural art.

Scripps College, founded 1926, remains women only. Architecturally, this is the exceptional campus of this group. Before buildings started to go up, two giants in their fields designed most of what is viewed today as a harmonious whole: architect Gordon B. Kaufmann and landscape architect Edward Huntsman-Trout. The Mediterranean style is expressed through creamy white stucco, green wood trim, red tile roofs, and lots of ornamentation with stone and modeled concrete. On the right side of your path, detour into the walled Fowler Memorial Garden. Amid the colonnades, there are frescos painted by Mexico's Alfredo Ramos Martínez. The view through a double row of elm trees toward the arched doorway of Balch Auditorium is sublime. Nearby, The Motley Coffeehouse is perfect for a break. The intimate courtyards of Balch Hall on the left hint at similar courtyards found throughout the original residence halls. Leave Scripps via a gate through the Graffiti Wall and enter the southwest quadrant of Harvey Mudd College. This college was founded in 1955 with a specialty in engineering, science, and mathematics, and the highly gifted students proudly refer to themselves as *Mudders*. Perhaps inspired by the engineering culture, the campus is highly linear, and most of the buildings hug either side of the half-mile-long Great Mall.

North of Foothill, the Claremont School of Theology is independent of the consortium. Next comes the United Methodist Church designed in 1968 by father-son architects Richard and Dion Neutra. The passage through the hedge might seem a bit uncertain, but it takes you to an urban farm and the captivating structures of Uncommon Good. At Indian Hill and Foothill Boulevard, U.S. Bank occupies a New Formalist–style building designed by artist Milton Sheets. A Sheets mosaic of ponies is on the south exterior. Sheets taught for decades at Scripps.

A sequence of blocks southwest of Indian Hill and Foothill display the consistent excellence of Claremont's residential architecture. Charming Pilgrim Place is a retirement home founded in 1915. It was originally designed to house Congregational Church missionaries between assignments. From Scrooby to Mayflower, the street names have historic American Pilgrim associations. Near the end of the hike, Claremont Packing House is an excellent example of adaptive reuse embracing the local citrus-growing history. A sawtooth roof provided natural light for fruit packers who would sort lemons and oranges for size and grade. The fruit was then crated or boxed and loaded on refrigerated boxcars for points east. Today that roof provides lighting for shops.

MILES AND DIRECTIONS

0.0 START at Claremont Station at the covered bus waiting area. Facing 1st Street turn right. Turn left on College Avenue.

0.4 Soon after crossing 4th Street, turn right into the grassy Marston Quadrangle of Pomona College. Head east to Bridges Auditorium. When directly in front of Bridges, turn left into a wide college path. Turn right on 6th Street. Turn left up several steps to pass through a narrow but impressive arched wooden gate. Frary Dining Hall, with the famous mural, is immediately to the right. Walk straight ahead, passing to the right of a grassy area known as Walker Beach, and aim for the exit out to 8th Street.

0.8 Cross 8th Street and leave Pomona College to enter Claremont McKenna. Immediately go up eight steps to a passage for Kravis Center. From the open area, pass to either side of the reflection pool that surrounds a glass and steel cube. Continue east in a wide quad area for 1,000 feet. Turn left in front of circular Bauer Center and then exit to an area with cars.

1.1 9th Street at Mills Avenue. Leave Claremont McKenna and enter Pitzer College. Turn right on 9th Street and locate the seven steps to an unpaved area that is signed as the Pitzer Multi-Species Commons. Turn left in front of McConnell Center with a two-story mural. As you reach a large area of native plants, turn left. Walk north. A greenspace, fittingly known as the Mounds, will be on your left. Walk toward the clock tower but turn left just in front of it. Walk to the left of a grassy field, pass another desert garden, and exit the campus through a gap to the left of the Broad Center.

1.4 Mills Avenue. Leave Pitzer and enter Scripps College. Directly across Mills Avenue from the Pitzer exit, take a pedestrian path that goes to the right of athletic facilities. Turn left when this path ends at a service road. Turn right into a wide campus path that begins at Tiernan Field House. Follow this path with residence halls on

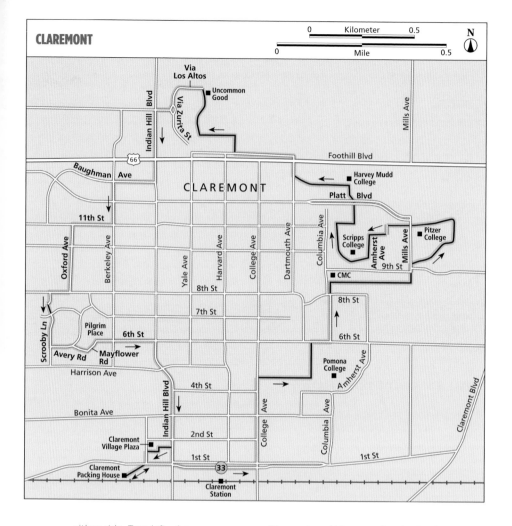

either side. Turn left when a gap appears. The enclosed Margaret Fowler Garden is on the right just after that turn. Continue south past a small parking lot and a bit of Amherst Avenue. When you have passed the Edwards Humanities Building, turn right to walk down the center or on the left side of Elm Tree Lawn. The Motley Coffeehouse (and restrooms) are reached in Malott Commons by going down steps on the left that are signed for Richard Dance Studio. From the tower of Malott Commons, the route goes almost due north past the ornamental steps and the lawns of Jaqua Quadrangle. When Toll residence hall blocks the path, turn right and then left to go around both Toll and a garden to reach the Graffiti Wall.

1.9 Scripps Graffiti Wall doorway. Leave Scripps and enter Harvey Mudd College. Cross Platt Boulevard and veer left into a ramp that merges into a wide entry plaza. Turn left in the Great Mall and aim for six-story Sprague Center. Pass to the right of Sprague and exit out to Dartmouth Avenue.

2.1 Turn right on Dartmouth Avenue. Cross to the north side of Foothill Boulevard, then turn left. Stay to the right of the main traffic lanes of Foothill, following the sidewalk.

2.4 Turn right up the wide steps into Claremont School of Theology. With the striking chapel straight ahead, turn left and pass to the right of the library. Aim for a stop sign across a parking lot and go down steps to reach there. Turn right on an access

The former Claremont lemon-packing house has been recycled into shops and restaurants.

road for Claremont United Methodist Church. Walk around the left side and then behind the church structure. Staying to the right of the school, pass through an obvious gap in the hedge. Walk through the gardens and buildings of Uncommon Good.

2.6 Uncommon Good. Exit to the parking lot. Turn left on Via Los Altos. Turn left on Via Zurita. In the unlikely event that the gate on Via Los Altos is locked, return to Foothill Boulevard by passing the church again. Turn right on Via La Selva. Turn left on Indian Hill Boulevard.

2.9 Indian Hill Boulevard at Foothill Boulevard. Cross twice to reach the southwest corner. Go south on Indian Hill. Turn right on Baughman Avenue.

3.1 Turn left on Berkeley Avenue. Turn right on 11th Street.

3.4 Turn left on Oxford Avenue. Turn right on 8th Street.

3.6 Pilgrim Place. Turn left on Plymouth Road. As Plymouth bends right, continue straight on a pedestrian path. From the path, connect to Scrooby Lane. Turn left on Avery Road. Turn left on Mayflower Road.

4.0 Turn right on 6th Street. Turn right on Berkeley Avenue. Turn left on Harrison Avenue.

4.1 Turn right on Indian Hill Boulevard.

4.4 Turn right into the Village Plaza at the Laemmle sign. Go west through the plaza.

4.5 Turn left on Oberlin Avenue. Cross to the south side of 1st Street.

4.6 Claremont Packing House. Enter to the right and make an interior loop. Return to 1st Street and head east.

4.9 End of hike at Claremont Station.

34 REDLANDS

Redlands has fairly been identified as the Jewel of the Inland Empire. Blur the modern cars out of your vision and much of residential Redlands reads as a prosperous Southern California town in 1905. It is the sort of place where a conservancy tour could spend an hour circling a single block. This sub-6-mile hike is an activity that blends views of many of those delightful blocks while stepping along briskly.

Start: Redlands Train Station, 389 Orange St., Redlands 92374
Elevation gain: 300 feet
Distance: 5.8-mile loop
Hiking time: 2.5 to 3.5 hours
Difficulty: Moderate
Best season: December–June
Trail surface: Sidewalks, paved paths, dirt
Other trail users: Park users, shoppers and diners

Restroom availability: Miles 1.7, 3.6
Canine compatibility: Dogs must remain on leash.
Parking status: Free street parking on Shoppers Lane. Alternative is 2,000 feet east near 6th Street and Stuart Avenue.
Rail transit accessibility: N/A
Trailhead GPS: N34° 03.54' W117° 10.97'

FINDING THE TRAILHEAD

Take I-10 east. Take exit 79 toward Orange Street/CA 38/Downtown Redlands. Remain on the frontage road (Pearl Avenue) until Orange Street, then turn right. Turn right into Shoppers Lane just ahead of FedEx.

WHAT TO SEE

If you cannot see the mountains clearly before beginning this counterclockwise loop, save this hike for another day. The 1910 Redlands station building is very formal, with a Classical pedimented temple front. Imagine arriving from the Midwest in the early 20th century to step off the train into the open, Doric column–lined loggia of this station on a warm winter day with the fragrance of orange blossoms in the air. Not only have the trains ceased stopping here, they've removed the rails.

At Orange and Redlands Boulevard, admire the Millard Sheets mosaic on the south side of the bank building that he designed for Home Savings in 1980. The magnificent Smiley Public Library has an interior that is pure 19th century. It is well worth pausing the walk to go inside. The fascia of the Redland Bowl stage reads, *Without vision, a people perish.* Two blocks of Olive Avenue, from Grant to Buena Vista, are lined with landmarked homes built within a decade after 1899. The favorite for most is the pink Mission Revival Holt House at 405 Olive. Redlands is the international home of Esri, the famous supplier of GIS (geographic information system). Some of that hometown talent has assisted in producing the excellent RAHS Explorer app. If you want to learn more about the town's historical and architectural heritage than this guidebook has space to tell you, follow along using the app while doing this hike.

Normandie Court is a delightful group of sixteen petite Châteauesque cottages built in 1926. There is a 1921 Pueblo Revival–style home at the northeast corner of Center Street and Fern Avenue. The 1891 Waite House at 556 Center St. is a real traffic stopper.

Orange Alley is a narrow outdoor shopping/dining corridor under an arbor of umbrellas.

The Holt House is a flamboyant example of the Mission Revival style.

The developer had high ambitions for this location and planted a deodar cedar tree on each corner. You will still see one of those trees on the southeast corner. Gerrards Market is an excellent choice to pause the hike after 1.7 miles. Just past the market, the LDS Church building on Center is wonderfully Mid-Century Modern amid all these homes that are more than a century old.

An 1887-built house and property at the southwest corner of Center and Palm Avenue attracts your attention. The property is still larger than 1 acre, but the low wall extends well beyond the current property lines, indicating how this estate was even grander before it was subdivided. The carriage house has a wonderful tower. On San Jacinto Street, a very impressive double row of palms begins when passing Walnut Avenue. West Highland Avenue was subdivided in 1886, and early Redlands liked to call it the Butler Belt for the grand houses that were built here. A plaque on the gate of Miraflores at 851 Highland tells you a bit of its story. Built in 1906 as an outsized English Tudor cottage, the massive shingled roof and the windows adorned by flower boxes are very pleasing.

Kimberly Crest House and Gardens and Prospect Park share a gate off Highland Avenue, and their stories are intertwined. The elderly Kimberlys moved into this 1897 mansion from their Wisconsin home in 1905. A half-century later, their daughter challenged the people of Redlands to fund the purchase of the adjacent hillside to make it a botanical park. She gifted her 6-acre estate to Redlands after the town met the challenge. Although these directions guide you directly over the park to the left of the mansion, you are encouraged to walk a few hundred yards up the driveway to take a look. Los Angelenos might be reminded of the Châteauesque-style Hollywood Magic Castle, and they would be correct. Architects Dennis and Farwell did both houses, and they are very similar. The hillside path of the park provides wonderful views over San Bernardino and beyond.

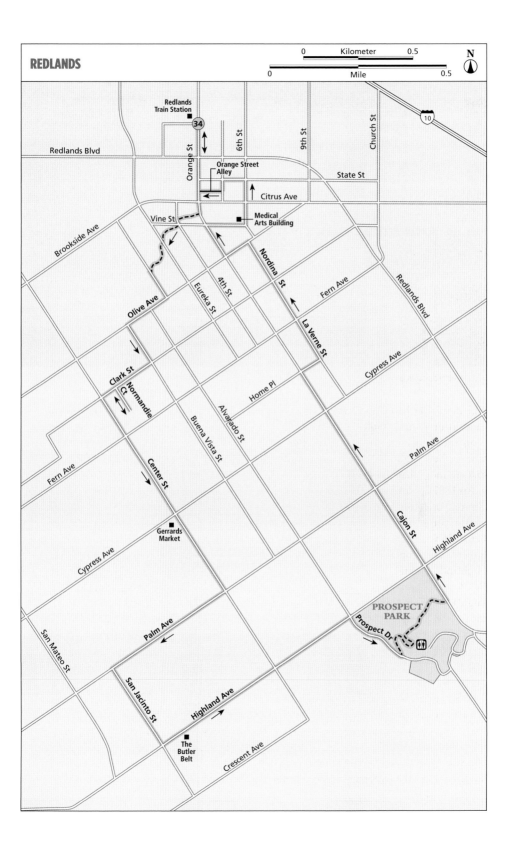

REDLANDS

0　Kilometer　0.5
0　Mile　0.5

N

Redlands
Train Station
34
Orange St
6th St
9th St
Church St
10
Redlands Blvd
Orange Street
Alley
State St
Citrus Ave
Vine St
Medical
Arts Building
Brookside Ave
Eureka St
4th St
Nordina St
Fern Ave
Redlands Blvd
Olive Ave
La Verne St
Cypress Ave
Clark St
Normandie
Ct
Home Pl
Palm Ave
Buena Vista St
Alvarado St
Fern Ave
Center St
Cajon St
Highland Ave
Cypress Ave
Gerrards
Market
PROSPECT
PARK
Palm Ave
Prospect Dr
San Mateo St
San Jacinto St
Highland Ave
The Butler
Belt
Crescent Ave

The way back to downtown Redlands is more of the same, and that's not a bad thing. There is an orange orchard at the base of Prospect Park. This guidebook features hikes in several other towns such as Monrovia, Whittier, and Claremont whose origin story is tied to citrus growing. Redlands is the one where the citrus groves can still be seen and where there is still a working Sunkist packing house. Turning from Vine to 6th Street near the end of the hike, you will notice a beautiful courtyard. This was built in 1927 as the Medical Arts Building, and it was originally configured as a shared waiting room and offices for eleven physicians and two dentists. State Street has been nicely scaled for foot traffic. A final highlight of the hike is Orange Alley, which is a narrow outdoor shopping/dining corridor under an arbor of colorful umbrellas.

MILES AND DIRECTIONS

0.0 START at Redlands Train Station. Turn right on Orange Street, walking away from the freeway.

0.3 Soon after passing Citrus Avenue, turn right into a park path by the El Camino Real bell. Pass to the right of the Redlands Historical Museum building and follow the path to the corner of 4th and Vine Streets. Cross twice to reach the front of the Smiley Public Library. Walk to the right of the library to Eureka Street. Cross Eureka mid-block to enter a park pathway that goes to the left of the Redlands Bowl seating. This path ends at Grant Street.

0.6 Turn left on Grant Street. Turn right on Olive Avenue.

0.8 Turn left on Buena Vista Street. Turn right on Clark Street. Turn left on Normandie Court.

1.0 Normandie Court. Walk to the dead end through the eclectic houses, then turn around and turn left on Clark.

1.2 Turn left on Center Street.

1.7 Gerrards Market. Continue on Center Street.

1.9 Turn right on Palm Avenue.

2.3 Turn left on San Jacinto Street.

2.6 The Butler Belt. Turn left on Highland Avenue.

3.3 Turn right into Prospect Park at the Kimberly Crest sign. Walk up the paved park road and pass a small parking lot. Go beyond a chain barrier to cars. Pavement continues straight toward the outdoor Redlands Theatre, but you are to follow Prospect Drive as it curves left. Climb a gentle slope on dirt road. Follow this road as it makes hairpin turns, first right, then left. The second turn goes around a group of rose bushes. The restroom building is concealed but only 150 feet to the right before making this turn. Remain on Prospect Drive to reach the exit at Cajon Street.

3.8 Turn left on Cajon Street.

4.6 Turn right on Home Place. Turn left on La Verne Street. Jog right on Fern Avenue and immediately turn left on Nordina Street.

5.0 Turn left on Olive Avenue. Turn right on Cajon Street. Turn right on Vine Street.

5.3 Medical Arts Building. Turn left on 6th Street.

5.4 Turn left on State Street. Turn left on 5th Street.

5.5 Turn right into Orange Street Alley.

5.6 Turn right on Orange Street. Use the crosswalk to reach the west side of Orange at Shoppers Lane. Turn right on Orange.

5.8 End of hike at Redlands Train Station.

35 **RIVERSIDE**

This hike visits a fascinating downtown area with high marks for architecture. You will go through lovely streets lined with homes built during the heydays of the 1910s and 1920s. The highlight is the walk up to historic Mount Rubidoux, 500 feet higher and a mile distant from downtown Riverside. You will get some understanding why the locals love the pathway to the peak so much.

Start: Starbucks, 311 Market St., Riverside 92501
Elevation gain: 550 feet
Distance: 6.7-mile loop
Hiking time: 3 to 4 hours
Difficulty: Moderate
Best season: December–June
Trail surface: Sidewalks, paved park paths, dirt trail
Other trail users: Tourists, shoppers and diners, bicyclists
Restroom availability: Miles 3.7, 5.6

Canine compatibility: Dogs must remain on leash.
Parking status: Free street parking available on 3rd Street; read the signs carefully.
Rail transit accessibility: Metrolink Riverside-Downtown Station. Walk 0.5 mile and intersect the loop hike in progress at the corner of Mission Inn Avenue and Lime Street.
Trailhead GPS: N33° 59.24' W117° 22.37'

FINDING THE TRAILHEAD

Take Highway 60–Pomona Freeway; eastbound or westbound, take exit 52A for Market Street toward Downtown. Follow signs off the exit for Downtown. Turn right on 3rd Street.

WHAT TO SEE

If you cannot see the mountains clearly beginning this counterclockwise loop, save this hike for another day. Beacon Way and Ladera Lane lead up and over a high spot known as Little Mount Rubidoux. The first house was built on this hill in 1903. The green thicket below is the Santa Ana River. Back down on Mount Rubidoux Drive, this vicinity has an additional historic name, Bankers Row. The charming 1931 stone-arch Buena Vista Bridge goes over Mission Inn Avenue. Notice the historic streetlights displaying Riverside's iconic symbol, the rain cross atop a mission bell in a trapezoidal frame. In the early days of the city, this road was the approach from the west.

The hike employs a bit of steep dirt trail to intersect the paved Mount Rubidoux road, saving about a mile of hiking. The road was built in 1907 for motorists; happily, wheeled use today means bikes and strollers. The artful design of the road draws many locals, and there is a feeling that this is a joyous civic gathering, not merely exercise. The summit has a rock amphitheater built for the nondenominational Easter sunrise services that began in 1909. Although the mountain park is owned by the city, a small portion with the cross on top was auctioned off to a private group to avoid a lawsuit. On the peak loop, the Testimonial Peace tower and bridge were built in 1925, modeled after a tower in Alcántara, Spain.

The transition from the Mount Rubidoux parking area with restrooms to the heart of downtown covers 1.3 miles, including some lovely houses and plantings around

View from Mount Rubidoux of downtown Riverside with San Gorgonio Mountain in the distance on the Riverside hike

Redwood Drive and 10th Street. The 1903 county courthouse was designed by architects Burnham and Bliesner. After the Mission Inn, the courthouse is Riverside's most admired building. It is one of the best examples of the Beaux-Arts style in California. The alley you walk through between 10th and 9th Streets is likely to have an art installation mounted on brick building walls; no promises. Main Street, between 6th and 10th Streets, was closed to cars in 1966. The mall is wonderfully done with a rich assembly of preserved buildings and public art. On the right, a building with balcony windows once housed the upscale Rouse's Store and is now the Center of the Arts. Just past that, an Art Deco building that once housed the S. H. Kress department store now is home for the California Museum of Photography. At University, there is a distinguished square building with a deep cornice. This was built as Riverside First National Bank, designed by Parkinson and Bergstrom in 1911.

Along University Avenue, an Italianate-style building was named for President Theodore Roosevelt when built in 1903. Next, the Arcade Building designed by Walker and Eisen is especially fine. Across the street, Back to the Grind is a cafe with a great ceiling and is one of several good options for a break in this vicinity. At the northeast corner of Lime Street and Mission Inn Avenue, notice the wood pergola over the sidewalk. In the heyday of the railroad traveler, vine-covered pergolas like this lined the avenue to shade the long walk from the train stations to the Mission Inn Hotel. The low Spanish-style building at that corner was built in 1923 as Arlington Heights Citrus Exchange. This would have been the critical link between local growers and the Sunkist cooperative. Riverside played a key role in California citrus and retains a vital connection to the industry 150 years since the first orchards. Eliza Tibbets was an activist and abolitionist

The Riverside County Courthouse is one of the best examples of the Beaux-Arts style in California.

who settled in Riverside. She is credited with the introduction of the Washington navel orange to California in the 1870s when she nursed two grafted orange trees that she obtained from Brazil by way of the United States Department of Agriculture. Although the first recorded orange orchards in Southern California were in 1834, the introduction of this species turned a nascent crop into the most prodigious symbol of California's agricultural bounty.

Three blocks of Mission Inn Avenue are the heart of the architectural legacy of this city. The Riverside Art Museum is in a building that Julia Morgan designed for the YWCA in 1929. At Lemon, First Congregational Church was one of the first regional appearances of the Spanish Colonial Revival style when designed by Myron Hunt in 1913. On the east side of Orange, the Metropolitan Museum was built in 1911 as the post office. The style is Italian Renaissance with a blend of Mission Revival. The west corner holds the old city hall building with the lovely low tower. Where Mission Inn Avenue is intersected by the Main Street Mall, notice the tower and arcades of the 1929 Fox Riverside Theatre.

The Mission Inn grew out of a boardinghouse that was begun in the 1870s by the pioneering Miller family. They had emigrated from Wisconsin and the son, Frank A. Miller, took over the boardinghouse and established the Glenwood Inn. In 1902 Miller found investors, including Henry Huntington, and created an eighty-two-room hotel in the Mission Revival style with Arthur Benton as his architect. Major additions were made by some famous architects over the next three decades. In the early 20th century, no other location in Southern California was so accomplished in projecting the allure of the winter warmth, orange groves, and the romantic myth of Old California. Doing this

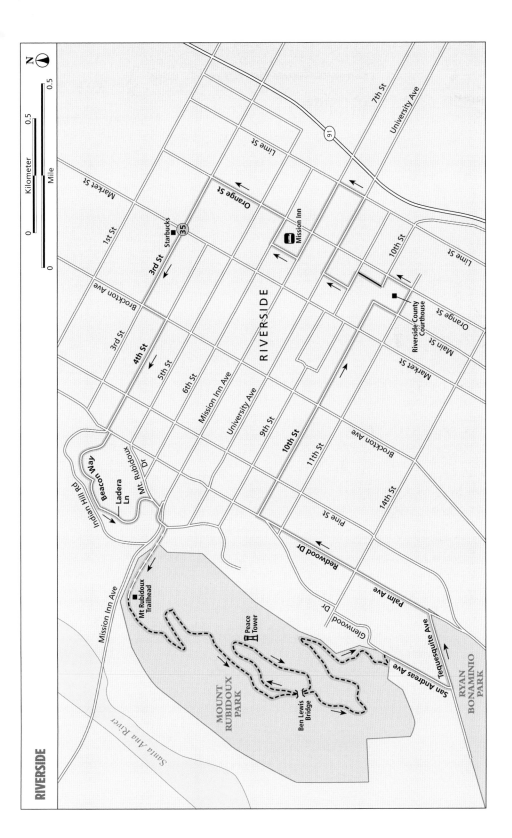

RIVERSIDE

hike should include a little time exploring some of the personality of the hotel. You walk around three sides of it before turning north on Orange to head back to the trailhead.

MILES AND DIRECTIONS

0.0 START at Starbucks. Walk away from Market Street, going west on 3rd. Turn left on Brockton Avenue. Turn right on 4th Street.

0.6 Cross Redwood Street and continue on Beacon Way the same direction that you have been going. A Y intersection has a street sign for Beacon going left as not a through street. Ignore that, and go down and right where it is not signed.

0.9 Turn left on Ladera Lane.

1.1 Turn right on Mt. Rubidoux Drive. Cross the Buena Vista Bridge and turn right on an unsigned service road on the other side of the bridge.

1.2 Trailhead. A trailhead sign reads "Buena Vista Trail." Ignore the use-trail at the foot of the sign and walk ahead to a proper junction. Paths go in two directions. Select the path on the left that immediately starts climbing. The correct way up is obvious; ignore several intersecting use-trails while hiking on several switchbacks and about one hundred railroad-tie steps.

1.5 Turn right onto the paved Mount Rubidoux trail from the steep dirt trail.

2.1 Ben Lewis Bridge. Go under the bridge and climb onto it from the other side. The Mount Rubidoux trail is a loop within a loop. The bridge takes you to the inner loop.

2.3 Peak area. When ready to start down, the departure path is a continuation of the arrival path, walking to left of the pinnacle with the American flag.

2.4 Pass under bridge of the Peace Tower.

2.6 End of inner loop. Just before returning to the Ben Lewis Bridge, turn sharply left to start down the outer loop.

3.2 Trail junction. Turn sharply right, remaining on paved path.

3.5 Mount Rubidoux trailhead. Turn right on Glenwood Drive, which turns into San Andreas Avenue. You will have lots of company.

3.7 Ryan Bonaminio Park. Turn left onto the near side of Tesquesquite Avenue. The restroom building is 100 yards to the right across the parking lot. Walk on the left side of Tesquesquite.

3.9 Veer left on Palm Avenue, which will blend into Redwood Drive.

4.4 Turn right on 10th Street.

5.0 Turn right on Main Street.

5.1 Riverside County Courthouse. Turn left into the Gabbert Judicial Plaza. Turn left from 11th Street to Orange Street. Turn left on 10th Street.

5.3 Turn right into an alley, located halfway between Orange Street and the Main Street pedestrian mall. Turn left at the end of the alley on 9th Street. Turn right into the Main Street pedestrian mall.

5.5 Turn right on University Avenue. Turn left on Lime Street.

5.7 Turn left on Mission Inn Avenue.

6.0 Mission Inn.

6.1 Turn right into the Main Street pedestrian mall. Turn right on Sixth Street.

6.3 Turn left on Orange Street.

6.5 Turn left on 3rd Street.

6.7 End of hike at Starbucks, 3rd and Market.

ORANGE AND SAN DIEGO COUNTIES

The hikes in this section are in communities along the southern 120 miles of coastline of Southern California. Average summertime high temperatures do not extend warmer than the mid-80s on any of these hike locations. It always seems comfortable.

San Diego likes to call itself "America's Finest City"; it is certainly the birthplace of the European epoch of California. In 1542, Juan Rodríguez Cabrillo claimed the harbor for Spain; it is the only natural harbor in California south of San Francisco. The first Spanish Presidio and mission in California were founded 225 years later. Of course, the area was already populated by an indigenous people that today call themselves the Kumeyaay. By area, Orange is one of the smaller California counties, but its population is greater than twenty-one US states.

The six hikes in the section are very different experiences. The short hike in City of Orange is all about a district built between 1890 and 1930 that has miraculously maintained its historical authenticity in a region that demolished and rebuilt everywhere else. Laguna Beach has a spectacular coastline of outcrops and coves, but the hike itself

Looking south to the San Clemente Pier while hiking on the San Clemente Pedestrian Beach Trail

Looking up the coast from Heisler Park in Laguna Beach

is less about that landscape and more about an eclectic flavor found here that is unique to California. San Clemente is very much themed to a single style. While chasing after examples of that style, the San Clemente hike is physically demanding with mileage and ups and downs, with lots of time near the beach. The La Jolla hike has a few ups and downs, but it is very much about a highly cultivated place with a variety of styles. The Rolando Village–La Mesa hike takes place in neighborhoods that are pleasant but are not remarkable; if you were not enthusiastic about exploring the stairways, there would not be much reason to go. Favorite hike in this section? That's an easy one. The Bankers Hill–Balboa Park hike could be the best in the entire book. It ticks all the boxes for what makes a great urban hike.

36 **CITY OF ORANGE**

The broad-minded City of Orange is remarkable because they did not condemn their past to demolition for the sake of new tracts, malls, and office buildings. The town square area is popular with visitors who come to enjoy a thriving shop and dining culture in an environment that looks like a movie set but is 100 percent authentic. On this short hike, you will be energized by all this commerce around the center plaza and you will ooh and ah on quiet streets full of well-preserved houses that date to the 1890s.

Start: Depot Park, 100 North Atchison St., Orange 92866
Elevation gain: 50 feet
Distance: 3.2-mile loop
Hiking time: 1.5 to 2 hours
Difficulty: Easy
Best season: Year-round
Trail surface: Sidewalks, paved paths
Other trail users: Shoppers and diners, park users, students
Restroom availability: Mile 2.1

Canine compatibility: Dogs must remain on leash.
Parking status: Free parking at station lot. When the lot is at capacity, there is a free parking structure immediately to the east.
Rail transit accessibility: Metrolink Orange Station is the start point.
Trailhead GPS: N33° 47.28' W117° 51.43'

FINDING THE TRAILHEAD

Travel to I-5 south of the 91 Freeway. Going south: Take exit 107C for the City Drive toward State College Boulevard. Turn left on Chapman Avenue. Pass the 57 Freeway and the destination will be on the left. Going north: Leave I-5 for the 57 Freeway north and use exit 1A for Chapman Avenue. Turn right on Chapman and the destination will be on the left. The start point is a park adjacent to a commuter rail station. There are restrooms at the station.

WHAT TO SEE

This clockwise loop begins in the shade of trees of Orange's oldest park. The depot dates to the 1930s, and it provides an early inkling for what you will experience of this town as you walk through it. There is a strong culture here of getting things right so far as preserving, restoring, and reinventing their inventory of old buildings. Across from the depot, the Hilbert Museum of California Art is free and open 5 days weekly. Their collection and exhibits specialize in California scene painting. An interesting assembly of buildings near the tracks help to tell the story of what once put food on the table in this town. California Wire Company specialized in weatherproof wire and built a complex of brick-clad industrial buildings that are now part of the Chapman University campus. Next to these and also an asset of Chapman is the historic Villa Park Orange packing house. Built in 1918, packing lines would operate under the north-facing skylights. Fruit was sorted for size and grade and loaded onto railcars. This was, for a time, one of the most productive houses in the Sunkist realm.

This town was born in the early 1870s, and the names of the founders, Glassell and Chapman, are remembered in the names of the town's spoke streets. They first called

The name of a brewery is the founding year of the plaza it is adjacent to.

their settlement Richland, but the post office turned that name down because California already had a Richland in Butte County. The next choice, Orange, was not as obvious as you might think. This was still Los Angeles County in the 1870s, and the citrus fruit would not become dominant in local agriculture for another 15 years, when a blight devasted the regional grape industry.

Although the institution has much older origins, Chapman College found a home here in the 1950s as the first four-year, accredited college in Orange County. A walk through some of the immaculate campus indicates that this is a well-endowed and successful university. On the left, just inside the campus gate, Fish Interfaith Center is noted for how the unusual fenestration has a magical effect on interior lighting. *California Gold* is an ongoing exhibition on the lower level of the Leatherby Library. Here you will find memorabilia and the archives of the famous regional booster, Huell Howser. The arrangement of Neoclassical college buildings around a grassy mall dates from 1913 to 1928. This was built as the old Orange Union High School. In this cluster of five buildings, Doti Hall is a pretty convincing imposter; it was built in 2013.

Plaza Park has been in use since the 1880s, and the landscape architecture and the community planning reflected in the ring of old buildings around this circular hub are almost unparalleled west of the Mississippi Valley. There is a bygone ambience here that people love. The shops and restaurants are a big hit.

The corner of Chapman and Grand presents an unusual pairing. On the northeast corner is a two-story Classical Revival structure from about 1905. Across Chapman from that, the Welton Becket Civic Center buildings from 1963 demonstrate that folksy Orange was ready to go all-in for what later would be called Mid-Century Modern. Most of this hike is spent walking south on Grand Street and north on Orange Street.

Full of old houses and mature streets, these are two of the best streets in the Old Towne Orange Historic District, as listed in the National Register of Historic Places. The houses that you hike past can roughly be identified as representatives of four successive design styles. They begin with pre-1900 Victorian and extend through Classical Revival then Craftsman or Bungalow styles and end with the taste for the Mediterranean Revival of the 1920s and 1930s. People who evaluate historic districts like to list the buildings found there as conforming and nonconforming to the overall historical theme of the district; you can see that Grand and Orange Streets have many hits and very few misses. Houses are in full view, close to the sidewalk, with many front porches. This is a fantastic pedestrian environment.

At La Veta Avenue, corner towers of arroyo stone announce the beginning of the distinct neighborhood of Nutwood Place. This was laid out in 1906. Notice how the streets become narrow. This tract had the town's first paved streets; even the circle around Plaza Park was still dirt at that time. Nutwood Place segues to W. O. Hart Park by the means of ornamental stairways that show off arroyo stone as the gate posts did. The park is obviously a big recreation space with lots of parking, but it is also important, as it includes the course of Santiago Creek. This creek is the drainage of the area around Santiago Peak, which is the highest point in Orange County and a prominent object in the views of north Orange and south Los Angeles Counties. There are bike paths along Santiago Creek that pass some good examples of the riparian zone a bit east of Hart Park. Admire the old-school pool structure. There is also a charming outdoor performance shell a bit to the left.

On River Avenue between Grand and Orange Streets, a huge sycamore tree towers over the large 1904 house on the property. The tree was studied by the National Geographic Society in the mid-1900s and guessed to be 350–500 years old. The hike back to Depot Park via the southwest corner of Plaza Park goes quickly. There are artifacts of a different age everywhere you look.

MILES AND DIRECTIONS

0.0 START at the base of the clock on the east side of the tracks and on the Chapman Avenue side of Depot Park. Walk through the park past the depot building. You are going north on the left side of Atchison Street. Turn right on Maple Street.

0.2 Turn left on Cypress Street. Turn right on Sycamore Avenue.

0.6 Enter Chapman University where Sycamore Avenue ends at the Schmid Gate. Walk between the Fish Interfaith Center on the left and the oval Attallah Piazza on the right. Turn right to walk in front of the Leatherby Library building. When you are in front of Oliphant Hall, turn right to follow the paths out the great lawn in the center of the much older buildings. Exit to the west to Glassell Street, walking along the large grass courtyard surrounded by Memorial Hall and four other buildings.

0.9 Turn left on Glassell Street.

1.2 Plaza Square Park, Walk to the left of the plaza and turn left on Chapman Avenue.

1.3 Turn right on Grand Street.

1.9 Turn diagonally left on River Avenue.

2.0 Enter Hart Park. Go down a few steps and turn right into a park path before reaching the parking lot. Turn right on the path at the swimming pool. Continue straight to locate the park restrooms, which are next to the play equipment. Return to this

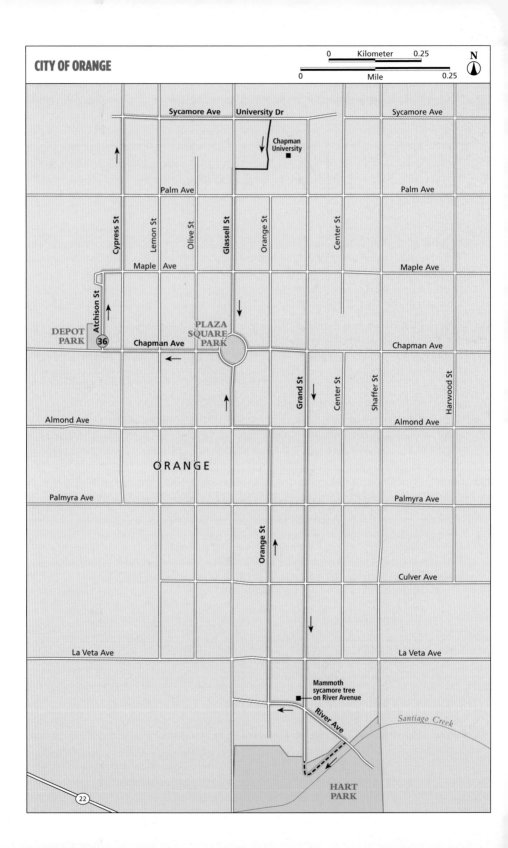

The National Geographic Society guessed that this sycamore tree could be 350–500 years old.

spot. From near the northeast corner of the pool, go up an ornamental stairway to exit the park for the dead end of Grand Street. Turn left on River Avenue.

2.2 Mammoth sycamore tree on River Avenue. Turn right on Orange Street.

2.7 Turn left on Almond Avenue.

2.8 Turn right on Glassell Street.

2.9 Walk to the left of Plaza Square Park and turn left on Chapman Avenue.

3.2 End of hike at Depot Park.

37 LAGUNA BEACH

Laguna Beach has a cachet that goes beyond even the best of the classic Southern California beach towns. The eclecticism in the built environment is nearly as strong a characteristic of Laguna as is the stunning natural environment. The city is historically associated with painters, potters, and sculptors. This 4-mile hike is a treasure hunt seeking out locations where the character of this magical place has not been washed away by Laguna's more recent identity as a resort destination.

Start: The Greeter's Corner, 329 South Coast Hwy., Laguna Beach 92651
Elevation gain: 300 feet
Distance: 4.0-mile loop
Hiking time: 1.5 to 2.5 hours
Difficulty: Easy
Best season: Year-round
Trail surface: Sidewalks, coastal path and boardwalk, pavement without sidewalks, stairs
Other trail users: Tourists, shoppers and diners

Restroom availability: Mile 2.4
Canine compatibility: Dogs must remain on leash.
Parking status: Pay parking in lots. The starting point is 0.4 mile from the popular Forest/Laguna Canyon parking lot #11. If you park here, walk from the Laguna Beach city hall on Forest Avenue. The hike will pass this spot 10 minutes before it ends.
Rail transit accessibility: N/A
Trailhead GPS: N33° 32.51' W117° 47.01'

FINDING THE TRAILHEAD

Take I-5 to exit 95 or I-405 to exit 2. From either, take Highway 133 toward Laguna Beach/Laguna Canyon Road. Highway 133 becomes Broadway Street. Turn left on Highway 1/Coast Highway. The Greeter's Corner is 650 feet ahead on the right-hand side of the road across from where both Forest and Park Avenues terminate at Coast Highway.

WHAT TO SEE

Greeter's Corner commemorates Eiler Larsen, the man who was the first impression that Laguna visitors had for 20 years beginning in the 1940s. A stairway takes you up to Cliff Drive. Across from Cliff Drive and Coast Highway is the Laguna Art Museum. Founded in 1918, this evolved from a small gallery into one of the first art museums in the state. Urth Coffee is housed in a 1917 Craftsman bungalow with both Japanese and Swiss flourishes. Duck under the arch of 414–22 North Coast Hwy. to appreciate a 1937 courtyard with fountain apartment arrangement that is now a group of gallery spaces. Across the street, the arched passage at Laguna Print was an auto court of guest cottages in the 1930s.

At the 1-mile mark your hike leaves the sidewalks for the coastal path to join a walking zone favored by tourists. Topography sets Laguna Beach apart from the typical Southern California beach town. Here there is no pier or long stretch of beach sand. The 8.5-mile length of Laguna has thirty individual coves, each separated from the others by cliff, rock, and tide. After the Heisler Park gazebo, there are stairs down to the boardwalk. The

The unusual lifeguard tower was once part of a gas station before being moved to the beach in 1937.

historic and unusual lifeguard tower was once part of a Union Oil gas station before being moved to the beach in 1937.

Hotel Laguna marks your return to sidewalks alongside traffic. It has been here since the 1920s, and it replaced another hotel built on this spot in the 1800s. This was a favorite spot in the era when Hollywood celebrities were a Laguna staple. The Whaling Wall mural occupies an oversized 1902 blufftop board and batten house that is now Wyland Galleries. At 901 Coast Hwy., there is a Tudor Revival building that embodies the eclectic flavor of the good commercial structures found in Laguna Beach. This one was built in 1936. William Mortensen located his studio and School of Photography here. He was the most famous practitioner of the pictorial style in early-20th-century photography. By the time Coast Highway intersects Thalia Street, many hikers will be looking for a stopping point with restrooms as the hike departs Coast Highway and turns inland in 2 blocks. Just before turning, the Streamline Moderne style of the 1930s is displayed where an automobile fuel kiosk shares a lot with an apartment building.

Even without so many individual landmarks, the views and the residential personality found inland from Coast Highway could be the most enjoyable part of the hike. Don't miss tiny Saint Francis by-the-Sea American Catholic Church. It was built in the 1930s on a narrow lot. The mixture of architectural styles displayed include Mediterranean Revival, Romanesque, Gothic, Byzantine, and Craftsman. 3rd Street heading into downtown is so steep that you can be thankful for the sidewalk steps. As 3rd Street meets Forest Avenue there are some charming municipal buildings. Next to the firehouse is *The People's Council* sculpture by artist Linda Brunker. In it are figures representing universal youth, a woman and man sitting around an obelisk. Across the street, the Laguna Beach Lumber Company, designed by architect Yann Egasse in 1919, is one of those odd and wonderful Laguna buildings. The city would be a poorer place if it were knocked down to build something modern.

MILES AND DIRECTIONS

0.0 START at the Greeter's Corner. Go north on Coast Highway and cross it to reach Ocean Avenue. Take Ocean Avenue away from the coast. Turn left on Beach Street. Cross Broadway Street and walk an alley named Broadway Place. Curve left and watch for the steps on the right that lead to Lower Cliff Drive. Then go up more steps to Cliff Drive.

0.3 Turn left on Cliff Drive. Walk to a grassy triangular park where Cliff angles into busy Coast Highway.

0.5 Across from Laguna Art Museum. Take the crosswalk on the right and proceed northwest on Coast Highway.

0.8 Turn left on Myrtle Street. Walk on the left side of Myrtle and take a crosswalk across Cliff Drive.

1.0 Enter the Heisler Park pedestrian paths at Cliff Drive and Myrtle Street. The path begins with a brief section that goes to the right. Then there is a three-way junction where you are to turn left. The goal from here is to follow bluff paths southeast for 0.5 mile to then enter the boardwalk at Main Beach. This will go past the top of the Recreation Point stairway and the gazebo. The route does not go down to beach level until the final sixty-six steps that come after passing the Inn at Laguna Beach. There is a web of path options here. The intent is for hikers to stay toward the coast and away from the parked cars, but not to head down the other stairs that lead to the sand.

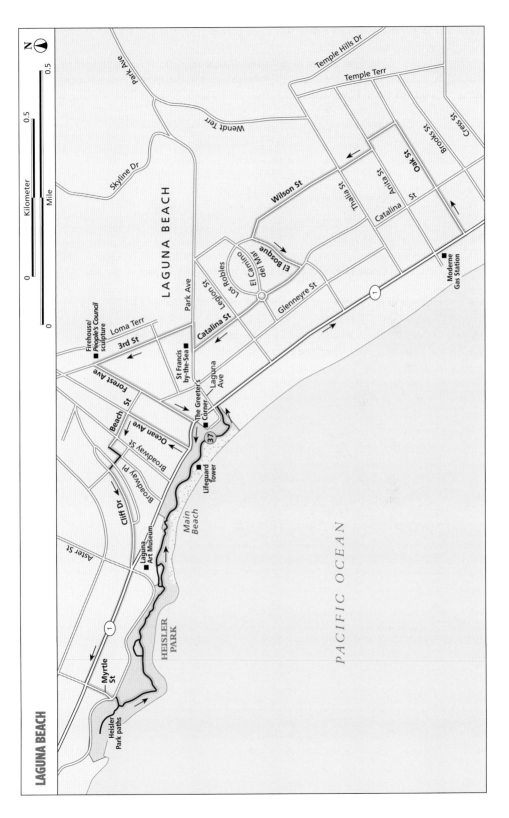

LAGUNA BEACH

LAGUNA BEACH

PACIFIC OCEAN

HEISLER PARK

Main Beach

Heisler Park paths

Myrtle St

Aster St

Cliff Dr

Laguna Art Museum

Broadway Pl

Broadway St

Ocean Ave

Beach St

Forest Ave

3rd St

Loma Terr

Firehouse/ People's Council sculpture

St Francis by-the-Sea

Catalina St

Laguna Ave

The Greeter's Corner

Lifeguard Tower

Park Ave

Legion St

Los Robles

El Camino del Mar

El Bosque

Glenneyre St

Wilson St

Skyline Dr

Wendt Terr

Park Ave

Temple Hills Dr

Temple Terr

Oak St

Thalia St

Catalina

Anita St

St

Brooks St

Cress St

Moderne Gas Station

Kilometer

Mile

0.5

0.5

N

A Streamline Moderne gas station and apartment building of the 1930s

1.2   Pass Heisler Park gazebo.

1.5   Pass the Historic Lifeguard Tower. Follow the boardwalk as it turns left in front of the hotel.

1.6   Turn right on Coast Highway at Laguna Avenue.

2.1   Moderne gas station at Anita Street.

2.2   Turn left on Oak Street.

2.5   Turn left on Wilson Street. At Anita Street, turn left and then right to resume on Wilson Street.

3.0   Turn left on El Bosque.

3.1   Turn right on Catalina Street.

3.2   Go around the traffic circle and remain on Catalina Street.

3.4   Saint Francis by-the-Sea. Turn right on Park Avenue. Make the first left onto 3rd Street.

3.6   Firehouse/*People's Council* sculpture. Turn left on Forest Avenue.

4.0   End of hike at the Greeter's Corner.

38 **SAN CLEMENTE**

San Clemente was founded with a singular purpose: to create a Spanish village by the sea. Here there are buildings dressed in iconic white stucco walls with red tile roofs nestling in hills that sweep to the sea. On this hike, you climb from the sea to the town center. Then you walk back to sea level at a state beach to enter a popular beach trail that passes the pier. However, there's one more climb away from the sea to add some in-town charm and history. You return to the beach trail again to finish the hike.

Start: San Clemente Metrolink Station, 850 Avenida Estacion, San Clemente 92672
Elevation gain: 300 feet
Distance: 7.5-mile loop
Hiking time: 3 to 4.5 hours
Difficulty: Difficult
Best season: Year-round
Trail surface: Sidewalks, paved paths, dirt, stairs
Other trail users: Beachgoers, shoppers and diners
Restroom availability: Miles 1.0, 4.1, 6.3

Canine compatibility: Dogs must remain on leash.
Parking status: Pay parking lot at station that serves both transit and beach users. Free street parking might be available more than 1,000 feet from the start point and in the direction that the beginning of the hike travels.
Rail transit accessibility: Metrolink San Clemente Station is the start point.
Trailhead GPS: N33° 25.94' W117° 37.98'

FINDING THE TRAILHEAD

Take I-5 to exit 76, Avenida Pico. Turn toward the coast. Turn right onto El Camino Real. Turn left onto Avenida Estacion. This is the entrance to a pay parking lot.

WHAT TO SEE

San Clemente did not unfold gradually like most Southern California beach towns. It was invented and willed into existence on empty pastureland that the founder, Ole Hanson, described as a clean canvas. His plan was announced in the press at the end of 1925. By 1927 the core buildings were opened. Some buildings that you pass at the beginning of this clockwise loop hike exhibit what Hanson had in mind. The beautiful beach club opened in 1927. It displays the white stucco walls and locally handmade red roofing tile that the founder required of all of San Clemente's first buildings. The hike walks around the 1937 Casino San Clemente before turning on Calle Deshecha to go past an old bowling center from the 1940s on the left. Turning left at the traffic circle, you see the faded tower of the San Clemente Theatre.

Bonita Park is an opportunity for a break early in the hike before you head to the commercial center of San Clemente. The hike today follows about a half-mile of El Camino Real. That term relates to royal roads of the era when California was owned by Spain. It is generally used to describe a 600-mile route that connects the twenty-one Spanish missions between San Diego and Napa. El Camino Real as a name became popular in

One of the early buildings of San Clemente, built in 1929 along El Camino Real

the early 20th century. This was a time when there was a mythic adoration of the mission age and there was a wave of automotive-related boosterism. From here, it would be an 8-mile walk to Mission San Juan Capistrano. In recent years, some strong hikers have developed a passion to hike a route that connects all twenty-one missions. Pedro's Tacos occupies a fanciful building that was built in the 1950s as a real estate office.

The town center around Avenida Del Mar has more great examples of the original Spanish-style buildings. The best is the one with the Moorish arches at 101 El Camino Real. It was designed by architect Virgil Westbrook, who also did the beach club. This building opened in 1929 with a bank and offices that enjoyed views directly to the sea. On either side of Del Mar are two more original 1926 buildings; one houses a chocolate shop and the other a Baskin-Robbins. The U-shaped San Clemente Apartments on the right side was the original Hotel San Clemente when it opened in 1927. From this commercial center, you hike more than 1.5 miles following Ola Vista. Well into this stretch, notice the medians on both Esplanade and Avenida Valencia and on Ola Vista itself. These indicate locations of bridle paths. In its early years, San Clemente had a major equestrian theme.

Calafia State Park has a beach cafe. This is the southern terminus of the 2.3-mile beach trail. T-Street Beach is famous with surfers, and San Clemente has been a surfing mecca since the 1930s. At the pier, you leave the beach path and turn inland to explore more of the architectural heritage of the town. An adorable, terraced row of rooflines on Avenida Victoria is the 1947 Beachcomber Inn. Also, look at four houses on Pasadena Court and Cazador Lane; each of them dates to San Clemente's first few years. Casa Romantica is open to the public, although it is often booked for events. Behind the moon gate doorway is a magical, blufftop Spanish mansion. Most of the fourteen rooms are built around

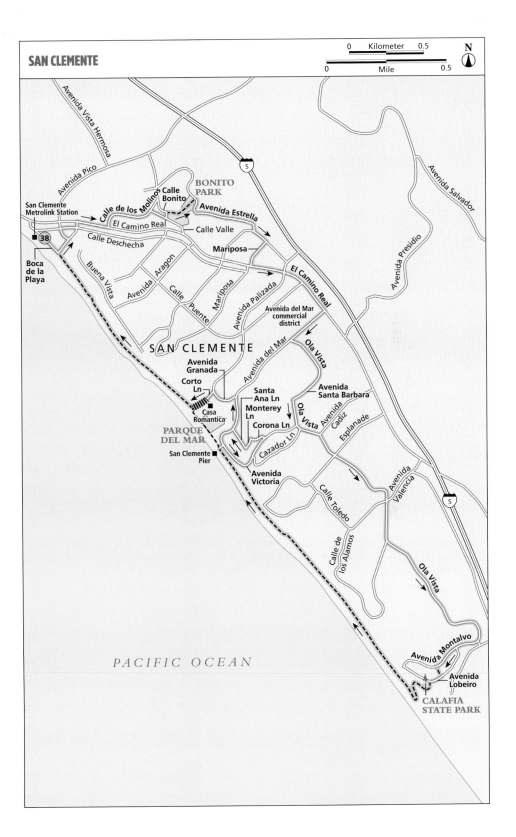

a central courtyard. This was Ole Hanson's own house. He only lived here 4 years before the Great Depression wiped him out. Sadly, when he died in Los Angeles in 1940, he was bankrupt and far removed from the town that he invented. You head back to the beach trail via the steep Corto Lane stairway and walk the final mile back to the start.

MILES AND DIRECTIONS

0.0 START at San Clemente Metrolink Station. Facing away from the ocean and the platform, turn right. Walk along the parking lot as it parallels the beach. Go up a ramp toward the white stucco buildings. This takes you to the cul-de-sac of Boca de la Playa.

0.2 From Boca de la Playa, turn left on Avenida Pico. Turn right on one-way Calle Deshecha. Turn left on Boca de la Playa.

0.4 Turn right on El Camino Real. Turn left on Calle de los Molinos.

0.7 Turn right on Calle Valle. Turn left on Calle Bonito.

0.8 Turn right into a dirt track that leads to the Bonito Park baseball field. Walk to the left around the field, passing between the bleachers and the backstop. From the backstop area, walk along the baseline, aiming for the Teen Center doorway. Turn left on the pavement toward the restrooms.

1.0 Bonita Park Restrooms. Proceed up a finger extension of the park, walking first on dirt, then on grass. As the grass ends, turn up the dirt bank on the left then turn right to leave the park at Avenida de la Estrella.

1.3 Turn right on Mariposa. Turn left on El Camino Real.

1.8 Avenida Del Mar commercial district. Turn right on Avenida Del Mar.

2.0 Turn left on Ola Vista. Remain on this street as it curves right and briefly becomes Avenida Santa Barbara.

2.2 Turn left to resume Ola Vista. The route follows Ola Vista for more than 1 mile as it curves through many intersections. Keep following the bike route signs before finally departing the bike route at a traffic island.

3.8 Turn right on Avenida Montalvo. Opposite address 238, turn left down a connecting path with some steps. Turn right at the bottom onto Avenida Lobeiro.

4.0 Calafia State Park. Turn left into the first park path. You should curve right then go down steeply on ramps and stairs. Pass a parking lot and the Calafia Beach Café. On the inland side of the train tracks, meet the beach trail at the end of the parking area.

4.2 Enter the San Clemente Pedestrian Beach Trail (SCPBT).

5.5 San Clemente Pier. Turn inland, taking the pedestrian subway under the train tracks. Turn right on Avenida Victoria. At Cazador Lane, detour to the right about 250 feet to see the landmark houses at 402 Pasadena Court and at 412–420 Cazador Lane. Return to Avenida Victoria and continue to walk inland and uphill.

5.9 Take the next left turn on one-way Corona Lane, which might not be signed. Turn left on Monterey Lane. Turn right on Santa Ana Lane. Turn right on Avenida Del Mar. Turn left on Avenida Granada.

6.3 Casa Romantica Cultural Center and Gardens, 415 Avenida Granada. Continue on Avenida Granada. Turn left on Corto Lane. Go down the beach access stairs.

6.5 Rejoin the SCPBT going northwest.

7.5 End of hike at San Clemente Metrolink Station.

Terraced rooflines of San Clemente's historic Beachcomber Inn

Idyllic La Jolla is famous for its dramatic coastline, its affluence, and its cultural credentials. Most of the buildings are tasteful, and there is some stellar architecture. You will walk above Windansea Beach and through an eclectic and intimate inland zone along a bicycle path. Wealth and isolation create an aura of exclusion here, but this hike will make La Jolla seem very approachable.

Start: La Jolla Recreation Center, 615 Prospect St., La Jolla 92037
Elevation gain: 200 feet
Distance: 5.9-mile loop
Hiking time: 2.5 to 3.5 hours
Difficulty: Moderate
Best season: Year-round
Trail surface: Sidewalks, paved paths, dirt, stairs
Other trail users: Shoppers and diners, beachgoers

Restroom availability: Mile 1.9
Canine compatibility: Dogs must remain on leash.
Parking status: Street parking for more than 2 hours in the immediate vicinity is limited. Parking without time limits can be sought out east or south of the starting point.
Rail transit accessibility: N/A
Trailhead GPS: N32° 50.62' W117° 16.68'

FINDING THE TRAILHEAD

From I-5, take exit 28 for La Jolla Village Drive. Turn west onto La Jolla Village Drive. Turn left onto Torrey Pines Road. Slight right to stay on Torrey Pines Road. Turn right onto Ivanhoe Avenue East. Turn left onto Silverado Street. Turn left onto Prospect Street. The Recreation Center is on the left-hand side, across the street from the Museum of Contemporary Art San Diego.

WHAT TO SEE

La Jolla was already part of the city of San Diego in the 1850s. One key name is behind much of the cultural pedigree of the place. Ellen Browning Scripps moved to this community, population 350, in 1896. Already in her 60s with a self-made fortune, she was a cultivated woman who never married. She graced the region with her philanthropy during 35 years in La Jolla. Ms. Scripps was an energetic supporter of the work of Irving Gill, who eventually would be regarded as one of the great architects of California history.

Your clockwise loop hike begins in a part of the village where nearly everything that you see was touched by Scripps. She engaged Gill to build the Recreation Center in 1915, and the architect employed his skill at trimming down the Mediterranean style into simple line, cube, and arch expressed in austere stucco. Scripps was a great advocate for public recreation, for children's causes, and for women and the suffrage. Her memoirs commented that early 1900s La Jolla was very much "a woman's town." The 1914 La Jolla Woman's Club is another Irving Gill work, and the Silverado Street side illustrates how he would use pergolas to fuse interior and exterior living space. St. James-by-the-Sea Episcopal was England-born Scripps's place of worship; the architect was Irving Gill's nephew, Louis. Standing at the point in front of the church, look across Prospect to the Museum of Contemporary Art. A crosswalk points directly to a prominent arch with a symmetrical rectangular volume behind it. That was the home that Gill built for

The Arcade Building was built to connect with a trolley that ran to San Diego until 1940.

Ocean Lane is a stairway connecting Prospect Street in downtown La Jolla to the beach.

Scripps in 1915. The facade is authentic, but the building has morphed into the museum. A block farther, the Park Prospect Condominiums is a cube-shaped residential block designed in 1964 by local Modernist Russell Forester. The Arcade Building was built to connect with the Arcade station of a trolley that ran to San Diego until 1940. After the arcade, your energy turns to descending to near the shore twice so that you can climb back via public stairways. Leaving the second stairway/alley, La Valencia Hotel is on the right. It was designed by architect Reginald Johnson and known by many as "The Pink Lady." It has witnessed nearly a century of prestigious guests.

On Ivanhoe Avenue, the New Deal–era post office has an interior cubist-style mural by San Diego artist Belle Barranceanu that depicts La Jolla village. On Kline Street, the ivy-covered Kinsella Library is open during the week with a collection ranging from California plein air paintings to a red Elton John piano. After that, Mary–Star of the Sea Church displays a strong Mission Revival image created by architect Carleton Winslow. Facing Girard Street, the church has a dynamic mural painted by Alfredo Ramos Martínez, who is considered by many to be the father of Mexican Modernism. After Kline Street, the hiking become quicker with less narrative. Much of this hike lacks obvious restroom opportunities. Even though you have not hit 2 miles yet, a pit stop in the Vons Market or somewhere else on Girard Avenue is highly recommended.

Irving Gill's La Jolla Christian Fellowship at the corner of Genter and Draper is bold Mission Revival style. This hike does 0.4 mile of the 1-mile La Jolla bike path. This pleasant rails-to-trails corridor is great for hikers, but perhaps too short for many cyclists. San Diego Electric Railway trolleys ran here for 16 years, ending in 1940. Just right of where you leave the bike path, enjoy the immaculate 1959 Monsees Building designed by Liebhardt and Weston.

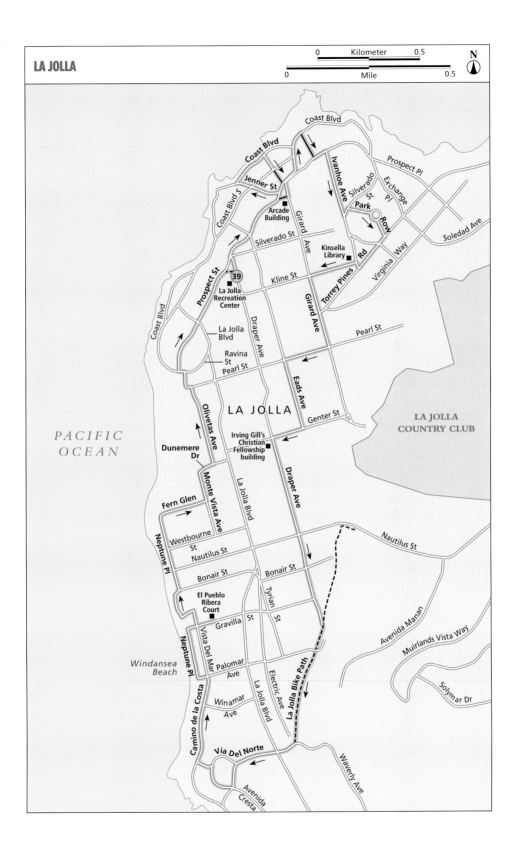

N

0   Kilometer   0.5

0   Mile   0.5

Coast Blvd

Coast Blvd

Coast Blvd

Prospect Pl

Jenner St

Coast Blvd S

Ivanhoe Ave

Silverado St

Exchange Pl

Arcade
Building

Park
Row

Soledad Ave

Girard Ave

Silverado St

Kinsella
Library

Torrey Pines Rd

Virginia Way

Prospect St

39

La Jolla
Recreation
Center

Kline St

Girard Ave

Coast Blvd

La Jolla
Blvd

Ravina
St

Pearl St

Pearl St

Draper Ave

Eads Ave

LA JOLLA

Genter St

LA JOLLA
COUNTRY CLUB

PACIFIC
OCEAN

Dunemere
Dr

Olivetas Ave

Irving Gill's
Christian
Fellowship
building

Draper Ave

Fern Glen

Monte Vista Ave

La Jolla Blvd

Westbourne
St

Nautilus St

Nautilus St

Neptune Pl

Bonair St

Bonair St

El Pueblo
Ribera
Court

Tyrian St

Gravilla St

Avenida Manan

Muirlands Vista Way

Vista Del Mar

Neptune Pl

Palomar
Ave

Windansea
Beach

Camino de la Costa

Winamar
Ave

La Jolla Blvd

Electric Ave

La Jolla Bike Path

Solymar Dr

Via Del Norte

Waverly Ave

Avenida
Cresta

At the corner of Avenida Cresta and Avenida Cortez, there is a Spanish-style house with an elegant red-tile gateway. The architect Cliff May is known as the father of the California Ranch–style house; this is one of his early romantic haciendas. Neptune Place brings Windansea Beach, a legendary surfing break. Here you can drop down toward the beach to locate the surf shack. It was built by returning World War II surfers in 1947. Destroyed by waves in 2015, locals rebuilt it. Devotees of Modern architecture, especially from Europe, go to great lengths to come see El Pueblo Ribera Court. This was built in 1923, still early in the career of architect Rudolph Schindler. These are individual, outdoor-oriented living units with courtyards and roof terraces. There is much online content available to help you understand their importance in Modern design history. Just before Neptune Place ends with a right turn onto Fern Glen, 7040 Neptune is an elegant villa designed by Santa Barbara's favorite architect, George Washington Smith. Imagine, this is 5 years newer than the Schindler courtyards that you just passed. Near the end of the hike, the landmark Bishop's School campus includes four Irving Gill buildings; of course the school was endowed by Ellen Browning Scripps.

MILES AND DIRECTIONS

0.0 START at La Jolla Recreation Center; stand at the entrance and look toward Prospect Street. Turn right in the pathway in front of the building through the park space to Draper Avenue. Cross Draper mid-block and turn left. Turn right on Prospect Street.

0.3 Arcade Building. Veer right in the arcade passage after passing Drury Lane; walk through the Arcade Building to the Girard Avenue side. Turn left on Girard. Take the crosswalk to the other side of Prospect toward Coldwell Banker.

0.4 Turn left on Prospect Street. Turn right on Jenner Street. Pass Coast Boulevard South then turn right on Coast Boulevard at the ocean front. Turn right on Ocean Street and continue up the steps of Ocean Lane to land next to that same Coldwell Banker.

0.8 Turn left on Prospect Street. Cross to the other side of Girard Avenue and turn left. Turn right on Coast Boulevard. Turn right in the public stairway adjacent to 1133 Coast.

1.0 Turn left on Prospect Street. Turn right into the next crosswalk and continue straight on Ivanhoe Avenue. At Silverado Street, jog left then cross Silverado to enter Park Row. Walk to the right of Union Place Circle and turn right on the continuation of Park Row.

1.4 Turn right on Torrey Pines Road. Cross East Ivanhoe Avenue at the signal and keep going on the right-hand side of Torrey Pines. Next cross Ivanhoe Avenue in the crosswalk and then turn right and then immediately go left on Kline Street.

1.5 Kinsella Library. Continue west on Kline Street.

1.9 Turn left on Girard Avenue. Turn right on Pearl Street.

2.1 Turn left on Eads Avenue. Turn right on Genter Street.

2.4 Irving Gill's Christian Fellowship building. Turn left on Draper Avenue. At the dead end, veer left up a connector path.

3.0 La Jolla bike path

3.4 Leave the bike path, turning right on Via Del Norte. This is not signed, but it is the first cross street encountered on the bike path that goes both right and left. Turn left to take La Jolla Hermosa Avenue briefly to admire a group of architectural offices. Turn around. Turn left on Via Del Norte.

Mary–Star of the Sea Church has a mural painted by Mexico's Alfredo Ramos Martínez.

3.6 Turn left on Avenida Cortez. Turn right on Avenida Cresta. Turn left on Via del Norte.

3.9 Turn right on Camino de la Costa. Turn left on Palomar Avenue.

4.2 Windansea Beach. Turn right on Neptune Place. Turn right on Gravilla Street.

4.4 El Pueblo Ribera Court, between 230 and 248 Gravilla Street. Turn around. Turn right on Vista del Mar. Turn left on Playa del Sol.

4.6 Turn right on Neptune Place.

4.9 Turn right on Fern Glen where Neptune ends. Turn left on Monte Vista Avenue. Turn right on Dunemere Drive.

5.2 Turn left on Olivetas Avenue. At Pearl Street, jog left to remain on Olivetas.

5.5 Turn left on Ravina Street. Immediately turn right on Prospect Street. Stay on the right side of Prospect while crossing La Jolla Boulevard.

5.9 End of hike at La Jolla Recreation Center.

40 BANKERS HILL–BALBOA PARK

West to east and back again, this hike is a cross section of a glorious part of San Diego just north of downtown. The route is studded with highlights: Maple Canyon trail, Quince footbridge, the green fields of Balboa Park, the historic and cultural El Prado corridor, the native landscape of Florida Canyon, the city views of Bird Park, bungalow- and brewery-rich North Park, and the iconic Spruce Street Suspension Bridge.

Start: Moe Coffee, 2542 State St., San Diego 92101
Elevation gain: 600 feet
Distance: 7.4-mile loop
Hiking time: 3.5 to 4.5 hours
Difficulty: Difficult
Best season: Year-round
Trail surface: Sidewalks, paved paths, dirt, stairs
Other trail users: Tourists, scooters, shoppers and diners

Restroom availability: Miles 1.1, 1.8, 3.9, 6.1
Canine compatibility: Dogs must remain on leash.
Parking status: Free curbside parking is not plentiful, but typically available on State Street.
Rail transit accessibility: N/A
Trailhead GPS: N32° 43.88' W117° 10.19'

FINDING THE TRAILHEAD

From the east or south: Take I-5 to exit 17A to merge onto Hawthorn Street. Turn right onto India Street. Turn right on Laurel Street. Turn left on State Street. From the north: Take I-5 to exit 18A toward Sassafras Street and San Diego Airport. Merge onto Kettner Boulevard. Turn left onto Laurel Street. Turn left on State Street. Moe Coffee is on the left side. This is a walk-up beverage vendor without restrooms. The hike will first pass restrooms at 1.1 miles in Balboa Park.

WHAT TO SEE

Begin this counterclockwise loop hike by going up Marble Canyon. This canyon stays relatively level as it slices through the bluff. The First Avenue Bridge crosses the canyon 100 feet above you. It is the only steel-arch bridge in the city. The bridge was erected in 1931, assembled from pieces that were shipped from the Midwest. The memorable Quince Street wooden-trestle bridge was built in 1905, and hikers have the good fortune to walk both under it and over it.

In the 1860s, the then-tiny city of San Diego set aside land for a public park half again larger than New York's Central Park. Even in the early 1900s, it was called City Park and envisioned as a green expanse without buildings. San Diego became the smallest city ever to host a world's fair when Balboa Park became the site of the Panama–California Exposition of 1915–1916. The impetus for the event was the completion of the Panama Canal, a project to which San Diego felt personally invested as it was the nearest US Pacific port to the canal. For its buildings, the Panama–California Exposition famously turned away from the fashionable Beaux-Arts architectural style to embrace Spanish Colonial Revival, with Mexico as the principal model. The chief architects were Bertram Goodhue and his associate, Carleton Winslow.

The hike goes both under and over the Quince Street wooden-trestle bridge.

Florida Canyon was preserved to represent the original landscape of Balboa Park. The 150 acres of coastal sage scrub provide an important habitat for native wildlife. Your route walks through Texas Canyon on trails from the intersection of Park Boulevard and Zoo Place down to just west of the intersection of Morley Field and Florida Drives. On maps the route appears more straightforward than it is in person because of the many use-trails. Supplement these directions with your instincts; one thing that you don't want to do is drop nearly all the way down in the canyon and inadvertently curve back up to Park Boulevard.

Bird Park, at the northeast corner of Balboa Park, was thoughtfully designed in the 1990s to integrate well with the North Park neighborhood that you are now entering. The city view here is marvelous. North Park is a cool place with small houses, walkable streets, and a unique retail identity. The hike is designed for a stop in this area; good choices will be near 30th Street and Myrtle Avenue. Great coffee, fresh craft beer, pizza, waffles: There is lots to pick from here. Going west on Dwight Street, notice the house at 3614 28th St. where you turn left. This is a 1916 example of a bungalow built by renowned San Diego builder-architect David Owen Dryden. There are many more nearby here in the Dryden Historic District.

The area near Myrtle Avenue and Vermont Street has graceful, lacy palm trees and Spanish-style houses. Back in Balboa Park, cross the other bridge over Cabrillo Canyon; no automobiles allowed on this one. Back near the vehicle streets, the Marston House Museum is 100 yards to the right and offers tours, if you are interested. West of Balboa Park, Spruce Street shows off some of the residential quality of Bankers Hill. The Spruce Street Suspension Bridge will bring out the kid in anyone. Built in 1912, it is 375 feet long and passes over Kate Sessions Canyon, 70 feet below. You transition from Dove and

The Balboa Park Botanical
Building behind the lily pond

Palm Streets to Reynard Way using a stairway. Not far from the Moe Coffee trailhead, restaurants and taprooms are nearby and waiting for you in Little Italy.

MILES AND DIRECTIONS

0.0 START at Moe Coffee. Facing the street from the walk-up coffee window, turn left on State Street. Immediately turn right on Maple Street. Follow pavement for 0.2 mile before it becomes foot trail. Pass under the landmarked steel arch bridge, then the wooden bridge. Here the trail climbs steeply to the left on rustic steps. This ends at an alley, which is Third Avenue. Turn left in this alley.

0.7 Cross Quince Street Pedestrian Bridge. Continue east on Quince. Cross Sixth Avenue. Enter Balboa Park and turn right on a paved park path between Sixth and Balboa Drive. Follow this path as others veer off. Cross to the south side of El Prado.

1.3 Turn left on El Prado. Walk across Cabrillo Bridge on the south side, passing through the West Gate.

1.6 Museum of Man is on the left side of El Prado. Walk through the arcade on the right side. At 250 feet from the West Gate, turn left into a crosswalk over El Prado that is located immediately after East Gate. Turn right to walk through the arcade on the left-hand side of El Prado.

1.8 Plaza de Panama Fountain. Continue due east on El Prado. After passing to the right of the Natural History Museum, the path goes up ten steps to arrive at a circular fountain. Veer left to take the footbridge over Park Boulevard. At the end of the bridge, the path is a circular curve down to Park Boulevard.

2.1 Turn north on Park Boulevard, the direction that bridge ramp has pointed you. Walk on the right side of Park Boulevard, either on pavement or on a faint path. Cross Zoo Place at the signal.

2.3 Enter the trail into Florida Canyon. The trail begins as an unpromising narrow dirt path going diagonally down the hillside immediately after the crosswalk over Zoo Place. Look for the most obvious path that first curves left (without reclimbing the slope) then angles down and right. You should land just west of the junction of Morley Field and Florida Drives. The correct way is indistinct; follow your instincts.

3.0 Turn right on Morley Field Drive. Turn left on Florida Drive. Notice vehicular Upas Street on the left. Opposite that, turn right, walking steeply up the pedestrian path that is a continuation of Upas Street. Continue east on Upas after it becomes a vehicle street at Alabama Street. Walk either on the left side of Upas where there is sidewalk or on the right side where there is grass.

3.5 Bird Park. Veer left to stay on Upas Street, across from Pershing Drive.

3.8 30th Street–North Park. Turn left on 30th Street.

4.0 Turn left on Dwight Street. Jog left twice as needed to remain on Dwight Street.

4.7 Turn right on Alabama Street. After passing four houses, turn left down the steps to Cypress Avenue. Go west on Cypress, which ends at Albert Street.

5.2 Turn left on Albert Street. Turn right on Brookes Avenue.

5.4 At Richmond Street, turn right then cross to the west side of the street at the stop sign. Turn left on Richmond. Turn right on Myrtle Avenue. Turn left on Vermont Street. Cross over the vehicular dead end of Upas Street to reach a park path.

5.7 Turn right, walking downhill on paved park path.

5.8 Cabrillo Canyon pedestrian bridge over Highway 163. Cross the bridge. On the other side, ignore a dirt bridle path going left and remain on paved path that switchbacks to climb out of the canyon.

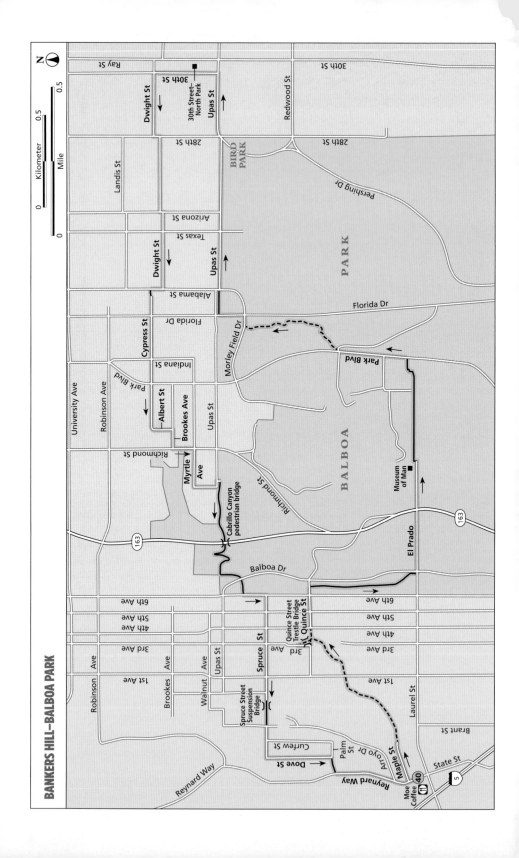

BANKERS HILL–BALBOA PARK

Spruce Street Suspension Bridge will bring out the kid in anyone.

6.0 Seventh Avenue at Upas Street. Turn left to walk due south on a paved park path. Balboa Drive approaches on the right. Turn right to cross it. Walk past the children's play structure and the park restroom out to the park boundary at Sixth Avenue.

6.2 Turn left on Sixth Avenue. Turn right on Spruce Street.

6.6 Spruce Street Suspension Bridge. Continue west beyond the bridge, walking downhill on Spruce.

6.8 Turn left on Dove Street.

7.0 Turn right down a stairway where Dove meets Palm Street. Descend group of steps, cross Eagle Street, and continue down more steps to bottom. Turn left on Reynard Way. Reynard becomes State Street.

7.4 End of hike at Moe Coffee.

This hike captures some of the flavor found east of coastal San Diego and near San Diego State. It includes the pre–World War II neighborhood of Rolando Village and the independent city of La Mesa. The main attractions here are the clusters of public stairways. The stairs offer charming pedestrian cut-throughs in Rolando. In La Mesa both the stairways and the views are breathtaking.

Start: Campus Plaza Shopping Center, 6155 El Cajon Blvd., San Diego 92115
Elevation gain: 700 feet
Distance: 5.9-mile point-to-point
Hiking time: 2.5 to 3.5 hours
Difficulty: Moderate
Best season: Year-round
Trail surface: Sidewalks, stairways
Other trail users: Stairway enthusiasts
Restroom availability: Mile 2.5
Canine compatibility: Problematic; not a loop hike

Parking status: Free street parking can be found on Acorn Street behind the shopping mall.
Rail transit accessibility: San Diego MTS Orange Line trolley, La Mesa Boulevard station. This is the end of the point-to-point route. You would take the bus before the hike, not at the end as described below for those who drive to the trailhead.
Trailhead GPS: N32° 45.67' W117° 03.92'

FINDING THE TRAILHEAD

Take I-8 eastbound from San Diego Downtown or from Highway 163, I-805, or I-15. Take exit 10 for College Avenue. Keep right at the fork and follow signs for Alvarado Road/College Avenue South. Merge onto College Avenue. Cross El Cajon Boulevard. Campus Plaza Shopping Center is the designated starting point on the left.

WHAT TO SEE

This hike is a point-to-point going west to east. Rolando Village is a charming neighborhood of low rolling hills with a street plan that departs from a rigid north-south grid. Enjoyment of this place comes from the assembly of modest homes built in the 1940s and 1950s and by the obvious pride that the residents have in their community. For walking enthusiasts, the thing that sets Rolando apart is the network of mid-block passages. There are eight; one is just sloping sidewalk, but the others have between seven and sixty-five steps. The locals identify these as their *catwalks*. Each of these Paseos has a name that is displayed in colorful tile laid into the cement. Passing through here by foot, you are entertained by nicely kept gardens, flags and pennants, quirky signs, and healthy street trees, including many jacaranda.

Notice how concealed Rolando Park is in the curving maze of streets and homes. This is the best place on the hike for a restroom. Fewer than 10 minutes after leaving Rolando Park, 70th Street is like a barrier. A gap in traffic will come, but don't push it. There is a crosswalk 1,200 feet to your left if needed. After leaving rude 70th Street, delightful Stanford Avenue is one of a dozen streets in this part of La Mesa that are named for prestigious colleges. A stairway with pastel stripes pops up on the left and, of course, your

Paseo de las Palmas is the only Rolando Village catwalk built with wood.

route leaves Stanford Avenue to check it out. At the top of these stairs on West Point Avenue, there is a good view east toward the top of Mount Nebo, where you are headed.

After crossing University Avenue, pass Helix High School. This school has produced several NFL stars, but the best-known alumni are probably actor Dennis Hopper and basketball's Bill Walton. La Mesa was incorporated in 1912, but the most famous aspect of the city today might be the stairways, which were built as early as 1927. They draw many enthusiasts, and the stairs are now labeled on maps, on signs, and even on the city website as the *Secret Stairs*. The view from the peak, elevation 850 feet, is impressive. The way down has many more stairs and some interesting houses. It takes no time at all from Mount Nebo to arrive in a bustling area near the trolley station. The quickest walking route back to the starting point is a flat and very boring 3 miles, mostly on El Cajon Boulevard. Suggested is a 16-minute bus ride back to the start.

MILES AND DIRECTIONS

0.0 START at Campus Plaza Shopping Center. Leave the west side of the shopping plaza near Jersey Mike's. Turn left on College Avenue.

0.2 Turn left on Estelle Street. Turn right on Laco Drive.

0.5 Paseo de las Palmas. Follow this stairway down from Lorca Drive to Rodrigo Drive. Continue on Rodrigo as it veers left at a Y. Turn left on Lorca Drive.

A late-May shower of jacaranda blossoms in Rolando Village

0.7 Near 6324 Lorca Dr., turn right down a ramp signed as Paseo de los Pinos. The ramp becomes a stairway. Turn right at the bottom on Bonillo Drive and veer left at a Y to remain on Bonillo. Turn left on Malcolm Drive.

1.0 Turn left up a stairway signed as Paseo del Halcon. On top, proceed straight ahead on Marraco Drive. Near the address 4411, turn right down a stairway signed as Paseo de los Coyotes. At the bottom, turn left on Lerida Drive. Immediately turn right on Revillo Drive.

1.4 Turn left on Malcolm Drive. Across from address 8491, turn left up a stairway signed as Paseo de los Agaves. At the top, turn right on Aragon Way and continue straight as Aragon Drive intercepts from the right. Turn right on Rolando Boulevard. Pass a single yellow house and turn down a long ramp with seven steps signed as Paseo del Colibri.

1.7 At the bottom, turn left on Mataro Drive. Near address 4575, turn right down a pedestrian passage signed as Paseo de la Naranja. At the end of this passage, cross Alamo Drive.

1.9 Paseo de Papagayo. Take these stairs from Alamo Drive up to Valencia Drive. Turn right on top.

2.0 Turn right on 67th Street. Veer left at the Y. Now on Patria Drive, turn left on Alamo Drive.

2.3 Turn left on Vigo Drive. Enter Rolando Park on the left, walk to the corner of the parking lot, and find green space just outside a baseball diamond.

2.5 Rolando Park. Exit the park near the restrooms to the cul-de-sac of 68th Street.

2.7 Turn right on Alamo Way.

2.9 At 70th Street, wait for a safe time to cross to the other side of the street. Turn right on 70th. Immediately turn left on Stanford Avenue.

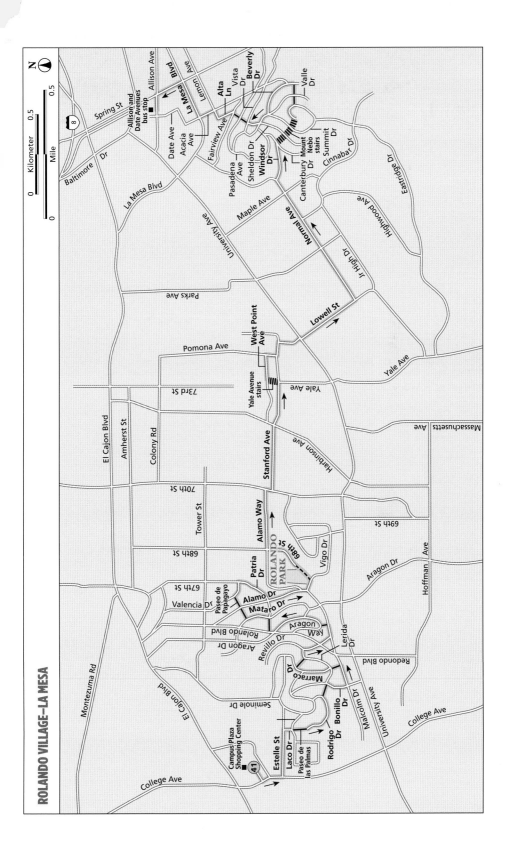

ROLANDO VILLAGE–LA MESA

The start of three consecutive flights of stairs to reach Mount Nebo in La Mesa

3.3 Yale Avenue stairs. Turn left up these stairs where Stanford is intersected by Yale Avenue. Turn right at the top onto West Point Avenue. Turn right on Pomona Avenue. Turn left on Stanford Avenue.

3.6 Turn right on Lowell Street. Cross busy University Avenue at the signal.

4.0 Turn left on Normal Avenue.

4.5 Turn diagonally right on Windsor Drive, which comes just after Avon Drive.

4.7 Mount Nebo stairs. Go up three segments from where Windsor and Canterbury Drives meet to Summit Drive. Turn left at the top.

4.9 Turn left down a well-signed stairway. This has two segments for a total of 184 steps crossing Valle Drive on the way to Beverly Drive. Turn left at the bottom.

5.2 Turn right from Beverly Drive to Summit Drive. Turn right on Sheldon Drive. Where Sheldon ends at Vista Drive, proceed straight to enter a relatively concealed pedestrian ramp by a utility pole. This is the start of a stairway in two segments that crosses Pasadena Avenue and ends at Fairview Avenue. At the bottom, turn right on Fairview and turn immediately left on Alta Lane. Turn right on Lemon Avenue. Turn left on Acacia Avenue.

5.5 Turn right on La Mesa Boulevard. At the trolley tracks, cross to the other side of Spring Street.

5.7 Turn left on Spring Street, walking on the opposite side of the street as the trolley station. Turn left on Allison Avenue.

5.9 End of hike at the Allison and Date Avenues bus stop. GPS N32° 45.97' W117° 01.32'. The suggested return is a 16-minute ride back to the start on San Diego bus route 1, signed for Fashion Valley. It runs every 15 minutes on weekdays and every 30 minutes on weekends. Exit the bus at College Avenue and cross to the diagonal corner for Campus Plaza, where the hike began. The bus does not take cash; a San Diego MTS Compass Card is needed. It can be purchased and loaded at the La Mesa Boulevard trolley station.

HIKE INDEX

MEET YOUR GUIDE

Bob Inman has lived just about his whole life in the Los Angeles area. His life of hiking began with the Boy Scouts when he began doing summer Sierra backpacks. He hiked more than half of the John Muir Trail when he was 16. His foot travels have taken him on continued excursions to the Sierras as well as repeated trips to the Desert Southwest, Switzerland, and the British Isles. His favorite place to hike is Scotland, and in 2016 he did a 9-day thru-hike across the Scotland Highlands from Perth to Fort William.

While he has retired from a career in produce transportation logistics, Bob has written two books on walking in Los Angeles and was the revising coauthor of a famous guidebook to architecture in Los Angeles. He is the cofounder if the Inman 300, America's first urban thru-hike. Bob also leads free urban hikes as an avocation. More than 6,000 people have participated in his events. He was the 2016 recipient of the Ray Bradbury Community Walking Champion award presented by the advocacy group Los Angeles Walks.

THE TEN ESSENTIALS OF HIKING

American Hiking Society

American Hiking Society recommends you pack the "Ten Essentials" every time you head out for a hike. Whether you plan to be gone for a couple of hours or several months, make sure to pack these items. Become familiar with these items and know how to use them. Learn more at **AmericanHiking.org/hiking-resources.**

 1. **Appropriate Footwear**

 6. **Safety Items** (light, fire, and a whistle)

 2. **Navigation**

 7. **First-Aid Kit**

 3. **Water** (and a way to purify it)

 8. **Knife or Multi-Tool**

 4. **Food**

 9. **Sun Protection**

 5. **Rain Gear & Dry-Fast Layers**

 10. **Shelter**